RETHINKING UNEQUAL EXCHANGE

The Global Integration of Nursing Labour Markets

Rethinking Unequal Exchange traces the structural forces that have created the conditions for the increasing use, production, and circulation of temporary migrant nurses worldwide.

Salimah Valiani explores the political economy of health care of three globally important countries in the importing and exporting of temporary migrant nurses: the Philippines, the world's largest supplier of temporary migrant nurses; the United States, the world's largest demander of internationally trained nurses; and Canada, which is both a supplier and a demander of internationally trained nurses. Using a world historical approach, Valiani demonstrates that though nursing and other forms of caring labour are essential to human, social, and economic development, the super-exploitation of care workers is escalating. Compiling statistical data gathered from various countries and time frames, Valiani cogently shows how the global integration of nursing labour markets is deepening unequal exchange and has the potential of substantially widening inequality between the core and periphery of the world system.

SALIMAH VALIANI is Associate Researcher with the Centre for the Study of Education and Work, University of Toronto.

Rethinking Unequal Exchange

The Global Integration of Nursing Labour Markets

SALIMAH VALIANI

With a Foreword by Samir Amin

UNIVERSITY OF TORONTO PRESS
Toronto   Buffalo   London

© University of Toronto Press 2012
Toronto Buffalo London
www.utppublishing.com
Printed in Canada

ISBN 978-1-4426-4366-6 (cloth)
ISBN 978-1-4426-1213-6 (paper)

Printed on acid-free, 100% post-consumer recycled paper with vegetable-based inks.

Canadian Cataloguing in Publication Data

Valiani, Salimah, 1970–
Rethinking unequal exchange: the global integration of nursing labour markets / Salimah Valiani ; with a foreword by Samir Amin.

Includes bibliographical references and index.
ISBN 978-1-4426-4366-6 (bound). – ISBN 978-1-4426-1213-6 (pbk.)

1. Nurses – Supply and demand.   2. Nurses, Foreign.   3. Nurses – Employment.   4. Labor market.   I. Title.

RT86.7.V34 2012   331.12'91362173   C2011-906626-2

This book has been published with the help of an award from the Ursuline Sisters of the Chatham Union, and donations by various individuals.

University of Toronto Press acknowledges the financial assistance to its publishing program of the Canada Council for the Arts and the Ontario Arts Council.

University of Toronto Press acknowledges the financial support of the Government of Canada through the Canada Book Fund for its publishing activities.

Contents

Tables

Figures

Foreword

SAMIR AMIN

Translation from the French by Salimah Valiani

Salimah Valiani's study traces the relations underlying international nurse migration from circa 1990 to the present. The richness of her analysis lies in her use of the grand synthesis approach of world historical political economy. Through this approach, Valiani is able to expose the overlapping processes of the global North and the global South that are relevant to the particularities of international nurse migration in the late twentieth and early twenty-first centuries – a moment now well-understood to be one of major restructuring and reorganization in the world capitalist economy.

In this study of one instance of restructuring in the world capitalist economy, Valiani combines a description of little known, labour migration policy discussions currently in play among states around the world; a reading of the post-1950 political economy of health care in key countries of the global North to uncover the causes of a shift in northern employer demand for internationally trained nurses; a reading of the post-1950 political economy of development in a key country of the global South to uncover the cause of increased world supply of temporary migrant nurses; and an interpretation of what the flow of predominantly female, caring labour from the periphery to the core of the world system means in terms of unequal exchange, a concept first elaborated in the 1960s. In contradistinction to most studies of contemporary migration, this study underlines the rise of temporary migration via 'work permits' and the concomitant attenuation of permanent migration in immigration policies of the global North. This shift signifies the loss of the moderately redistributive function of permanent migration whereby certain numbers of workers of the global South, from about the 1960s to the 1990s, were able to migrate permanently to the global North, along with their families, and draw from relatively better social and economic conditions.

The ability to combine several elements, time frames, and layers of analysis is surely not unrelated to Valiani's multiple vocations as a multidisciplinary academic researcher, trade union based policy analyst, and advocate. She pointedly raises and draws connections between issues relating to labour markets, class struggles, gender inequality, super-exploitation in the labour process, unequal exchange, and the historically uneven development of countries in the world capitalist system that is fundamental to all of these issues.

The capitalist strategies of monopolists, whose goal is to collect imperialist rent, consist of two complementary vectors: the control of the flow or migration of workers, and the control of the flow of capital. I will focus my remarks on the first of these vectors, which is the subject of this study. While Valiani provides what I will call a *micro-structural perspective* of migration on a global scale, I provide here a *macro-structural* perspective of migration on a global scale.

1.

The constituting of the world capitalist system, as it exists today – which may also be called *historical capitalism* – has occurred over the past five centuries, as rendered through the conquering of the Americas.

For Europe, the initial core of the world capitalist system, this historical process involved massive migrations of Europeans who conquered and populated the Americas, in addition to Australia, New Zealand, and a significant portion of South Africa. The mass migration of Europeans increased the proportion of world population represented by those of European origin from 18 per cent in the year 1500, to 36 per cent in the year 1900. The migration of Europeans occurred in two historical moments. The first was the mercantilist period of 1500 to 1800. The second was the industrial revolutions in Europe and the United States of America – circa 1800, and again from the early twentieth century to the Second World War – during which emigration from Europe accelerated.

These waves of European migration were part and parcel of the agrarian capitalism of early historical capitalism. Agrarian capitalism was based on the adoption and application of the principle of private property with regard to the control of agricultural land. The 'modern' notion of private property replaced the previously existing 'feudal' form of controlling land, with the bourgeoisie now determining the rules and regulations around access to land for the peasantry. Inherent in the new form of private appropriation of land was the exclusion of a large and growing proportion of peasants with regard to access to land. Now landless, these peasants became 'poor,' or in more exact terms, they were impoverished.

Along with all this came accelerated urbanization in the centres of capitalist development of the time – Europe and the United States of America – at a slower pace before 1850 and quicker thereafter. Considerable numbers of peasants were absorbed in the new urbanization, thus becoming the new working classes. The relatively gradual, labour intensive nature of the processes of industrialization in Europe and North America allowed for such absorption to occur.

There were, however, limits to the absorption of 'surplus rural population,' as the language of neoclassical economics would have it. A colossal 'oversupply' of displaced peasants fed massive waves of emigration to the Americas. Without the outlet of the Americas, the cities of Europe would have been overpopulated by the 'unemployed,' taking on the characteristics of the 'planet of slums' that is the reality of cities in the global South today. It is impossible to know the consequences for Europe had there not been the outlet of migration to the Americas. Also impossible to know is how or whether the massive impoverishment of the peasantry would have been sustained within the logic of capitalism. What we can say is that the democratic management of European societies of the time would have been an unfathomable challenge.

2.

Due to the history of the constitution of world capitalism as described above, peoples of the periphery of the world system have not benefited from the 'advantage' of accessing alternative destinations to dispose of 'surplus rural populations.' As in Europe a few hundred years ago, the current 'surplus rural population' in the global South has been created through the class-determined transformation of peasant agriculture into capitalist agriculture.

It is indeed unforeseen within 'really-existing capitalism' if the development path of agriculture in the periphery will unfold any differently from the way it unfolded in Europe. This development path, based on the private appropriation of agricultural lands, is at the origin of the massive migration of rural peoples to the slums of urban centres in the global South today.

The agrarian question cannot be resolved on a global scale within the logic of world capitalism. The world capitalist system has resolved it in a limited manner, that is, for the core of the system, which constitutes 15 per cent of the world population. It cannot do so for the periphery, which constitutes 85 per cent of humanity. In the global North, a comprehensive grasping of the global agrarian question is non-existent within economistic and other dominant perspectives. These perspectives can do no better than to approach the symptom of the problem – rural-urban migration within countries of the global South – from a prejudiced perspective that may be called naïve, at best.

Given all this, I do not hesitate to conclude that historical capitalism has 'done its time' and is rendering itself obsolete. The alternative suggests an entirely new vision for the organization of agriculture, a vision that is necessarily outside of the realm and logic of capitalism and its profit motive.[1]

3.

The discourse of neoliberalism does not even address – much less respond to – these fundamental issues at the roots of world inequality. Neoliberalism is little other than propaganda of a most vulgar form. If the proponents of neoliberalism were true to the logic of liberalism, they would insist that the 'globalization' they so intimately expound be applied consistently – such that all borders be eliminated for all flows: flows of capital, flows of goods and services, and the flows of human beings.

The proponents of neoliberalism, however, cannot be true to their own logic because capitalism, as it exists today, is structured on the monopolistic ownership of the means of production – a structure which is in complete contradiction to the liberal notion of 'free markets.' The free movement of displaced peasants and others from the global South to the global North is not in the best interests of monopolists, most of which are employers, and is therefore not permitted. Impoverished people of the global South are in turn further excluded from the benefits of 'development' as we know it.

Beyond the proponents of neoliberalism, it is clear that human civilization as a whole still lacks the capacity to imagine or accept the free movement of all human beings, across all borders. Given this, it would follow that we refrain from propounding upon the notion of 'global citizenship.' This notion is particularly advanced by the 'bobos,' or 'bourgeois bohemians,' of the opulent urban centres of the global

North. The 'bobos' of various countries seem to be in denial of the fact that the movement of most 'others' is subject to the policing inherent in immigration instruments such as the 'visa' and the 'work permit.' To put it slightly differently, global citizens cannot come into being in the world of today, a world which has not yet disentangled itself from the contradictions of historical capitalism. Recalling the contradictions of past and present migrations, Bolivian president Evo Morales points out that European immigrants who appropriated lands and embattled indigenous peoples in the Americas did not carry visas.

Given the current lack of free movement for peoples of the global South, the latter should resist the dictates of neoliberal globalization as it exists today. Peoples of the global South must protect their own home-grown forms of social and economic development. In other words, peoples of the global South must take and deepen control of their collective production, thereby subverting the flow of migration to the global North. This is one of the conclusions and principal 'policy prescriptions' that may be drawn from Valiani's analysis of the causes and consequences of the global integration of nursing labour markets.

4.

The discourse of states of the global North on the question of migration is one of 'security,' as illustrated by the policies of the European Union (EU). The EU is currently attempting to impose policing policies upon states of the global South – especially African and Arab states – in the name of collaboration.

On the whole, the totality of strategies of monopolistic capital in the world economy today – which continues to be in crisis – allows for the extraction of monopolistic rent, or profit, based on the labour power of workers of both the global South and the global North.[2] On a global scale, this rent may be considered an imperialist rent that reproduces and deepens the inequality between societies of the current imperialist core of the world system (i.e., the United States of America, Canada, Australia, Western Europe, and Japan) and societies of the periphery dominated by countries of Africa, Asia, and Latin America.[3] As Valiani demonstrates in this study, the deepening of unequal exchange between the global North and global South is particularly salient in the absorption of predominantly female caring labour of the global South by the global North.

In addition to deepening inequality between the global North and the global South, the current strategies of monopolistic capital and other employers, including states, simultaneously allows for the possibility of new forms of super-exploitation of workers in the imperialist core of the world system. In particular, this is occurring through increasing underemployment as well as long-term unemployment for growing proportions of workers in the global North. The casualization of work of registered nurses in Canada, as portrayed in chapter 4, is one instance of this phenomenon. This, in turn, is increasing inequality between various categories of workers within the global North.

The overall effect of the totality of strategies of monopolistic capital in the world today is the creation of the possibility of a 'fifth international' of workers and peoples of the world – a global integration of solidarity more necessary now than ever before.

Preface and Acknowledgments

This study is an academic inquiry into questions which began arising during my first round of work as a policy analyst and advocate within the trade union movement. Through the Public Service International report *Women and International Migration in the Health Sector* (Van Eyck: 2004), I became aware that temporary migration was a trend in the health sector, particularly nursing, dating as far back as the early 1990s. As the outcome of a participatory action research project in which Public Service International (PSI) brought together health union representatives from sixteen of the world's major source and destination countries of migrant health workers, the report is rich in description, tracing the flows, contractual agreements, and working conditions of health workers in these sixteen countries.

From my vantage point as an advocate located in the central labour body of Canada, the Canadian Labour Congress (CLC), the key questions arising from the PSI study were, *What were the causes of increasing employer demand for temporary migrant nurses, and what made for the supply of temporary migrant nurses internationally?* From my vantage point as a political economist, the key questions arising were, *What does international nurse migration in the late twentieth century reveal about restructuring in the world economy, and how might we rethink 1960s theories of unequal exchange in light of liberalizing labour markets and the essential role of female caring labour in capitalist production?*

In answering these questions I have been inspired and supported by several communities of thinkers and activists. For the habit of searching for the not-so-apparent political motivations of policy pronouncements, I am indebted to members of the CLC Training and Technology Committee (2005–08). For the access to key decision makers in the

Philippine public service, I am indebted to General Secretary Annie Geron and the staff of Public Services Labor Independent Confederation (PSLINK), and Secretary-General Jossel Ebesate of the Alliance of Health Workers. For the methodology of tracing the overlapping of social processes and world economic relations over long historical periods, I am indebted to the intellectual community of world systems analysts, a giant of which is the late Giovanni Arrighi, who was one of my mentors at the State University of New York – Binghamton. Without the painstaking work of countless, anonymous civil servants, I would not have had the range of statistical data used in this study. Finally, and most crucial to the completion of this study, which is a combination of elements of several inquiries over time, I am indebted to Wallace Clement (Carleton University); Zebun Valiani; Hugh Armstrong (Carleton University); Manfred Bienefeld (Carleton University); Roland Schneider (Trade Union Advisory Committee to the Organisation for Economic Cooperation and Development); Colin Lewis (London School of Economics); Gareth Austin (London School of Economics); Chi Chi Hodgson (Canadian Labour Congress); and Frank Ruiz, Neelam Sandhu, Jean-Paul Prévost, Jean Wolff, Lindsey McKay, Jean Ann Ledwell, the Ursuline Sisters of the Chatham Union, and Samir Amin (Third World Forum) for the consistent, reflective, critical, and caring support they provided.

RETHINKING UNEQUAL EXCHANGE

The Global Integration of Nursing Labour Markets

1 Introduction

Over the past fifteen years, *international migration* has emerged as a topic of widespread discussion among academics, policy analysts, states, activists, migrant workers, and unions. As far back as 1949, the International Labour Organisation (ILO) coined the term *migrant for employment* to refer to 'a person who migrates from one country to another with a view to being employed otherwise than on his (*sic*) own account' (ILO: 1949). Concerned about the protection of migrant workers' rights, the ILO created Convention 97, *Migration for Employment*, which from the early 1950s established – at least in terms of international law – the fundamental principle that migrant workers merit the same wages, working conditions, and other rights as workers in the countries in which they are employed. The lack of such equal treatment in practice is an issue of central concern today for migrant workers, activists, and unions.

Academics and policy-oriented researchers are concerned with what is argued to be a large increase of *international migrants*[1] in the world in recent decades. The Department of Economic and Social Affairs (DESA) of the United Nations Secretariat, for example, reports that in the past forty-five years, the total number of international migrants has 'more than doubled,' rising from an estimated 75 million in 1960 to 191 million in 2005 (DESA: 2006, 1). As defined by the UN, international migrants are persons who have resided outside of their country of birth or citizenship for twelve months or more, regardless of the reason for moving or of their legal status abroad.

Martin, Abella, and Kuptsch – leading policy thinkers on contemporary migration – assert that there is a rising number of international migrants and that this figure has grown at a faster rate than global population growth. As an explanation, they cite the fall of communism in Europe, refugee-producing wars such as those in Yugoslavia and Afghanistan, regional trade agreements incorporating measures for specific types of labour mobility, and the 'Asian economic miracle' (Martin et al.: 2006, 4).

A statistic cited in a report of the Bureau for Workers' Activities of the International Labour Office brings out the rather politicized nature of discussions stressing the rising numbers of migrants. In the report entitled *In Search of Decent Work – Migrant Workers' Rights*, it is highlighted that the proportion of migrating workers relative to total world population remains stable at slightly less than 3 per cent (International Labour Office: 2008, 34; International Organization for Migration: 2005, 394, 396). The Bureau for Workers' Activities stresses that this proportion has changed little since 1965. This suggests that narrow nationalism and xenophobia – and attempts to counter them – lie at the heart of much of the current academic and policy focus on migration. Along the same lines as the Bureau for Workers' Activities argument, historians stress that migration is not a new phenomenon and that the movement of people is a recurring element of human history (Moses: 2006; Kardulias and Hall: 2007).

Taking a cue from feminist policy analysts addressing rights issues of migrant domestic workers and highlighting gender and other structural aspects of migration from the early 1990s (see the discussion of Heyzer et al. [1994] later in this section), feminist academics and others in recent years have begun stressing the feminization of migration flows. Nicola Piper (2008), for example, in an edited volume entitled *New Perspectives on Gender and Migration*, sees the feminization of migration flows from the late 1990s as connected to 'at least four phenomena': improved statistical visibility of women as migrants; increasing participation of women in most migration streams; growing unemployment among men in migrant-sending countries; and increasing demand for labour in feminized sectors in migrant-receiving countries (Piper: 2008, 2–3). According to DESA figures, female international migrants constituted almost 50 per cent of all migrants in 2005, as compared to 47 per cent in 1960 (DESA: 2006, 3).

Bringing a regional lens to female migration, Piper outlines variations between Africa, Latin America, and Asia. In terms of emigration from Latin America, Piper points out that feminization is particularly evident in flows of migrants destined for Southern Europe. In terms of the continent of Africa, according to Piper, high levels of poverty, disease, and rising male unemployment explain the relatively quicker pace of feminized emigration from Africa. For Asia, labour migration has sharply increased since the 1970s, with female workers clearly dominating in some cases (Piper: 2008, 3). Also from a regional and gender approach to migration, the International Council of Nurses highlights the over-representation of female health worker emigration from sub-Saharan Africa to countries of the global North (Buchan and Calman: 2004, 26–7). Overriding all of these flows, Piper observes that a yet higher proportion of female migration remains invisible due to the undocumented flows of sex trade workers and other workers of female-dominated sectors (Piper: 2008, 4).

In the introductory chapter of his edited volume entitled *The International Migration of Health Workers*, John Connell asserts that health labour migration is 'demand-driven' and related to the 'growing global integration of health care markets' (Connell: 2008, 2). Highlighting developed countries as the drivers of demand for international health care workers, Connell further asserts – in tandem with the analysis of the international federation of public sector unions, Public Service International (Van Eyck: 2004) – that 'income differentials' and 'employment conditions' are the principal factors pushing health workers to migrate from developing countries (Connell: 2008, 11–12).

Explanations for labour migration of most contemporary analysts as exemplified by Martin et al. (2006) and in the edited volumes of Piper (2008) and Connell (2007) may be described as *push and pull* formulations. 'Demand pull' in receiving countries of migrants, as Martin et al. put it, is the recruitment of international labour for specific jobs and sectors by employers and states claiming domestic labour shortages. Meanwhile, unemployment, underemployment, and low wages in the origin countries of migrants create the 'supply push' for emigration. And 'network factors' – for example, job and wage information flows that are built through communities and generations – allow for expanded and successive migration flows (Martin et al.: 2006, 7).

What remains inexplicit in all of these perspectives on migration, including in the ILO term *migrant for employment*, is the distinction between workers migrating on a *temporary*, legally limited-time basis, and workers migrating on a *permanent*, or legally unlimited-time basis. As Martin et al. rightly point out – without adequate explanation – labour migration schemes of the 1990s and thereafter in 'the USA, Germany, and other industrial democracies' have been aimed to fill specific job vacancies in particular niches for limited periods (2006, xii). These arrangements, Martin et al. argue, are to ensure that migration of guest workers is truly temporary, thereby correcting what has come to be perceived as the 'mistake' of previous decades: little state control over which migrating workers remain permanently in their destination countries (2006, xii).

Indeed, in terms of statistics, perhaps more remarkable than any of the figures mentioned thus far is the proportion of *temporary migrants* relative to *permanent migrants* in the world's wealthiest countries in recent years. In 2006, the number of migrants entering countries of the Organisation for Economic Co-operation and Development (OECD) on a temporary basis – some 2.5 million – was three times the number of those entering on a permanent basis (OECD: 2008a, 22).[2] In 2008, the number of temporary migrant workers in OECD countries was approximately 2.3 million while permanent labour migrants numbered about 1.5 million (OECD: 2010, 30). Between 2003 and 2007, temporary labour migration was the fastest-growing form of migration to countries of the OECD, increasing at an average rate of 7 per cent (OECD: 2010, 30).[3] In terms of the migration of highly skilled, internationally trained workers to countries historically built on permanent migration, the OECD reports a growing trend of temporary migration leading to permanent residency in recent years. In 2007, 33 per cent of highly skilled, permanent residents in Australia were previously temporary migrant workers. In New Zealand for the year 2005, 66 per cent of highly skilled permanent residents were previously temporary migrant workers. And for the United States of America in recent years, more than 80 per cent of highly skilled permanent residents were previously temporary migrant workers (OECD: 2009, 104).

The edited volume of Heyzer, Lycklama à Niejeholt, and Weerakoon (1994) – which was the outcome of a 1992 regional policy dialogue held in Colombo, entitled 'Foreign Female Domestic Workers: International Migration, Employment and National Policies' – offers the conceptual beginnings required to understand the phenomenon of *temporary labour migration*. Focusing on temporary labour migration to Malaysia and Singapore from the Philippines, Indonesia, and Sri Lanka, Rita Raj-Hashim argues that policies of countries of destination restrict the entry of labour through temporary contracts in order to meet specific demands for labour while keeping social and economic costs for the receiving country to a minimum (Raj-Hashim: 1994, 119).

In beginning with an analysis of state policies facilitating temporary labour migration, Heyzer et al. (1994) take a structural approach to questions of migration. Building on the structural approach of Heyzer et al., this study postulates that the emerging, *global integration of labour markets*, based on temporary labour migration, is an under-analysed, key element in the restructuring of the *capitalist world economy*. Reconstructing historically the rise of temporary migration of nursing labour to countries of the *global North* – a phenomenon which can be traced back to the late 1980s in government statistical data – this study poses the following primary research question: *What accounts for the increased use of temporary migrant nursing labour in the global North, circa 1990, sparking the beginnings of the global integration of nursing labour markets?* Temporary labour migration is defined here as the entry of internationally trained workers into a country on the basis of temporary work authorizations rather than permanent resident status. As nursing and domestic care labour markets were among the first labour markets to shift from functioning on a national scale to integration on a global scale, the second major question posed in this study is: *How can the dynamics of the global integration of caring labour markets be interpreted with regard to restructuring in the capitalist world economy?*

The North/South focus is selected here due to the growing inequality between the world's wealthiest nations and the rest of the countries of the world (ILO: 2008; DESA: 2005), as well as the rapidly increasing shortages of nurses and other health workers in the global South (Buchan and Calman: 2004; Van Eyck: 2004). While the average nurse-to-population ratio in Western Europe and North America is 1,000 nurses per 100,000, in Africa, South-east Asia, and Latin America it is merely 100 nurses per 100,000, and in Central and South-eastern Europe it is 750 nurses per 100,000 (Buchan and Calman: 2004, 11–12). Perhaps the most salient illustration of the overlap of inequality and health migration is the following statistic: From the continent of Africa alone, 20,000 health workers migrate to North America and Europe annually, though African health workers represent only 3 per cent of the world's health care labour force. Meanwhile, one-quarter of the world's deaths due to illness occur in Africa (Blanchet and Keith: 2006, 13).

Before elaborating on the arguments of this study, various areas of discussion from which this study draws and to which it aims to contribute are explored below. These areas of discussion are unpaid caring labour, female labour, and capitalist production; globalizing care economies and female labour migration; and global capitalism in historical perspective.

Unpaid Caring Labour, Female Labour, and Capitalist Production

In a friendly critique of Marx and Marxian economists from the late 1960s, socialist feminist thinkers consider the role of unpaid female labour in the capitalist production process, defining it as the principal source of women's oppression. Dalla Costa and James speak of a 'community of housewives' forming 'the other half of capitalist organization' and 'the hidden source of surplus labour' (Dalla Costa and James: 1972, 7). Lerguia and Dumoulin delineate the functions of housework in the maintenance of capitalist society, arguing housework to be the 'invisible' economic base of 'visible' producers of commodities (Lerguia and Dumoulin: 1972, 44). These functions include biological reproduction; education and caring for children, the elderly, and the ill; and reproduction of the labour power consumed daily in capitalist production (Lerguia and Dumoulin: 1972, 42).

Making the link between the oppression of women underlying unpaid female labour in the home and the 'super exploitation' of wage-earning women working outside the home, Terry Fee stresses that the historical stamp of wage-less housework as trivial laid the roots for women's secondary place in the paid labour force (Fee: 1975, 8). This link is especially relevant when analysing nursing labour, a form of caring labour which was performed primarily in the home in the first half of the twentieth century and later moved into the productive sphere of hospitals.

Building on feminist discussions of the ethics of care, philosopher Eva Kittay underlines the fundamental role of caring labour in human societies.[4] Kittay begins with the idea that human beings are mutually dependent and involved in an inevitable variety of interactions, thereby rejecting the presumption of society as an association of self-contained, self-centred equals only voluntarily interacting with one another (Kittay: 1999, xi–xiii). Given the long maturation process of humans, the common phenomena of illness and old age, and the 'decidedly' human capacities for moral feeling and attachment, Kittay sees human dependency and interconnectedness – and in turn the act of providing care – as foundational to human survival and the development of culture itself (Kittay: 1999, 29).

Bringing the discussion of female labour and women's oppression into the realm of late twentieth-century capitalism and adding a North/South dimension, Saskia Sassen (1998) outlines three principal ways in which women's inequality is reinforced through what she terms *economic globalization*. First, the expansion of export-oriented, cash-crop production puts further pressure on women, whose labour in subsistence agriculture and household production subsidizes the wage labour of men in cash-crop production. Second, the internationalization of manufacturing is directly dependent on the unregulated, exploitative use of female labour, in particular, rural women previously not integrated in industrial production. And third, economic globalization is causing new patterns of migration in which female migrant workers face the *double disadvantage* of sex and class in terms of remuneration, job opportunities, and legal status (Sassen: 1998, 112–16).

Globalizing Care Economies and Female Labour Migration

Following the lead of advocates identifying the growing numbers of women migrating beyond national borders to perform domestic work, feminist researchers over the past decade have elaborated on a 'new' global service or care economy within which an expanding trade in domestic workers is increasingly internationalized (Hochschild: 2000; Parreñas: 2001; Briones: 2009; Yeates: 2009). Without making explicit theoretical links with earlier discussions of the role of caring labour in capitalist production, it is acknowledged in this largely descriptive discussion that the increasing use of migrant domestic workers builds on existing 'divisions of labour,' including patriarchal structures in both the source and destination countries of domestic workers (Yeates: 2009, 22).

The migration of domestic workers is seen as 'both caused by and a response to' global economic restructuring or systemic changes in the social organization of production (Yeates: 2009, 16). An array of factors is thus listed as propelling the internationalization of the trade in domestic workers. Demand for domestic workers in wealthier countries of the world economy is identified as growing due to aging populations, changes in family structure, feminization of the labour force, 'masculinization' of women's employment patterns, and restructuring or/and shortages of public care services (Parreñas: 2001; Briones: 2009; Yeates: 2009). Making some connection with growing world inequality, Yeates stresses that this increasing demand is 'an indication of a sizeable affluent population unable or unwilling to provide for its own domestic needs' (Yeates: 2009, 21).

The supply of domestic workers in the global service economy is provided predominantly by less wealthy countries. Employing basic categories of early world systems theory (see the next section for a broad discussion of the world systems approach), Parreñas (2000) asserts that women from *peripheral countries* migrate to *core countries* to undertake reproductive labour as one of many responses to the problem of uneven development. In Yeates's interpretation of world systems theory, capitalist expansion necessitates supplementary household labour reproduction strategies, which may involve the geographical dispersal of household members (Yeates: 2009, 16). The migration of women as care workers is thus an extension of household labour by female caregivers to help support social reproduction at home through financial contributions rather than unpaid caring work within the family.

Without tracing the processes leading to the implementation of structural adjustment programs in the global South and in formerly communist states, these programs are underlined for their particular impacts on women, leading to increased numbers of women migrating for employment (Sassen: 2000; Briones: 2009; Yeates: 2009). Yeates (2009, 17) emphasizes how reductions in public sector employment affect female workers in particular, many of whom serve as teachers, nurses, and administrative workers. Sassen (2000) discusses how the adoption of market policies, the opening of economies to foreign firms, and the elimination of state subsidies have created enormous social costs, including high unemployment. She links late-1990s unemployment rates of 70 per cent in Armenia, Russia, Bulgaria, and Croatia to increased trafficking of women, whereby women are sold by impoverished families to brokers for employment in the sex trade (Sassen: 2000, 504, 516).

Along with migrant domestic workers, Sassen (2000) includes trafficked sex trade workers, mail-order brides, and migrant nurses within a continuum of *alternative global circuits* upon which the survival of households, the earning of profits (i.e., by organized criminal gangs and recruitment agencies), and state collection of foreign exchange are increasingly based. Yeates (2009), on the other hand, focuses on the international migration of nurses, painting a picture of *global nursing care chains* and locating them as part of what she terms *the globalization of care*.

Though she points out that it is difficult to delineate the extent of nurse migration due to a lack of internationally standardized data,

Yeates argues that there has been a growth of global nursing care chains and includes within them a series of countries and institutions under various structures of governance. More specifically, global nursing care chains consist of nurse-employing institutions in countries hosting migrant nurses; nurses who migrate; possible intermediate nursing situations in a third country; nursing training institutions; recruitment companies; and companies dealing with the travel, training, and legal issues of migrant nurses. Governance structures include state immigration services, nursing licensing authorities, and bilateral or international mobility agreements (Yeates: 2009, 75).

The flow of nurse migration reflects global inequalities in power and wealth, with the position of countries in global nursing care chains reflecting their position in the *world system*. Not only do nurses migrate from countries of the *periphery* to countries of the *core*, Yeates (2009, 78) argues there are 'distinct regional processes and divisions of labour' whereby nursing labour moves from weak core countries to strong core countries, and from weak peripheries to strong peripheries. Without making a distinction between permanent and temporary migration, Yeates cites various flows of nursing labour through which countries at the top of nursing care chains are supplied by those lower down. Nurses thus migrate from Canada, the United Kingdom, and Ireland to the United States; nurses migrate from the Philippines, Egypt, Bangladesh, India, and South Africa to states of the Arabian Gulf; nurses migrate from South Africa to the United Kingdom, Australia, and New Zealand; and nurses from Swaziland and Zambia migrate to South Africa (Yeates: 2009, 78, 80). Without providing an explanation but naming the Philippines as an example, Yeates points out that the countries at the bottom of nursing care chains may supply international markets without replenishing stocks through the importation of health workers from other countries. Along with the Philippines state, Yeates identifies the states of Bangladesh, Pakistan, India, Sri Lanka, Thailand, and Indonesia as having created dedicated agencies for the export of nurses (Yeates: 2009, 85).

Global Capitalism in Historical Perspective

As in most studies of globalization, studies of globalizing care economies take economic restructuring and global integration as relatively new phenomena and assume them to be given, rather than attempting to trace the processes leading to economic restructuring and global integration. In contrast to this approach, the *world systems* or *world historical* approach maps expansion and change in world capitalism over the long run, historically tracing the production and reproduction of a minority of countries as the *core* of the *world system*, and a majority of countries as *peripheral* in the world system. Such an approach is useful to move beyond descriptions of the direction of global flows of caring labour (i.e., from periphery to core, weak peripheries to strong peripheries, and so on), the reason for which is fairly obvious: relatively higher wages, working conditions, and standards of living. Additionally, the world historical approach allows for the reconstruction of key *processes* giving rise to the global integration of nursing labour markets, the heart of the primary research question posed in this study. Given all this, as well as the fact that world systems categories tend to be used in abbreviation – without elaboration of underlying historical processes – by those examining globalizing care and other economies, the world historical approach is elaborated on below.

Drawing upon discussions of imperialism and colonialism in Africa and Latin America in the 1960s, as well as upon Fernand Braudel's conceptualization of *la longue durée*, Terence Hopkins and Immanuel Wallerstein conceived of the notion of *historical capitalism* to begin understanding long-term, large-scale, global social change. Hopkins and Wallerstein proposed the task of identifying continuities and breaks in time, beginning circa 1492 – the moment that Europeans arrived in the Americas – an event which they argue led to a series of processes that created the world economy as we know it today (Hopkins and Wallerstein: 1982). Various forms and flows of migration are an element of this series of processes (Hopkins and Wallerstein: 1982; Kardulius and Hall: 2007; Sassen: 1988).

For Braudel, *la longue durée* is a means to understand *social time*, which is of particular interest in the disciplines of economic history and historical sociology. Contrasting with the study of *social time* is the study of *ebbs and flows* in economics and the study of *historical time* in the discipline of history. While *social time* involves the tracing of '*les conjonctures*' – rhythms of life and growth of science, technology, institutions, and concepts – the study of *ebbs and flows* typically involves the far narrower tracing of cycles of economic boom and bust, while the study of *historical time* involves detailing from archival records what Braudel calls 'explosive' events occurring within the shorter time span (Braudel: 1980, 27, 31).

Braudel delineates three layers of *social time*: *the anti-market, the market*, and *material life*. Rather than identifiable sites in lived realities, these layers are conceptual categories that facilitate analysis. The conceptual layer of *the anti-market* is defined by what Braudel terms *monopolistic relations*: relations of states possessing monopolies over the means of violence, and those of capitalists possessing monopolies of capital. The layer of *the market* is defined by relations of supply and demand, thus smaller-scale social relations in which competition is more or less perfect, as in the idyllic vision of neoclassical economics. The layer of *material life* consists of all other social relations of production and exchange.

Taking only Braudel's layer of the anti-market – the layer of relations of states possessing monopolies over the means of violence, and of capitalists possessing monopolies of capital – Giovanni Arrighi identifies four *systemic cycles of accumulation*, beginning circa 1450, within what he calls 'historical capitalism as a world system' (Arrighi: 1994, 6).

Following from Hopkins and Wallerstein, Arrighi defines capitalism as a historical process which began unfolding in the fifteenth century. For Arrighi, the first-time fusion of the state and capitalist elements such as money-changers, merchants, brokers, and wholesalers marked the beginning of *historical capitalism*. While Arrighi concedes that capitalist elements had existed in Eurasian and other trading systems prior to the fifteenth century, he underlines that it was only in Europe that they came together with states. This powerful fusion propelled European states into the territorial conquest of the world, leading to the development of the *capitalist world economy* (1994: 11).

Arrighi's four systemic cycles of accumulation are the first (Genoese) cycle circa 1450–1640; the second (Dutch) cycle circa 1640–1790; the third (British) cycle circa 1790–1925; and the fourth (U.S.) cycle circa 1925 and continuing to the present. Each systemic cycle of accumulation consists of a phase of *material expansion* followed by a phase of *financial expansion* (see figure 1.1). The phase of material expansion is one of continuous change, whereby the capitalist world economy grows steadily along a well-defined path. During this phase, the activity of capitalists tends to be in productive sectors, as aggregate demand and profit rates increase steadily and investment follows in pace. A phase of financial expansion is one of discontinuous change, whereby the established path of economic development has reached its limits,

Figure 1.1: Systemic Cycles of Accumulation*

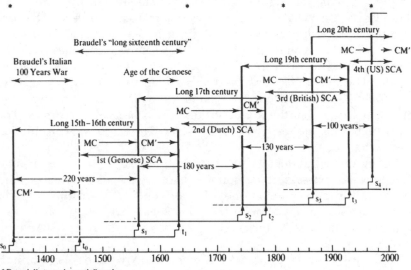

*Systemic cycles of accumulation (SCA), with arrows marking material expansions (MC) and financial expansions (CM).
Source: Arrighi (1994, 364).

and the world economy shifts onto another path via radical restructuring and reorganization. During the latter phase – given the ongoing nature of the pursuit of profit – the largest of capitalists tend to invest in speculative activity because demand and rates of profit in the productive sectors in which they have typically invested shift to a downward curve.

The central agents in Arrighi's formulation, then, are states and capitalists. For each systemic cycle of accumulation and each phase of expansion within them, Arrighi traces economic, political, and military relations between what are now conceived of as *Western Europe*, and by extension, North America, and the *global South*. Arrighi argues that these relations are key in the establishment, by the twentieth century, of a stratified world economy composed of a small number of wealthy states (*the core of the world system*) and a large majority of impoverished states (*the periphery of the world system*).[5] The layers of economic and military relations over multiple centuries connote, in the world historical approach, that all of these states figure into a *single whole*, both in abstract and concrete terms.

Within this structural framework for the understanding of *historical capitalism*, Philip McMichael (1990) offers the *incorporated comparison* as a tool of analysis. Through the incorporated comparison, *instances* of world processes may be studied to arrive at a fuller understanding of the whole. McMichael makes clear that the incorporated comparison differs from the methodology of Wallerstein, often labelled functionalist or teleological in that it takes as a precept that the whole determines the parts, or that the location of a country (i.e., core or periphery) in the world system defines its role and fate in the world economy. McMichael contrasts the incorporated comparison with Wallerstein's *encompassing comparison* in order to explain his tool of analysis:

> Rather than using 'encompassing comparison' – a strategy that presumes a 'whole' that governs its 'parts' – it progressively *constructs* a whole as methodological procedure by giving context to historical phenomena. In effect, the 'whole' emerges via comparative analysis of 'parts' as moments in a self-forming whole. I call this *incorporated comparison*. (McMichael: 1990, 386; emphasis in the original)

McMichael uses the term *parts* while Hopkins (1979) uses the term *instances*; these two are synonymous. Both bring into question the concept of *cases* in modern social scientific inquiry, a concept which is employed in most studies of globalization, hence the frequent listing of *factors* leading to a globalizing outcome. Encapsulated in the notion of *cases* are a series of assumptions: that there is an ensemble of cases or units of observation; that the same set of properties can be used to understand each of the cases or units; that each case contains a certain degree of each property which may be measured qualitatively or quantitatively; and that while each unit may be compared, given that they are individual units, their processes are generally not interrelated.

The conceptualization of *parts within a whole*, or of *instances of world historical processes*, begins from an opposite set of assumptions. Instances chosen for study must be justified both historically and logically within periodizations and categories of world historical analysis. Each instance is assumed to be different, and its precise unfolding can be historically specified in relation to other instances within processes of world systemic scale.

Taking the topic of international trade as an example, in standard social science, two countries (cases) become interrelated through the exchange of goods and services. Prior to this, economic processes of each country (case) are assumed to function completely separately. In world historical inquiry, two or more instances (countries, which themselves are an ensemble of spatio-temporal relations) are assumed to be interrelated from the onset of the inquiry (given historical capitalism), and specific forms of the unfolding of world processes shape the pattern of trade between the countries under study.

Translating world historical method into Marxian terminology, instances or countries, as expressed above, are the *object* of inquiry and a form of *abstraction*. The *object*, as Marx discusses in *Grundrisse*, is one-sided until it is placed within the context of the whole. Only then can the abstraction be seen in its multi-dimensions (1973: 105–7). Marx lays out five consecutive layers of analysis – including migration – required to understand what he calls *the capitalist mode of production* – the ensemble of which, it may be argued from Marx's perspective, amounts to the whole:

> The order obviously has to be (1) the general, abstract determinants which obtain in more or less all forms of society . . . (2) The categories which make up the inner structure of bourgeois society and on which the fundamental classes rest. Capital, wage labour, landed property. Their inter-relation. Town and country. The three great social classes. Exchange between them. Circulation. Credit system (private). (3) Concentration of bourgeois society in the form of the state. Viewed in relation to itself. The 'unproductive' classes. Taxes. State debt. Public credit. The population. The colonies. Emigration. (4) The international relation of production. International division of labour. International exchange. Export and import. Rate of exchange. (5) The world market and crisis. (Marx: 1973, 108)

Marx's method of *historical materialism* is not unlike the world historical approach elaborated here; each inquiry begins with a broad notion of world capitalist processes (Braudel's *anti-market*) which are then historicized through social agents. However, a major rift between Marx's historical materialism and the world historical method is around the conceptual divergences between cases and instances. As cited above, for Marx there are 'general, abstract determinants which obtain in more of less all forms of society,' while in world historical method each instance or part is assumed to be different, given particular spatio-temporalities within the unfolding of the whole. Marx's approach must itself be placed in historical context: both a critic and a part of eighteenth- and nineteenth-century debates of classical political economy, Marx was functioning within a Eurocentric language and world view which sub-consciously modelled all societies on the self-perceptions of Western Europe.

Apart from this shortcoming, many of Marx's categories are useful for world historical inquiry. Tracing the underpinnings of the *Grundrisse* through three cycles of analysis arguably presented by Marx, key sets of social relations and agents may be identified: *capital* as key social agent, *capital* and *labour* as co-determined, and *labour* as key agent. One significant social agent recognized by Marx but analysed more explicitly in world historical method is *the state*. In world historical method, the category of the state is itself traced historically and relationally given that the *interstate system* developed in conjunction with the de-velopment of the capitalist world economy.

Coloniality is a defining feature of the *interstate system,* whereby emerging states became linked through a hierarchy in which the lower rungs consisted of formal colonies (Quijano and Wallerstein: 1992, 550). As formal colonization ended and states became politically inde-pendent, coloniality has persisted in the interstate system as a socio-cultural hierarchy of *European* and *non-European* states. *Ethnicity* and/ or *race* – social constructions and ever-malleable – emerged as 'building blocks' of the capitalist world economy, delineating social boundar-ies connected to the division of labour (Quijano and Wallerstein: 1992, 551). The justification of multiple forms of labour control in relation to ethnicity for the interrelated purposes of production, world trade, and capitalist accumulation occurred first in the Americas, and later elsewhere in other, sometimes similar forms. *Black Africans* were thus constructed as slaves, *Native Americans* as various forms of coerced cash-crop labour (for example, repartimiento, mita, peonage), and *Eu-ropeans* as wage labour. On a global scale, then, the state is an agent within the interstate system, while on a national scale, the state is a site of agency contested by various social groupings combining class, eth-nicity, and other constructed traits.

Thesis of the Study

Using the structural formulation of *historical capitalism* presented by Giovanni Arrighi (1994) in *The Long Twentieth Century*, the thesis of this study is that historically rooted contradictions in the material expansion of the fourth (U.S.) systemic cycle of accumulation led to (re) intensified exploitation of female caring labour. One element of this reintensification is the global integration of nursing labour markets, which is conceived as part of the radical restructuring and reorganization of the financial expansion of Arrighi's fourth (U.S.) systemic cycle of accumulation.

Stated in concrete terms, the increased circulation of temporary migrant nurses around the world was put in motion by monopoly driven hospital cost escalation, the restructuring of nursing work, persistent undervaluing of nursing labour, and concerted state efforts to produce nursing labour for export. Working with categories and concepts elaborated in the previous section, these structural forces are historically reconstructed through three spatio-temporal instances, using the incorporated comparison. Reconstructing processes of the United States, Canada, and the Philippines, it is argued that processes unfolding in these national spaces were of world systemic consequence in setting in motion the global integration of nursing labour markets. The worldwide context of the dismantling of trade unions as a political force, from the 1980s onward, is shown to be interrelated with increased employer demand for temporary migrant nursing labour – a theoretical link not made thus far in studies of late twentieth-century health labour migration.

Processes of the Philippines, United States, and Canada are drawn out as particularly important, given that the Philippines was the first country to make a steady supply of temporary migrant nurses available, and that the United States and Canada were the first states of the global North to begin importing temporary migrant nurses in relatively large numbers (circa 1990). Following from these processes, given a tight world supply of nurses, the increased use, circulation, and production of temporary migrant nurses began to unfold on an international scale, a global process which is still emerging.[6]

This is not to suggest that the use of temporary migrant nursing labour in United States and Canada has been consistently on the rise from the early 1990s. As will be demonstrated, the use of relatively large numbers of temporary migrant nurses in both countries has occurred in waves from the late 1980s on, for various reasons. Nevertheless, it is these two countries of the global North which first adopted the practice of importing relatively large numbers of internationally trained nurses as temporary migrant nurses rather than as permanent residents, a practice which was then taken up by the United Kingdom and various other countries of the global North, leading to an upward shift in world demand for temporary migrant nursing labour.[7]

Evidence in this study is drawn from a combination of primary and secondary sources: government and inter-governmental policy documents, official statistical data, interviews with government and trade union officials, trade union pamphlets, trade journals, health industry-commissioned reports, and academic studies. The use of different types of evidence is necessary here due to the tensions arising from discussing the global integration of nursing labour markets, a process in its early stages of formation, and the imperfect nature of statistical data available on international labour migration.

Outline of the Book

As the country of the global North (core) that imports the most significant number of internationally trained nurses, the post–Second World War hospital market of the United States is the first spatio-temporal instance examined, in chapter 3. It is argued that, by the early 1990s, internationally trained nurses entering on temporary work authorizations became viewed by U.S. employers as a strategic new source of nursing labour. This is demonstrated to be part of an attempt on the part of U.S. hospitals to respond to escalating costs. The growth of various sectors of capitalists, employers, and organized labour within the U.S. health care market are mapped and related policy discussions are examined. The monopoly structure of medical technology production is identified as the driving force behind the escalation of costs in U.S.American hospitals, rather than labour costs, as is often assumed.[8] The development of this monopoly structure, as well as the monopoly structure of the pharmaceutical industry, are seen as contradictions of the material expansion of the fourth systemic cycle of accumulation leading to the restructuring of nursing labour in the U.S.

The post–Second World War health care system in Canada is the second spatio-temporal instance examined, in chapter 4. Though it is a country built on the *permanent migration* of internationally trained workers, including considerable numbers of nurses, Canada began importing temporary migrant nurses in the late 1980s. Canada is also a source country of temporary migrant nursing labour, particularly to the United States. The Canadian instance provides a measure of contrast to that of the U.S. due to its post-1960 history of public, rather than private, health care insurance and delivery. Through an examination of the labour process in Canadian hospitals – the primary location of medical service delivery – it is argued that undervalued nursing labour has formed the fundamental basis of universal public health care in Canada, and that the increased supply and demand of temporary migrant nursing labour is one of several developments arising from this contradiction. That a public health care delivery system, one of the foundations of the welfare state, could be built on such a contradiction is viewed as another inherently limiting element of the material expansion of the fourth (U.S.) systemic cycle of accumulation of the capitalist world economy.

As the largest exporter of temporary migrant nurses worldwide, the Philippines is the third spatio-temporal instance examined, in chapter 5. The building of a state architecture and practices facilitating the exportation of health care and other labour are traced within the restructuring of Philippine labour legislation, circa 1970. It is demonstrated that the Philippine state set a trend whereby peripheral states, international financial institutions, and other elites began conceiving of labour exportation – and the accompanying remittances – as a new path of development to pursue in the global South and what was formerly communist Europe. The historically entrenched structure of the Philippine state is argued to be at the root of both the collapse of domestically oriented capitalist development in the Philippines, and state dependency on foreign exchange generated through the export of labour. The inability of the Philippines to shift from export-oriented capitalist development to domestically oriented capitalist development is conceived as another contradiction unfolding in the material expansion of the fourth (U.S.) systemic cycle of accumulation.

As implied in the above synthesis of the three spatio-temporal instances, the period of major concern here spans from the 1950s to the early 2000s. This is the primary span of Arrighi's *fourth* (U.S.) systemic cycle of accumulation, during which the world economy grew through the world historical process of Keynesianism – Arrighi's *material expansion* – reaching its limits circa 1970. This process led to a phase of radical restructuring, or financial expansion. The birth of *health care* as it is known today, including state health care programs and the rise of medical technology, is reconstructed in this study as part of the material expansion of the fourth (U.S.) systemic cycle of accumulation, as is the development path of the Philippines, from about 1950 to 1960.

The 1970s restructuring of Philippine labour legislation, the 1970s health care expenditure crisis in the United States, the late-1980s restructuring of nursing work in the United States, and the withdrawal of Canadian nursing labour from the Canadian health care system – are all traced as outcomes of contradictions percolating between 1950 and 1970, during the material expansion of the fourth (U.S.) systemic cycle of accumulation. In turn, the emerging global integration of nursing labour markets, based on temporary migration, is traced as part of the post-1970 radical restructuring and reorganization of the financial expansion of the fourth (U.S.) systemic cycle of accumulation. Each instance, then, serves as a double-specification: concurrently revealing of both the parts and the whole.

In chapter 6, a preliminary response is provided for the second major research question posed in this study: *How can the dynamics of the global integration of caring labour markets be interpreted with regard to restructuring in the capitalist world economy?* Taking a methodological step back, insights from the global integration of nursing labour markets are drawn out with regard to the longer history of the capitalist world economy, including the radical restructuring which is currently unfolding. *Absolute* and *deepening unequal exchange,* new categories within Arghiri Emmanuel's (1972) theory of *unequal exchange,* are proposed as a conceptual means of delineating the social costs and production losses incurred through the export of caring labour. It is tentatively proposed that *world-stratified production and distribution of caring labour* is a *budding tendency* in the restructuring of world capitalism, given the global integration of nursing labour markets, the global integration of domestic labour markets, and the historically under-recognized role of unpaid female labour in capitalist production.

What follows in the next chapter is an elaboration of the central new concept proposed in this study: *the global integration of labour markets.* It is argued that *temporary labour migration* is the key policy instrument employed by both labour-importing and labour-exporting states in envisioning and shaping the global integration of labour markets. Temporary labour migration is traced as a more recent element of the post-1970 shift in which employers and states moved to weaken the social and political role of trade unions internationally. This analysis is followed by a presentation of the available, macro-level evidence allowing for the identification of nursing labour markets as an early instance of global integration. Statistical evidence is drawn, primarily, from documents of the Organisation for Economic Co-operation and Development, which have not previously received analytical attention in health labour migration literature.

2 Temporary Migration and the Global Integration of Labour Markets

Policy Shift: From Permanent Residency to Temporary Labour Migration

Temporary labour migration is the phenomenon of workers migrating on the basis of temporary work authorizations, which attach the legal status of workers to particular employers or/and particular positions of employment. Temporary labour migration schemes take on various forms: from bilateral and regional agreements for the exchange of labour between states, to changes in national legislation allowing employers easy and accelerated access to temporary migrant workers for varying time periods, to provisions in multilateral trade agreements such as Mode IV of the World Trade Organization's General Agreement on Trade in Services.

Given that the legal status of temporary migrant workers is bound to employers and the sanction of deportation contained within, protection of the rights of temporary migrant workers is at best unclear, and at worst non-existent. That workers' temporary legal status is bound to their employers translates into an inordinate degree of power in the employer's hands within the generally uneven power relationship between individual workers and employers. Due to temporary migrant workers' particular need to remain employed – to maintain legal status within the country of employment, to transfer remittances home, and to pay recruitment agency fees, which tend to be necessary to obtain employment away from home countries – employers may control to their advantage the terms of migrant workers' employment in ways they cannot vis-à-vis workers with permanent resident or citizen status in the country of employment.

Temporary labour migration on the basis of temporary work authorizations, or work permits, contrasts with *permanent migration* and the accompanying legal status of *permanent residency*.[1] In countries such as Canada, Australia, the United States, and Britain, permanent residency involves the right for all internationally trained workers to settle, including full legal protections, the right to live and work in the location of one's choice, the right to change employers, the right to family re-unification, and a path to citizenship and voting rights. In that internationally trained workers entering countries as permanent residents are entitled to virtually the same social, economic, and political rights as those already possessing citizenship, they become part of national labour markets. Temporary migrant workers, on the other hand, earn wages in countries of employment while transferring a significant proportion of these wages to family members in their home countries. As such, temporary migrant workers constitute the integrating links between labour markets of home and destination countries without enjoying full benefits in any of them.

In its 2007 publication, *Gaining from Migration: Towards a New Mobility System* (written by Dayton-Johnson et al.), the Organisation for Economic Co-operation and Development (OECD) – official think tank of the richest nations in the world economy – elaborates on a 'new mobility system' in which temporary migration is the central policy instrument:

> . . . within the new system, governments will make most decisions about permanent immigration after admission, thus using the early stages of work visas as *probationary periods. Temporary workers who demonstrate their ability to remain in the labour market, to abide by all rules,* to learn the national language at functional levels and to meet other reasonable requirements *can graduate into permanent status.* (Dayton-Johnson et al.: 2007, 25; emphasis added)

Though the OECD authors indicate that governments will be the decision-makers around 'permanent immigration,' the mechanics of the 'new system' imply that decisions to retain internationally trained workers would necessarily depend on evaluations by employers. More specifically, temporary work visas for limited periods of employment would serve as 'probationary periods' in which internationally trained workers are tested for their abilities to integrate in state-defined terms, as well as their abilities to remain employed (Dayton-Johnson et al.: 2007, 25).

Language in the 2007 budget of the Canadian government reflects the same vision; it rationalizes a $33.6 million budgetary allocation for the establishment of a new immigration program based on temporary labour migration as a path to permanent residency.[2] Additionally, the Canadian Experience Class, which came into effect in August 2008, quietly introduced first-time measures involving a strong role for employers in the selection of candidates for permanent residency:

> To ensure that Canada retains the best and brightest with the talents, skills and knowledge to meet rapidly evolving labour market demands, the Government will introduce a new avenue to immigration by permitting, *under certain conditions*, foreign students with a Canadian credential and skilled work experience, and skilled temporary foreign workers who are already in Canada, to apply for permanent residence without leaving the country. Recent international graduates from Canadian post-secondary institutions with experience and temporary foreign workers *with significant skilled work experience have shown that they can succeed in Canada* [sic], that they have overcome many of the traditional barriers to integration, and that they *have formed attachments to their* communities and *jobs*. (Department of Finance Canada: 2007, 218; emphasis added)

Given that, for the past fifty years, internationally trained workers with skills needed in the global North have entered several northern countries as permanent residents from the onset, the new approach exemplified in these policy pronouncements is a significant shift.[3] The OECD authors would not dispute such a claim. As they point out, the proposed system is 'no less ambitious than revising the social compact' (Dayton-Johnson et al.: 2007, 31).

Official policy statements of the second, intergovernmental Global Forum on Migration and Development (GFMD), held in October 2008, are no less plain in drawing immigration policy in line with imperatives of the market as determined by employers. The GFMD chair, Esteban B. Conejos Jr., Philippines Undersecretary of Foreign Affairs for Migrant Workers' Affairs, specified in his conclusions that bilateral 'labour migration arrangements' between governments, and *circular migration* – essentially, temporary migration programs assuring that migrants return to their countries of origin – are 'good practices' to ensure that 'labour mobility is managed flexibly between countries' (GFMD: 2008, 4). OECD recommendations for the flexible management of labour between countries include allowing employers to recruit migrant workers without testing employer claims of shortages; assigning work permits for limited durations; entry bonds for migrant workers; and lump-sum payment of migrants' pension contributions only upon exit from countries of employment[4] (Valiani: 2007b, 8).

Reflecting on state interests of the countries from which temporary migrants originate, Raj-Hashim (1994) and Heyzer (1994) stress that temporary labour migration policies embody a range of state goals, reaching far beyond that of relieving domestic unemployment and underemployment. More specifically, given the post-1980 situation of low commodity prices, rising foreign debt, and falling economic growth rates, these policies reflect 'sending' state efforts to raise foreign exchange through remittances of temporary migrant workers, and efforts to increase per capita national income through expanded savings and investment (Heyzer: 1994, xv; Raj-Hashim: 1994, 119).

This completes the picture in terms of revealing the confluence of state interests underlying the global shift to temporary migration policies. While the prime concern for labour-importing states is the flow of labour to fill market demand in the most flexible, least costly manner possible, the prime interest for labour-exporting states is the flow of remittances, which is at its fullest when workers migrate on a temporary basis, unaccompanied by family members. Lending weight to the connection between increasing remittances and temporary labour migration is the comparison of remittance flows before and after the 1990s, when temporary labour migration schemes became widespread. According to estimations by the International Fund for Agricultural Development (IFAD) – an agency of the United Nations – U.S. $300 billion were remitted in 2006 by migrant workers to their home countries (see figure 2.1, below) in Asia, Africa, Latin America, and Eastern and Central Europe (IFAD: 2007, 2).[5] This is about ten times the U.S. $31 billion remitted to developing countries in 1990, prior to the rise of temporary migration programs. Between 1990 and 2000, remittances to developing countries more than doubled from U.S. $31 billion to U.S. $84 billion (World Bank, as cited by Grabel: 2008, 5).

Temporary Migration and the Global Integration of Labour Markets: The Makings of Global Policy

As noted above by the OECD, the new approach of combining labour mobility with immigration policy as shaped by employers' interests is a matter of revising the social compact (Dayton-Johnson et al.:

Figure 2.1: Worldwide Remittance Flows to Developing Countries in 2006 (millions of USD)

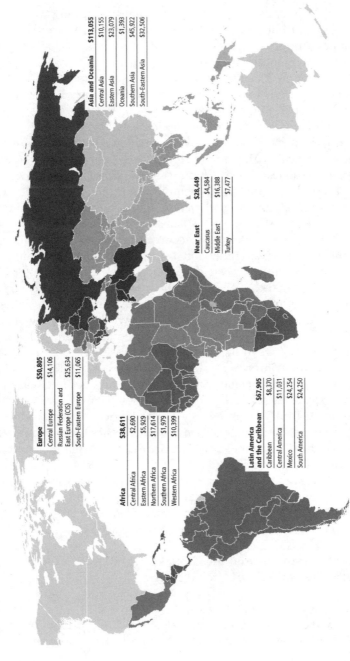

Europe	$50,805
Central Europe	$14,106
Russian Federation and East Europe (CIS)	$25,634
South-Eastern Europe	$11,065

Africa	$38,611
Central Africa	$2,690
Eastern Africa	$5,929
Northern Africa	$17,614
Southern Africa	$1,979
Western Africa	$10,399

Asia and Oceania	$113,055
Central Asia	$10,155
Eastern Asia	$23,079
Oceania	$1,393
Southern Asia	$45,922
South-Eastern Asia	$32,506

Near East	$28,449
Caucasus	$4,584
Middle East	$16,388
Turkey	$7,477

Latin America and the Caribbean	$67,905
Caribbean	$8,370
Central America	$11,031
Mexico	$24,254
South America	$24,250

Source: International Fund for Agricultural Development (2007, 3).

2007, 31). This statement bears underscoring. In order to fully grasp its meaning, what is required is a reconstruction of the origins of the social compact to which the OECD refers, and the social relations to which it gave rise.

Following the Great Depression of the 1930s and in the wake of the Second World War – both of which were outcomes of financial and trade liberalization in the third (British) systemic cycle of accumulation of the capitalist world economy – the Keynesian policy framework was adopted by elites in North America and Western Europe (Arrighi: 1994). Keynesianism, in the mid-1940s, was perceived by core states of the world system as a 'third way' to the laissez-faire capitalism of the nineteenth and early twentieth centuries, and the rising centralized planning of socialist China and the Union of Socialist Soviet Republics (Silver: 2003, 152).

Within the Keynesian framework, states committed to the policy of full employment and the use of fiscal and monetary policies that would help achieve and maintain it. In exchange for a share of increasing profits via gradually rising wages, organized labour was required to allow capitalists to manage production and investment so as to increase productivity and profitability. Capitalists were required to negotiate with workers on a regular basis via collective bargaining with unions. These formed some of the key social and political premises of the material expansion of Arrighi's fourth (U.S.) systemic cycle of accumulation of the capitalist world economy.

It is within this world historical context that the International Labour Organisation Conventions 87 and 98 – Freedom of Association and Protection of the Right to Organize, and Right to Organize and Collective Bargaining – were ratified by representatives of states, unions, and employers in the late 1940s. Along the same lines, capitalists and national federations of unions in countries of the global North were invited to engage in 'tripartite' policy-making at the national level through what Marxian political economist Leo Panitch (1981) calls 'corporatist structures of the bourgeois democratic state.'

During the 1950s and 1960s, there were varying degrees of success in achieving the Keynesian vision of full employment, based on cooperation among unions, capitalists, and states, in countries of North America and Western Europe. The common thread running through all of these national spheres was the constant tension between workers and capitalists over the *distribution* of rising profits.[6] The primary vehicle for trade unions to express the interests of workers was through wage pressure, using both industrial action (i.e., strikes) and their role in corporatist structures to help shape the determination of income policy (Panitch: 1981, 30–4).

By the 1970s, successful wage pressure by unions, along with other forces, led to inflation and unemployment, which in turn fuelled more labour militancy (Panitch: 1981, 36). Nominal wages continued to rise rapidly, though inflation eroded gains in real wages throughout the decade (Goldfield: 1987; Moody: 1988; Silver: 2003, 162). Responding to this layering and re-layering of capitalist contradiction, some core states – Britain, Sweden, and West Germany, for example – created new corporatist structures in the mid-1970s, attempting to rein in rank-and-file workers by providing means for decision-making directly at the level of the workplace. These new structures included legislation facilitating unionization in sectors not traditionally organized, collective bargaining at the local level, and legal frameworks for shop-steward, health and safety, and other workers' committees (Panitch: 1981, 37). Similarly, in Canada, legislative frameworks for the regulation of workplace health and safety were erected by the mid-1970s, following wildcat strikes in 1972 by workers of various sectors, beginning with miners in the province of Ontario (Heron: 1996, 149,159).

Much of this was short-lived, as by the end of the 1970s, large capitalists had adopted new investment and production strategies – and, in turn, core states had shifted to a neoliberal policy framework more amenable to the interests of large capital. The neoliberal policy package includes monetarism, balanced budgeting, minimal taxation, deregulation, privatization, liberalized trade and capital flows, and – most relevant here – flexible labour markets. Starting in the early 1980s, workers' rights to collective bargaining, industrial action, workplace decision-making, and even freedom of association came to be respected and enforced to a far lesser degree by capitalists and states of North America and Western Europe. As Silver explains, referring to core states as *metropolitan* states:

> . . . in the 1970s, when faced with . . . demands from capitalists for a restoration of favourable conditions for capital accumulation, metropolitan states attempted not to choose. In response, capital went 'on strike.' An increasingly mobile capital 'voted with its feet,' not only by intensifying and deepening the geographical relocation of productive capital to lower-wage areas but also by accumulating capital in liquid form in proliferating offshore tax havens . . . By the early 1980s, the shopfloor gains of core

labour movements had been largely overturned. Liberal corporatist structures either failed to deliver gains and lost most of their credibility with workers (e.g., as unemployment skyrocketed throughout Western Europe) or collapsed entirely with a shift in government strategy toward outright repression (e.g., with Thatcher's election in Britain). Workers fought to defend the established social contracts . . . The British miners' strike, the U.S. air traffic controllers' strike, and the showdown at Fiat in Italy are among the events contributing to the early 1980s surge of labor unrest reports. These strikes were largely defensive struggles (i.e., resistance to the undermining of established ways of life and existing social contracts) . . . They all met with defeat. (Silver: 2003, 163–4)

From the 1990s onward, there was a growing adoption of temporary labour migration policies. This may be seen as another major thrust in the shift by states to assure to capitalists the restoration of favourable labour market conditions for capital accumulation. All of this is part of the radical restructuring and reorganization of Arrighi's financial expansion of the fourth (U.S.) systemic cycle of accumulation.

To explain this in greater detail: By committing themselves to making labour markets flexible from the early 1980s, core states, followed by other states in the capitalist world economy, did all but formally abandon the Keynesian goal of full employment. In liberalizing labour markets through schemes of temporary migration, states not only provide further advantages to capitalists within the context of severely weakened workers' and trade union rights, they are also putting in process, perhaps even more crucially, *the global integration of labour markets* through the final abandonment of full employment as a social vision. As Panitch underlines in his analysis of the 1960s and 1970s, 'the general trend toward the structural strengthening of the working class' was the 'attenuation of the reserve army of labour' resulting from state commitment to, and the actual achievement of, nearly full employment in much of North America and Western Europe (1981, 30). By the same reasoning, the social and political power of trade unions, which are essentially nationally based, is rendered virtually nil when the *reserve army of labour* in a given country is expanded to potentially include workers from any country of the world.

The Marxian concept of the *reserve army of labour* refers to the pool of unemployed and underemployed workers in a given nation upon which employers may draw to displace existing workers. Employers might do this, for example, in cases where workers have organized and made workplace gains with which employers do not wish to comply. When the pool of this reserve army is broadened beyond national borders, more important than the quantity of workers imported is that employers have the option to draw new labour into a national market, particularly if this labour carries precarious legal status and weak access to rights protections. The ability to draw new labour with precarious migration status from other national markets translates into a downward harmonizing force, as wages and other terms of employment tend to fall in all national labour markets involved. This is likely the reason why the International Labour Organisation began addressing the issue of differential wages and working conditions of migrant workers as early as 1950, long before the generalized rise of temporary migration schemes, with the ratification of Convention 97, Migration for Employment.

The global integration of labour markets is thus the logical extension of the proliferation of temporary migration policies whereby states cooperate with the private sector to manage and coordinate the production, use, and circulation of labour within and across nations – without the participation of unions. Stressing the importance of private sector participation and not making any mention of trade unions, the proposal of the International Migration and Development Initiative[7] – precursor to the Global Forum on Migration and Development, established in 2007 – elaborates on the new labour market vision of states, taking temporary migration as given:

> Evidence shows that existing gaps between the supply and demand for labour are set to increase in coming years, with aging and declining populations in much of the industrialized world, and growing populations in much of the developing world.
>
> A hands-on approach is therefore needed to facilitate the mobility of labour, which until now has not benefited from the same level of liberalisation as capital and goods. A new approach, one which aims to facilitate the matching of labour demand and supply, should address the needs of all types of economic migrants, the skilled and less skilled, in sectors from health care to hotels, restaurants and construction, IT and education on both a temporary and permanent basis. (International Organisation for Migration: 2006, 2)

In further defining the 'hands-on approach' required to facilitate labour mobility, the proposal lists the creation of a globally centralized information source on regional and national migration regulations; 'capacity building' in the formulation of national labour policies and collection of statistics on nationals working abroad; and globally centralized research on 'migration opportunities and practices' (International Organization for Migration: 2006, 2).

At the second Global Forum on Migration and Development (GFMD), held in Manila in October 2008 and attended by delegates of 164 member countries of the United Nations, two working groups were formed with the aim of fostering such global coherence: the 'ad hoc Working Group on Data and Research on Migration and Development' and the 'ad hoc Working Group on Policy and Institutional Coherence' (GFMD: 2008, 5, 6). Some 600 official delegates attended the Forum – including UN Secretary General Ban Ki-moon; UN Secretary General Special Representative for Migration and Development, Peter Sutherland; and Sir John Kaputin, Secretary General of the Africa, Caribbean, and Pacific (ACP) Group of States – and for the first time, the decision was taken to hire a staff support unit to plan the third GFMD (held in Greece in November 2009). These are indications of a growing state commitment to the goal of the global integration of labour markets (Valiani: 2008a, 5).[8] Similarly, the GFMD is a venue for states to negotiate agreements matching labour demand with labour supply. By the close of the first GFMD, held in Brussels in June 2007, thirty-two bilateral agreements and memorandums of understanding had been signed by states for the temporary migration of workers of various skill levels.[9]

Clearly this new vision has far-reaching implications, perhaps most centrally for the array of policies relating to labour-force development: from the structuring of education systems, to the design and funding of skills training, to the recognition of credentials – all typically determined at national or subnational levels. Returning to the OECD language quoted at the beginning of this section, it is this entire package of re-envisioning and restructuring that the OECD authors refer to as the 'ambitious revising of the social contract.'

Nursing Labour Markets: An Early Instance of Global Integration

In a 2006 document entitled *Health Workforce and Migration Study: Preliminary Findings*, the Directorate for Employment, Labour, and Social Affairs Group on Health of the OECD refers to 'the internationalisation of the labour market for health workforce,' qualifying that 'significant barriers remain to such flows across frontiers' (2006, 8). A diagram from the study showing the countries and continents of origin for migrant nurses, their migratory paths, and their countries of destination helps to substantiate the assertion that, in comparison to most other sectors of production, the labour mobility of nurses is relatively high (see figure 2.2). The description of the diagram is worth citing at length:

> The movements of both doctors and nurses can be depicted as a cascade-type model of migration in which the United States appears to be at the bottom of the 'fall' (see Graph 3): it is the only net receiving country vis-à-vis all other OECD countries, with a net gain of 79,000 nurses (difference between OECD nurses in the United States and US-born nurses in other OECD countries) . . . Canada, Australia, and Switzerland are also positioned at the lower end of the cascade as they are net receivers of health professionals from most OECD countries. However, in the case of Canada, the intra OECD net migration is negative for nurses (-6 thousands), reflecting emigration of Canadian nurses to the United States. Migration flows from the 8 EU Eastern European countries (A8) to OECD countries is also illustrated in Graph 3. (Directorate for Employment, Labour, and Social Affairs Group on Health, OECD: 2006, 8)

Bringing out the global nature of the cross-border flow of nursing labour, figure 2.2 shows that nurses migrate from OECD countries as well as from countries in Africa, Latin America, and Asia. Within the global South, there is a hierarchy of nursing labour markets to which workers migrate, each flow giving rise to another. In Latin America, for example, Chile is a receiving country of nurses migrating temporarily from Peru, Ecuador, Cuba, and Argentina (San Martin: 2004). In the Caribbean, Guyanese nurses migrate to work in Jamaica, while Jamaican nurses migrate to work in the Virgin Islands, as well as Western Europe and North America (Connell and Stilwell: 2006).

Figure 2.3 reveals the South-North dimension of nursing labour migration: of the top ten countries of origin of internationally trained nurses working in OECD countries, six are countries of the global South, with the Philippines taking first place. These data also draw out the importance of including formerly communist countries of Europe in the category of periphery when analyzing labour migration from the periphery to the core of the capitalist world-economy. Of the twenty-two total countries of origin for internationally trained nurses working in OECD countries, a combined total of sixteen are countries of the global South and formerly communist Europe.

Figure 2.2: Migratory Routes of Internationally Trained Nurses, Continents and Countries of Origin, circa 2000

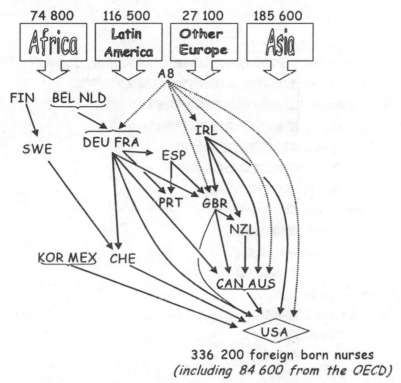

336 200 foreign born nurses
(including 84 600 from the OECD)

Source: OECD Census and Population Register; figure reproduced from Directorate for Employment, Labour, and Social Affairs Group on Health (2006, 8).

Though the study by the Directorate for Employment, Labour, and Social Affairs Group on Health makes little distinction between temporary and permanent migration, it includes figures (see figure 2.4) showing the increasing inflow of internationally trained health workers to OECD countries on the basis of temporary employment authorizations. This is indicative of growing awareness in policy circles of an emerging pattern of temporary migration in medical health labour sectors. From the 1990s, in Canada and Australia – countries built on a foundation of permanent migration – temporary migration of doctors and nurses

Figure 2.3: Internationally Trained Health Workers in OECD Countries by Countries of Origin, circa 2000

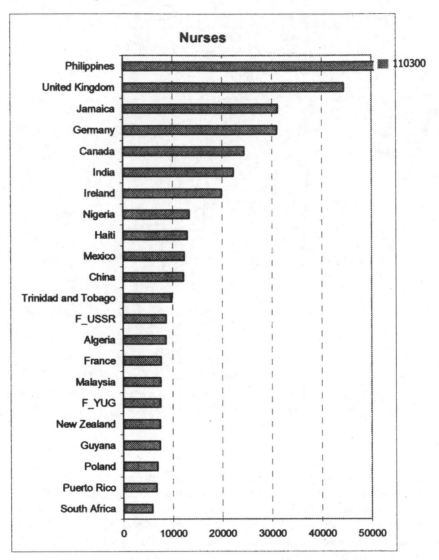

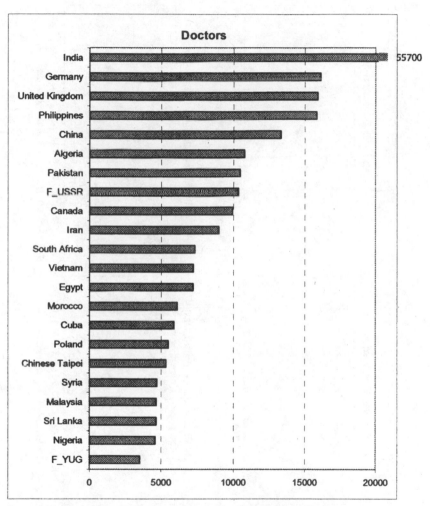

Source: Directorate for Employment, Labour, and Social Affairs Group on Health (2006,11).

Figure 2.4: Inflow of Internationally Trained Nurses and Doctors, Selected OECD countries, 1995–2000

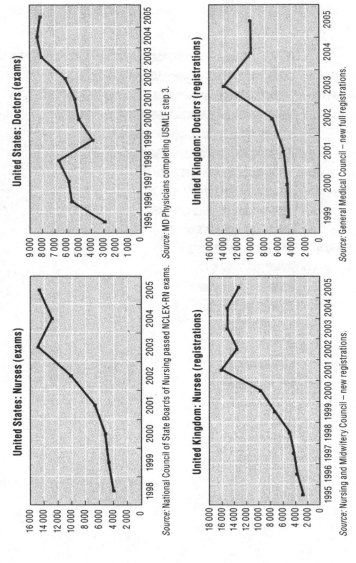

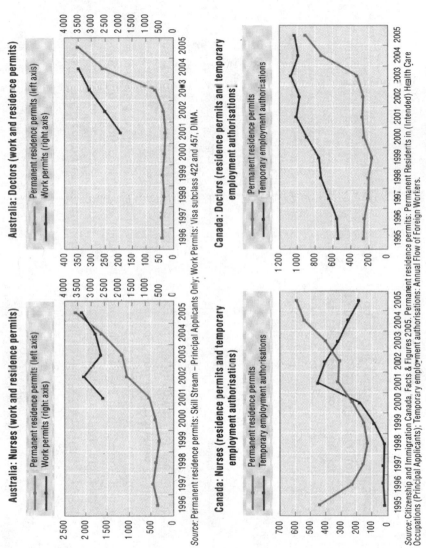

Australia: Nurses (work and residence permits)

Permanent residence permit (left axis)
Work permits (right axis)

Source: Permanent residence permits: Skill Stream – Principal Applicants Only; Work Permits: Visa subclass 422 and 457, DIMA.

Australia: Doctors (work and residence permits)

Permanent residence permits (left axis)
Work permits (right axis)

Canada: Nurses (residence permits and temporary employment authorisations)

Permanent residence permits
Temporary employment authorisations

Canada: Doctors (residence permits and temporary employment authorisations)

Permanent residence permits
Temporary employment authorisations

Source: Citizenship and Immigration Canada. Facts & Figures 2005. Permanent residence permits: Permanent Residents in (Intended) Health Care Occupations (Principal Applicants); Temporary employment authorisations: Annual Flow of Foreign Workers.

Source: Reproduced from Directorate for Employment, Labour, and Social Affairs Group on Health (2006, 15).

Figure 2.4: (*continued*)

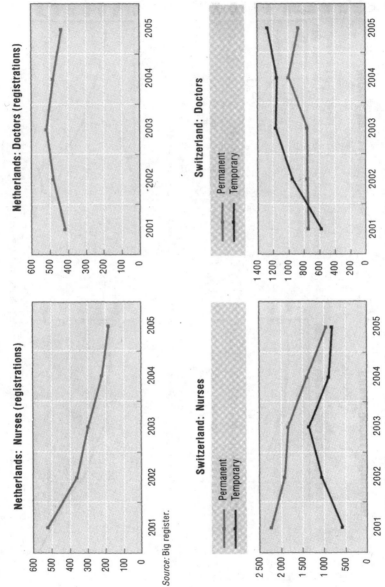

Netherlands: Nurses (registrations)

Netherlands: Doctors (registrations)

Source: Big register.

Switzerland: Nurses

Switzerland: Doctors

Source: Office fédéral des migrations ODM, Registre central des étrangers RCE.
Permanent: Holders of a permit valid for 12 months or more (settlement and residence permits plus short duration permit longer than 12 months).
Temporary: Holders of a short duration permit (valid for less than 12 months).

Figure 2.5: Legal Status of Internationally Trained Doctors in Canada, Permanent Residents and Temporary Migrants Compared, 1995–2005

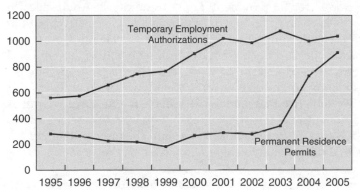

Source: Citizenship and Immigration Canada; figure reproduced from Organisation for Economic Cooperation and Development (2007, 182).

(i.e., on the basis of work permits) has been on the rise, despite a steady demand for doctors and nurses in both countries.

Despite a shortage of doctors, the number of internationally trained doctors entering Canada on temporary employment authorizations relative to that of doctors entering as permanent residents is remarkably high and worth underlining (see figure 2.5). It helps illustrate the nature of control which may be exercised over temporary migrant workers, regardless of skill level. Between 1995 and 2005, internationally trained doctors entered Canada primarily on temporary work authorizations, whereby employers could dictate the location of their employment.[10] Such a term of employment cannot be enforced on doctors with permanent resident or citizen status, given the mobility rights inherent in these legal categories. Temporary migrant doctors have thus been used in Canada to serve in rural and remote areas where domestic doctors, for the most part, do not choose to live and work[11] (Sharma: 2006, 125).

A 2008 study by the Directorate for Employment, Labour, and Social Affairs Health Committee of the OECD offers an explanation for the rise of OECD countries' dependency on internationally trained nurses. In its study, the Health Committee argues that the downswing in health labour-force training in the majority of OECD countries, which it argues occurred from the early 1980s to the early 1990s, led to shortages of health workers by the late 1990s. It was around this time that immigration to most OECD countries 'jumped sharply,' according to the Directorate (Directorate for Employment, Labour and Social Affairs Health Committee: 2008, 8). In order to explain the availability of internationally trained nurses for migration to the OECD, the Health Committee cites 'pull factors,' including 'better pay, professional development and career opportunities or a desire to work in a diverse environment,' as well as 'push factors in the origin country' and migration policies (29).

In a lengthy sentence that somewhat reflects the descriptive, rather than analytical, nature of this style of reasoning, John Connell emulates this methodology of listing factors to explain the rise of demand for 'skilled health workers' in 'developed countries' in the 1990s:

> . . . aging populations, growing demand and ability to pay, inadequate training programs, high attrition rates (for reasons ranging from patient violence to discontent with working conditions, etc.) as jobs in the health sector were seen in many developed countries as too demanding, poorly paid and lowly regarded (in line with reduced public sector funding, and disregard for the public sector). (Connell: 2008, 7)

Using a combination of world historical, Marxian, and socialist feminist analytic tools, the following three chapters offer quite a different set of explanations for international nurse migration in the late twentieth and early twenty-first centuries. Processes of the United States, the only net-receiving country of internationally trained nursing labour in the OECD (see figure 2.2), Canada, a major receiver of internationally trained nursing labour (located directly above the United States in figure 2.2), and the Philippines, the largest world supplier of internationally trained nurses (see figure 2.3) – all are shown to be of world systemic consequence in setting the global integration of nursing labour markets into motion on the basis of temporary migration.

3 The Global Integration of Nursing Labour Markets – The U.S. American Instance

This chapter examines the historical processes leading to the restructuring of the U.S. nursing labour market. The increasing use of temporary migrant nursing labour in the United States is identified as part of this restructuring. The key questions posed are: *What led to the restructuring of the U.S. nursing labour market? How did this restructuring occur? And which key social agents were involved?* It is argued that, although they are seemingly unrelated, the rising use of medical technology in hospitals starting in the 1940s led to ever-increasing hospital costs through to the 1980s. This, in turn, led to the decision by hospital administrators, circa 1990, to reduce hospital costs via the restructuring of nursing work. Labour market changes are traced as part of the contradictory outcomes of monopoly capital, of which the medical device and diagnostics industry is demonstrated to be one instance.

The analysis is divided into five sections. The first section presents Marxian and world historical approaches to global economic restructuring in the twentieth century, laying bare the theoretical framework for this chapter. The second section provides a sketch of the key historical developments in the post–Second World War U.S. hospital market, an element of the material expansion of Arrighi's fourth (U.S.) systemic cycle of accumulation of the capitalist world economy. This is followed by an overview of the health expenditure issues discussed by leading policy analysts through the 1970s and 1980s. The fourth section reveals that though not identified by policy analysts, one of the principal causes of U.S. hospital cost escalation was and continues to be the monopoly structure of medical technology production.

The final section traces the response of U.S. hospitals to continuing cost escalation in the 1990s. It is argued that, given the political impossibility of restraining hospital cost escalation inherent in the monopoly structure of medical technology production, hospital labour was restructured. This took shape in the reorganization of nursing work, including the increased use of temporary migrant nursing labour.

Analysing Global Restructuring: Marxian and World Historical Theoretical Tools

Beginning in the 1970s, long before the birth of the *globalization debate* and the coining of the term *neoliberalism*, Marxian economists and critical political economists postulated a structural change in the world economy. The varying explanations of structural change in the twentieth-century world economy offer the analytical scope required to begin understanding many of the changes associated with *globalization* and *neoliberalism*, including those related to workers' rights and labour migration. The key questions posed by these analysts are: *What is happening in the world economy? Why and how? Which key social agents are involved?*

Marxian economists identify structural change in the world economy through an analysis of profit rates over a thirty-to fifty-year time period, generalizing from the data of one or more core countries – or what they call *advanced capitalist economies*. Anwar Shaikh (1999), for example, identifies a secular fall in the profitability of U.S. American, Japanese, and German manufacturing from 1948 to 1982, due to a fall in the output/capital ratio – the effects of which surfaced globally during the 1970s and 1980s in the form of rising unemployment, inflation, business failures, and bankruptcies. Brenner (1998) cites 'unplanned for, unforeseen price competition' of Japanese and German manufacturers as the cause of a fall in U.S. manufacturing profitability between 1965 and 1973. The fall in one sector, according to Brenner, triggered a general fall in the profit rates of all advanced capitalist economies, leading to global economic decline.

Giovanni Arrighi (1994) offers a far more comprehensive explanation of shifting world capitalism by building on the thesis of *accumulation crisis*, or a crisis in profitability circa 1970, but identifying it as only one element of a structural change which continues to unfold today. In his seminal work, *The Long Twentieth Century*, Arrighi defines a *signal crisis* of economic, political, and military dimensions in the fourth (U.S.) systemic cycle of accumulation. As the latter term implies, Arrighi's notion of crisis is a systemic one, and is in turn defined from the point of view of the leading capitalist state, often referred to as the *U.S. hegemon* in the world historical approach.

In its economic dimension, the crisis involves the U.S. state's loss of control of world production and financial flows to U.S. American and Western European capital. This loss of control surfaced between 1968 and 1973, when currency markets in Western Europe saw a sudden, large increase in U.S.-dollar-based transactions, leading to the abandonment of the gold-dollar standard followed by the breakdown of the Bretton Woods system as a whole (Arrighi: 1994, 299). By the mid-1970s, the total value of monetary transactions carried out in offshore markets – that is, outside of the United States of America and therefore beyond the jurisdiction of U.S. law – amounted to several times the total value of world trade transactions. This swelling of financial transactions relative to trade transactions continued into the 1980s, such that by 1984 foreign exchange trading – once again, beyond the control of any state power – amounted to U.S. $35 trillion while total world trade amounted to a mere U.S. $1.8 trillion (Gilpin: 1987, 144; Arrighi: 1994, 299).

Arrighi attributes the massive accumulation of capital underlying the increase in financial transactions to the intensified investment and profitability of large capitals, predominantly via American and Western European corporations, in the 1950s and 1960s – the height of the material expansion within the fourth systemic (U.S.) cycle of accumulation. Clearly, this massive accumulation of capital could not continue indefinitely. Arrighi cites the outpacing of gains in labour productivity by rising real wages in North America and Europe, combined with 'strong upward pressure on the purchase price of primary inputs,' as the reasons for 'a major contraction in returns to capital' beginning in 1973 (Arrighi: 1994, 304).

As in the previous three systemic cycles of accumulation of the capitalist world economy, Arrighi identifies a full-blown shift of large capitals from investment in productive economic activity (i.e., material expansion) to investment in speculative activity (i.e., financial expansion) starting at the end of the 1970s. By this time, the contraction in profits became recognized by capitalists as a trend, leading to the continued ballooning of foreign exchange trading relative to trade transactions as detailed above.

Stated more figuratively, Arrighi's argument is that having paved the way for the rebuilding of Western Europe in its own image following the Second World War, the U.S. hegemon put in motion a dynamic whereby European and U.S. capital ultimately ceded control of the production and circulation of world profits from the U.S. hegemon and other core states. In turn, in an attempt to regain some control, by the early 1980s, the United States of America and other states began adopting policies amenable to the interests of the largest of capitals, marking the beginning of the global wave of neoliberalism. The neoliberal shift, including the adoption of flexible labour policies, is thus part of the radical restructuring and reorganization of the financial expansion of the fourth (U.S.) systemic cycle of accumulation in Arrighi's formulation of historical capitalism.

The restructuring of the U.S. nursing labour market, circa 1990, can be located within this phase of world economic and social reorganization. A historical reconstruction of the major developmental thrusts of the U.S. hospital market prior to 1990 allows for an understanding of the forces that led to the restructuring of nursing labour. The U.S. hospital market is of principal interest given that hospitals have been the principal employers of nursing labour since the 1950s, when medical care came to be delivered primarily in hospitals.

Material Expansion and the U.S. Hospital Market

One expression of Arrighi's material expansion in the fourth (U.S.) systemic cycle of accumulation is the development and spread of new medical technologies in the U.S. health care market, which began circa 1940. The rise of medical technology is part of the commodification of heath care, a social process which is subconsciously overlooked due to the predominance of scientific medicine in current North American conceptualizations of health. The beginnings of health care commodification in the United States of America may be traced back to the first decade of the twentieth century, when the American Medical Association, the American Pharmaceutical Association, the National Association of Retail Druggists, and the American Hospital Association came together to seize the delivery of health care away from women. Prior to the twentieth century, women delivered health care in the domestic sphere using past knowledge, medicinal herbs, and, by the 1860s, concoctions produced by the patent medicine industry (Weiss: 1997, 1–5).

Monopoly power in pharmaceutical production is widely discussed and well documented.[1] The rise and spread of the pharmaceutical industry began in the late nineteenth century during the financial expansion of the third (British) systemic cycle of accumulation. The implications of patented pharmaceutical products on health care costs in the U.S. are also well documented, affecting national health care expenditures as a whole (see figure 3.2, below). Particular to the period of focus in this study, however, and uniquely linked to rising hospital costs, is the rise, spread, and power of the medical device and diagnostics industry. The latter is traced in detail here to reveal the dynamics and impact of an under-examined corporate force in U.S. health care with particular relevance for hospitals and, in turn, hospital labour restructuring.[2]

As part of the deepening commodification of health care, kidney transplant and dialysis therapy – practices which are commonplace today – came into being in the early 1950s, followed by the spread of post-operative recovery rooms and mixed intensive care units in hospitals throughout the 1950s and 1960s. On a similar scale, respiratory therapy, diagnostic radioisotopes, and electroencephalographs spread through the 1960s and early 1970s (Russell: 1979, 41–84). Starting in the mid-1970s open-heart surgery technology was diffused, including electronic monitoring devices, defibrillators, respirators, pump oxygenators, and cardiac catheterization labs (Russell: 1979, 106–10).

Becton Dickinson, Baxter Laboratories, and a handful of other companies were key forces in this process of deepening commodification – not only in creating and patenting new medical technologies, but in reshaping cultural notions to favour their use and spread. For example, Baxter Laboratories notes in its company history that it was through convincing doctors of the safety and effectiveness of its intravenous solutions that intravenous therapy became widely adopted in the 1940s (Baxter: 2009). Established in the 1930s, Baxter was an early innovator in intravenous therapy and blood collection products. The company was the first to introduce commercially available dialysis technology, artificial kidneys, and blood plasma through the 1940s and 1950s. In 1962, Baxter created the first disposable blood oxygenator, the technology which made open-heart surgery possible (Baxter: 2009).

In response to a broad-based social struggle linked to the inability of a large proportion of U.S. Americans to meet the costs of technology-enhanced health care, Medicare and Medicaid were established by the U.S. federal government in 1965. By mid-1958, reflecting the social gain made by trade unions of employer-sponsored health insurance benefits, families in which the principal earner was fully and permanently employed had a 78 per cent probability of having some health insurance coverage. Where the principal family earner was only employed temporarily, however, the probability of a family having health insurance coverage was much lower at 36 per cent. Similarly, if retired, the probability of a person having coverage in 1958 was 43 per cent. For a housewife at the time, the probability was only 32 per cent, and for a person with a disability, the probability was 29 per cent (Anderson, Collette, and Feldman: 1963, 4–6).

The state-administered Medicaid program was thus designed to cover the costs of care for three major groups: low-income, elderly U.S. Americans; persons with long-term disabilities; and low-income children and families. Medicare was designed to cover most of the costs of medical care for the elderly and certain groups of people with disabilities, but in time came to cover the costs of medical equipment and supplies.[3] In 1973, for example, a law was enacted to extend Medicare coverage to hemodialysis, the new treatment for chronic renal failure, with an annual cost of U.S. $40,000 per patient in 1972 terms (Weiss: 1997, 132). Prior to Medicare, the federal government's Hill-Burton Program, established in 1947, provided grants, loans, and loan guarantees to hospitals and health care facilities through formula-directed financing.

Due to what Starr calls 'the politics of accommodation,' public health care programs in the United States were structured from their inception so as not to intervene with health industry interests (Feder: 1977; Starr: 1982, 376). This happened in three principal ways. First, under Medicare, hospitals received payment according to costs as defined by hospitals (i.e., fee-for-service payment) rather than through a state-determined or negotiated schedule of rates (Starr: 1982, 375). Second, through successful lobbying by the hospital industry, the Medicare administration agreed to pay depreciation on hospital assets, and this on an accelerated basis (Starr: 1982, 375).

Third, the federal government avoided assuming direct control of Medicare costs by allowing hospitals and other institutions delivering medical care to choose 'fiscal intermediaries' to provide reimbursements, consulting, and auditing services, thus permitting private insurance firms to administer Medicare (Starr: 1982, 375).

By 1974 – a time of high inflation in the U.S. economy as a whole – health expenditures in the United States had risen to 7.8 per cent of the gross national product (GNP), up from 4.6 per cent of the GNP in 1950 (Zubkoff: 1976, 1; Anderson and Ginsberg: 1986, 654). In the words of Michael Zubkoff, rapporteur of the Health Report to the 1974 White House Summit on Inflation, it had come to be 'generally recognized' that the health sector was 'both a hostage and cause of inflation' (Zubkoff: 1976, 1).

In 1975, despite mandatory economic controls imposed on the health industry in the previous year, health expenditures increased to 8.3 per cent of GNP, rising to 9.4 per cent of GNP by 1980. Of these increases, only some 4 per cent were accounted for by increases in the Consumer Price Index (Willis and Zubkoff: 1976, xiii; Anderson and Ginsberg: 1986, 654). In tandem with this, public expenditures on health care increased by 22 per cent in fiscal 1975, as compared to 12.3 per cent in fiscal 1974 (Willis and Zubkoff: 1976, xiii).

Within U.S. health care expenditures, hospital care constituted the largest relative portion in 1974: approximately 40 per cent (Social Security Bulletin: 1975, as cited by Altman and Eichenholz: 1976, 8). From 1950 to 1965, per capita expenditures on community hospitals rose by 8 per cent annually, almost doubling to 14 per cent annually between 1965 and 1970. Meanwhile, the inflation rate for all other services in the Consumer Price Index increased in the range of 2 per cent to 5.8 per cent annually (Starr: 1982, 384). It follows, then, to ask: What were the factors contributing to hospital cost increases for the period in question, 1950 to 1973?

As Altman and Eichenholz underline, the following key aspects of hospital cost increases may be drawn from the figures in table 3.1:

1. Although significant, wage increase in the post-Medicare period did not account for all of the growth in payroll expenses; much of the increase resulted from increases in the number of hospital employees.
2. Nonpayroll expenses grew more rapidly in the post-Medicare period than did payroll expenses. Price increases of supplies, services, and equipment also did not account for all of that increase. New technology, capital-for-labor substitution, and a higher level of usage contributed to the overall rise. (Altman and Eichenholz: 1976, 14)

How did hospitals cope with such cost increases, which pushed the price of hospital care to grow at a markedly greater rate than the prices of other commodities? Weiss notes, on the basis of U.S. General Accounting Office data, that during the 1980s hospital operating cost increases surpassed the general rate of inflation by 63 per cent (Weiss: 1997, 75). Hospitals increasingly could not cope with these rising costs, resulting in the closure and/or merging of hospitals, and the *centralization of capital* in the hospital sector as a whole.[4] Though Weiss does not

Table 3.1
Factors Contributing to Hospital Costs: Average Annual Percentage Increase

	1950–60	1960–5	1965–7	1967–9	1969–71	1971–3
Total Increase (%)	7.5	6.7	10.3	13.8	14.8	11.5
Increase in wages and price*	3.8	3.5	4.1	8.0	8.2	5.9
Wages	5.2	4.7	4.7	9.9	10.0	6.6
Prices	1.5	1.3	2.9	4.8	5.1	4.9
Changes in services	3.7	3.2	6.2	5.8	6.6	5.6
Labour	3.1	1.7	3.8	2.8	3.7	2.3
Other	4.6	5.6	9.6	9.8	10.3	10.2

*In health care cost accounting of this period, 'wages and prices' were considered the *inflationary components* of health care costs, while items in the category 'changes in services' were considered *real components* of health care costs.
Source: Consumer Price Index, Bureau of Labor Statistics, and Hospital Statistics; table reproduced from Altman and Eichenholz (1976, 15).

make this connection, he and others do provide substantial evidence for it.

For example, while there were five hospital consolidations in 1961, starting in 1973 there were some fifty hospital consolidations annually (Weiss: 1997, 70). By 1980, according to the Multihospital System Survey, non-profit, multihospital systems controlled 57.6 per cent of hospital beds, state and local public hospitals controlled 7.3 per cent, and investor-owned multihospital systems controlled 35.1 per cent of beds (Johnson and diPaolo: 1981, 80; Starr: 1982, 430).

Through the 1980s, 550 community hospitals failed and several hundred merged as a result of escalating costs as well as fiscal crises due to reductions in federal financing (Weiss: 1997, 67). Almost concurrently, between 1978 and 1984, the number of corporate-owned hospitals more than doubled, increasing from 445 to 955 (Lindorff: 1992, 49; Weiss: 1997, 71). By 1981, after several large mergers, close to three-quarters of the beds in investor-owned multihospital systems were operated by three companies: Hospital Corporation of America, Humana, and American Medical International (Starr: 1982, 432).

Through centralization, profitability in health care delivery was maintained. By the mid-1990s, the investor-owned multihospital systems Humana and American Medical Holdings – the latter of which had acquired American Medical International in 1989 – began ranking in the Fortune 500, generating U.S. $137.1 million (1994) and U.S. $176 million (1994), respectively, in after-tax profits (Fortune: 1995). A brief account of the expansion of Humana, one of the three largest investor-owned multihospital systems mentioned above, illustrates the nature of profitability and scale of growth attained by a decreasing number of such systems.

Humana was founded in 1961 when two lawyers opened a nursing home in Louisville. In 1968, with a chain of nursing homes and U.S. $4.8 million in revenues, Humana diversified into purchasing and building hospitals, as the co-founders learned that hospitals earned 'six times as much per patient from Medicare and Medicaid as nursing homes' (Kinkhead: 1980, 68). The company was noted, in a 1980 article in *Fortune*, as one perceiving itself as 'serving not patients but customers . . . wooing them aggressively with newspaper ads, elaborate food, fast service, and Holiday Inn-like private rooms' (Kinkhead: 1980, 68).

Ranking third among investor-owned multihospital systems, in 1978 Humana acquired its competitor, American Medicorp, which was ranked just above Humana in second place at the time. Humana increased savings as well as profits by cutting labour in its newly acquired American Medicorp hospitals and obtaining greater discounts on hospital supplies and medical technology, because of a greater volume of purchases under nationwide contracts (Kinkhead: 1980, 70). By 1980, Humana owned 90 hospitals, was earning U.S. $1.4 billion (1980) in revenues, and had a share value of U.S. $336, having risen from an original share value of U.S. $8 (Kinkhead: 1980, 68).

Policy Talk: Causes of U.S. Health Sector Inflation, 1970s and 1980s

Policy discussion of what was referred to as 'health sector inflation' in the 1970s and 1980s revolved around three principal explanations – most of which continue to be used today – in the U.S. and in other countries (Zubkoff: 1976, 1): first, that third-party health insurance causes increased demand for medical services, leading to rising health expenditures; second, that the payment system for medical care delivery encourages cost growth; and third, an argument arising in the 1980s that the increasing requirement for care of the elderly is a major source of health expenditure increases. Throughout the policy discussions of the 1970s and 1980s, neither the cost of medical technology nor the cost of health care labour were identified as key forces in explanations of health sector inflation.

An elaboration of the first major explanation is contained in the 1974 Health Report to the White House Summit on Inflation, as well as in papers of several experts who participated in the 1974 conference leading up to the Health Report.[5] Public and private health insurance were traced as major forces creating increased demand for medical care, especially care provided in hospitals (Zubkoff: 1976, 2; Russell: 1976; Newhouse: 1976; McMahon and Drake: 1976; Ginsburg: 1976). Individuals were seen as demanding increasing amounts of hospital care because the price they encountered was 'a small fraction of the cost of producing hospital care' (Ginsburg: 1976, 164). To a lesser extent, doctors were argued to be the key force behind increasing demand for hospital services, given the predominance of physician decision-making in determining a patient's need for hospital care (Dunlop and Zubkoff: 1976, 92). In both cases, increasing demand for hospital care was seen to be increasing medical care delivery prices as well as overall health expenditures.

Another major force in health care cost increases, identified as a corollary to third-party health insurance, was the 'fee-for-service' and 'cost-plus reimbursement' payment system for medical care delivery (Zubkoff: 1976, 1; Newhouse: 1976). As stated by Harvard health economist Joseph Newhouse in his paper for the 1974 conference, reflecting a consensus of experts and presented as such in the Health Report to the White House Summit on Inflation: 'continuing the present trend toward full or nearly full insurance coverage in the context of a nearly unregulated fee-for-service delivery system is likely to produce continued inflation in medical care' (Newhouse: 1976, 212).

Continuing with this logic, Newhouse argued that medical care providers, particularly 'the hospital sector,' were in the position to turn 'the terms of trade' in their favour if given full insurance coverage (Newhouse: 1976, 210–11). In turn, rather than resisting medical care price increases, 'intermediaries' – particularly health insurers – simply increased the price of health care insurance (Newhouse: 1976, 214).

Reflecting a hospital perspective, McMahon and Drake outlined various challenges faced by hospitals, stressing the 'value-loaded' nature of language that expressed hospitals as 'growth-oriented' and hospital costs as 'inflationary' (McMahon and Drake: 1976, 132). They raised the problem of increasing costs of new pharmaceutical products and the inadequacy of tools used to compute them into inflation calculations, all of which they claimed led to inflated figures attributed to hospitals (McMahon and Drake: 1976, 132). McMahon and Drake also raised the issue of costs related to care for the elderly. Though constituting only 10 per cent of the total population, McMahon and Drake argued, the elderly represented 20 per cent of hospital admissions at that time, accounting for one-third of total inpatient days (McMahon and Drake: 1976, 133). Over and above all of this, McMahon and Drake stressed that it was increased consumer demand for higher cost, 'style-medical care,' encouraged by greater insurance coverage, 'and not issues of technical productivity or organization of hospital services' that was 'crucial in explaining hospital cost inflation' (McMahon and Drake: 1976, 135).

By the 1980s, medical needs of the elderly were increasingly emphasized as a major force in rising national health expenditures (Mechanic: 1984; Davis: 1986; O'Cleireacain: 1989). Noting that the proportion of GNP devoted to health care had increased from 8 per cent in 1960 to 11 per cent to 1983, public health policy analyst Karen Davis, for example, highlighted that care for the elderly represented one-third of total health care expenditures in 1984 (Davis: 1986, 227, 229). With regard to public health care expenditures in particular, without citing earlier figures for comparison, Davis stated that 40 per cent of Medicaid expenditures in 1981 went to care for 3.5 million elderly people.

Comparisons of hospital costs of the elderly versus those of the young were also increasingly common in the 1980s. Davis argued that in 1981, the average annual per-capita hospital expenditure of persons over the age of 65 was $1,381, compared with $392 for the non-aged (Davis: 1986, 229). Less commonly brought to light were the effects of state-level cost containment programs focused on health care for the elderly. Carol O'Cleireacain, a New York trade union representative of public health workers, argued that the State of New York had been among the first to impose cost controls on hospitals, nursing homes, and home care in the 1980s, leading to increased use of emergency room services by elderly patients who were unable to access medical care elsewhere (O'Cleireacain: 1989, 178).

Finally, also in the 1980s, U.S. employers began uniting around what was identified as the 'runaway cost of employee medical benefits' (Richman: 1983, 95). According to *Fortune* magazine, some 100 business coalitions formed in the early 1980s to investigate 'what goes into the cost of health care' (Richman: 1983, 95). Medical insurance premiums had increased by 20 per cent or more in 1982, argued *Fortune*, and companies had spent some U.S. $67 billion, representing more than one-fifth of the 'total national health bill' (Richman: 1983, 95). One contention espoused by employer groups was that 'at least 25 per cent of all medical care paid for by third parties may be unnecessary' (Richman: 1983, 95).

The two principal policy solutions proposed in health sector inflation discussions of the 1970s and 1980s were to provide cost-restraint incentives to hospitals, doctors, and health insurers; and to increase competition in health service delivery. Beginning in 1983, the prospective payment system for hospitals was introduced under Medicare through which hospitals received fixed per-patient amounts based on a standardized schedule of diagnoses (Anderson and Ginsberg: 1986). The new system, known as the Diagnosis Related Group, was aimed – among other things – at discouraging what were perceived to be unnecessarily lengthy hospital stays and the excessive use of expensive testing by doctors (Davis: 1986, 237). Similarly, health insurers were mandated, in several states, to implement utilization review programs whereby health insurance enrolees and their doctors were evaluated for the appropriateness, efficacy, and efficiency of health services consumed.

The increased use of health maintenance organizations (HMOs) was the primary method, both recommended and implemented, to encourage competition in health service delivery. HMOs were seen as capable of reducing costs through fixed, prepaid health plans offering a range of medical services while minimizing the use of hospitals. Reflecting the enthusiasm around free-market solutions, a 1986 article in *Policy Studies Review* reported that between 1970 and 1984, the number of HMOs in the United States had risen from 29 to 337, with 'more competition expected from private insurers and health care providers' (Anderson and Ginsberg: 1986, 658).

Organizations representing physicians' interests struggled with these reforms, stressing the challenge posed to the autonomy – and ultimately the power – of physicians, as well as the altering of the physician-patient relationship. As summarized by medical sociologist David Mechanic, an active member of the National Academy of Sciences' Institute of Medicine:

> Current efforts to control the escalation of cost often involve modification
> of two basic conditions of the traditional physician-patient relationship.
> First, they often seek to lock in care to a particular category of providers

or to restrict choice to a provider who becomes a gatekeeper to more specialized and expensive services. Second, cost-control efforts modify the definition of the provider's role from sole agent of the patient's welfare to a role of balancing the patient's wants and needs against the aggregate population and a fixed budget. (Mechanic: 1984, 65)

The 1990s: Health Care Cost Escalation Continued

It was not until the 1990s that medical technology was identified as an important source of health care cost escalation, but only by a small minority of analysts in academic journals. The following citation from David Mechanic's article in the trade journal *Health Affairs* reflects the dominant, largely unquestioning view of cost growth caused by medical technology:

> The most profound choices we face in the decades before us are not the management of new and amazing technologies such as Positron Emission Tomography or diagnostic Nuclear Magnetic Resonance Spectrometry, but rather how we manage sickness, disability, and functioning in old age. (Mechanic: 1984, 67)

In contrast, in a 1992 article published in the *Journal of Economic Perspectives*, Joseph Newhouse contended that economists 'need to pay more attention to technological change,' criticizing in part his own earlier focus on health insurance coverage and medical care providers in explaining cost growth (Newhouse: 1992, 5). Similarly, in his *Yale Law Journal* article, physician Paul Kalb discussed the rise of an emerging but weak consensus around the need to control technology in order to control the 'alarming rate' of health care expenditure increases (Kalb: 1990, 1109).

Presenting an analysis of time series data, Newhouse made a methodological critique of health economists' reliance on single-period models taking technology as given (Newhouse: 1992, 5). In considering the forces widely held to be the major reasons for the growth, over time, in real health care expenditure (see table 3.2), Newhouse attributed 'well under half – perhaps under a quarter' of this growth to increasing insurance coverage, increasing income, ageing of the population, and physician-driven demand (1992, 10–11).

In terms of the link between the spread of health insurance coverage and increasing demand for medical services, Newhouse underlined

Table 3.2
Growth in Real Health Care Expenditure and GNP, by Decade (percentage per year)

Period	Growth in real health care dollars, per capita	Growth in real GNP, per capita	Health care share of GNP at end of period
1929–40	1.4%	0.0%	4.0%
1940–50	4.0%	3.1%	4.5%
1950–60	3.6%	1.5%	5.3%
1960–70	6.5%	2.5%	7.3%
1970–80	3.8%	1.7%	9.1%
1980–90	4.4%	1.7%	12.2%

Source: Health Care Financing Review, Office of National Cost Estimates, Economic Report of the President, Statistical Abstract; table reproduced from Newhouse (1992, 4).

that the average coinsurance rate for hospital services was 'essentially constant' at approximately 5 per cent through the 1980s, while 'real hospital expenditure rose over 50 per cent during the decade' (Newhouse: 1992, 7; Levit et al.: 1991). In terms of the impact of the aging U.S. population, Newhouse pointed out that the proportion of elderly people in the total population had increased by only 4 per cent over three decades, rising from 8 per cent in 1950 to 12 per cent in 1987 (Newhouse: 1992, 6). Using 1987 data on medical spending for those over 65 years of age, Newhouse reported that the increased proportion of elderly people could account for an increase of 15 per cent of total health spending from 1950 to 1980, while real per capita health expenditure grew by more than a factor of five over the same period (refer to table 3.2).

With regard to rising income as a major cause of increasing health expenditures, Newhouse looked at a cross-section of U.S. household data (holding health insurance constant) for the years 1940 to 1990. Using an estimate of income elasticity for medical care of 0.2–0.4, Newhouse calculated that income growth accounted for approximately 35 to 70 per cent of increased medical care expenditures, which increased by a total of 780 per cent over the period (Newhouse: 1992, 7).[6]

Tracing the growth in the number of doctors per person from 1930 to 1990, Newhouse demonstrated, by way of 'simple correlation,' that there was little evidence for the argument that doctors bring about

Table 3.3
Growth in Number of Doctors Per Person, by Decade

Year	Percentage Change
1930–40	0.6
1940–50	−0.1
1950–60	−0.1
1960–70	1.1
1970–80	2.4
1980–90	2.0

Source: 'Health United States,' 'Physicians for a Growing
America: Report of the Surgeon General's Consultant';
table reproduced from Newhouse (1992, 9).

considerable health expenditure increases by increasing demand for
medical services to protect their own incomes (see table 3.3). More specifically, he argued that 'the lack of any obvious change in the rate of
expenditure growth after 1970, when physician supply increased, is
striking' (Newhouse: 1992, 8).

Taking these forces together and holding medical technology constant, Newhouse argued that if increased demand from more elderly
people, more health insurance coverage, more per capita income,
and physician-driven need were major causes of rising hospital
expenditures – still the single largest component of U.S. health expenditure in the 1990s – their combined effect should have resulted in increased hospital days. Instead, while hospital admission rates had barely
increased since 1960 and the average length of hospital stays had decreased, real hospital cost per day rose by a factor of four (see table 3.4).

As Newhouse explained, '. . .what is being done to and for people
who are in the hospital is affecting hospital costs, not an increasing
number of people at the hospitals' (Newhouse: 1992, 12). In turn, he
pointed to the 'march of science' – defined as new types of physical
capital and new procedures – as accounting for the bulk of health expenditure increases for the period from 1940 to 1990. By the year 2000,
citing Newhouse's study as well as nine disease-specific studies of
medical technology, the Technical Review Panel on the Medicare Trustees Reports found that 'the primary long-run determinant of real health
care spending has been the development and diffusion of new medical
technology' (2000, 31).

Table 3.4
Utilization of Short-Stay General Hospitals

Year	Admissions per 1000	Length of stay (days)	Days/ 1000	Adjusted Cost/Day (1982 dollars)
1950	110.5	8.1	895.1	n.a
1960	128.9	7.6	980.0	114
1970	144.9	8.2	1188.1	172
1980	160.4	7.6	1219.2	282
1986	135.4	7.1	961.3	437
1989	134.6	n.a	n.a	n.a

Source: American Hospital Association, Statistical Abstract, Health Care Financing Review; table reproduced from Newhouse (1992, 12).

The next logical question, though it was not posed by Newhouse or in other studies, is: *Why does the march of science cost so much?* Kalb alluded to this question when he highlighted that, while most drugs and medical devices in the United States 'are assessed for safety and efficacy . . . most medical and surgical procedures are not formally evaluated at all' (Kalb: 1990, 1113). Though Kalb, Newhouse, and others do not suggest it, a look at the industry structure – and the pattern of profitability of medical device and diagnostic producers – helps uncover the reasons why the march of science, or medical technology, is so costly.

From the mid-1960s to the early 1990s, corporations producing measuring, scientific, and photographic equipment (United States Industry Code Number 38) – among them, medical technology producers Becton Dickinson, Baxter International, and Bausch and Lomb – figured high in the top rankings of the Fortune 500 (see tables 3.5 and 3.6). For most of the years sampled between 1966 and 1991, the industry figured within the top ten industries in Fortune's listings of 'Total Returns to Investors' as well as 'Changes in Profits.' In comparison to the pharmaceutical industry – the only other health-related industry to appear in Fortune's top twenty industries over the same period – the measuring, scientific, and photographic equipment industry realized a greater profit growth rate in most of the years sampled between 1966 and 1991 (see table 3.6).

Taken individually, of the nineteen companies in the measuring, scientific, and photographic equipment industry category for the year 1991,

Table 3.5
Total Return to Investors, Medical Technology Industries, Selected Years (percentage change)

Year	Industry	Increase %	Rank***
1966	Measuring, scientific, photographic equipment*	14.7	6/22
	Pharmaceuticals**	18.4	1/22
1968	Measuring, scientific, photographic equipment	13.0	7/22
	Pharmaceuticals	17.0	1/22
1970	Measuring, scientific, photographic equipment	13.1	6/28
	Pharmaceuticals	15.5	2/28
1973	Measuring, scientific, photographic equipment	−22.8****	n.a.
	Pharmaceuticals	−18.89	n.a.
1975	Measuring, scientific, photographic equipment	44.01	16/28
	Pharmaceuticals	16.26	24/28
1980	Measuring, scientific, photographic equipment	14.44	5/28
	Pharmaceuticals	6.91	15/28
1983	Measuring, scientific, photographic equipment	23.79	17/27
	Pharmaceuticals	7.18	21/27
1985	Measuring, scientific, photographic equipment	17.93	17/25
	Pharmaceuticals	45.13	4/25
1989	Measuring, scientific, photographic equipment	5.2*****	6/21
	Pharmaceuticals	8.8	1/21
1990	Measuring, scientific, photographic equipment	2.9	15/21
	Pharmaceuticals	13.1	1/21
1991	Measuring, scientific, photographic equipment	50.2	6/24
	Pharmaceuticals	61.5	3/24

*United States Industry Code No. 38.
**United States Industry Code No. 42.
***The total number of top industries featured in the Fortune 500 varies from year to year, hence the different denominators.
****In the year 1973, total return to investors decreased in all industry categories of the Fortune 500, except the 'petroleum' and 'mining' industries. This is an outer expression of the accumulation crisis identified in Marxian political economy.
*****For the years 1989 and 1990, the Fortune 500 'Return on Assets' is used here instead of 'Total Return to Investors.'
Source: Fortune 500 Industry Median Ratings, 1966–91.

Table 3.6
Change in Profits, Medical Technology Industries, Selected Years (percentage change)

Year	Industry	Increase %	Rank***
1966	Measuring, scientific, photographic equipment*	49.1	1/21
	Pharmaceuticals**	16.2	13/21
1968	Measuring, scientific, photographic equipment	15.2	8/22
	Pharmaceuticals	9.8	14/22
1971	Measuring, scientific, photographic equipment	13.3	7/19
	Pharmaceuticals	9.9	10/19
1973	Measuring, scientific, photographic equipment	18.2	17/28
	Pharmaceuticals	16.6	19/28
1975	Measuring, scientific, photographic equipment	11.0	8/11
	Pharmaceuticals	9.2	9/11
1980	Measuring, scientific, photographic equipment	24.6	3/18
	Pharmaceuticals	13.8	7/18
1983	Measuring, Scientific, Photographic Equipment	-2.8	n.a
	Pharmaceuticals	13.5	12/19
1985	Measuring, scientific, photographic equipment	11.2	6/12
	Pharmaceuticals	9.1	7/12
1990	Measuring, scientific, photographic equipment	-36.8	n.a
	Pharmaceuticals	18.8	3/8
1991	Measuring, scientific, photographic equipment	16.3	2/24
	Pharmaceuticals	16.0	3/24

*United States Industry Code No. 38.
**United States Industry Code No. 42.
***The total number of top industries featured in the Fortune 500 varies from year to year, hence the different denominators.
Source: Fortune 500 Industry Median Ratings, 1966–91.

twelve were producers of medical technology. These included Eastman Kodak,[7] which ranked first in total sales within the category of nineteen; Baxter International,[8] which figured fourth; Becton Dickinson, which ranked seventh; Bausch and Lomb,[9] which figured ninth; and United States Surgical,[10] which figured fifteenth (Fortune: 1992, 282). In terms of growth of profits for 1991, medical technology producers Baxter

International ranked first in the category of nineteen, Millipore ranked fourth, and United States Surgical ranked fifth. Rankings within the Fortune 500 can be traced back to the 1960s for medical technology producers Becton Dickinson and Eastman Kodak. For Baxter International and Bausch and Lomb, rankings within the Fortune 500 date back to the 1970s.

Why were producers of medical devices and diagnostic equipment doing so well circa 1960 to 1990? The posing of this question is crucial to uncovering the reasons behind centralization in health care delivery through the 1970s and 1980s, as well as to revealing why health care costs were escalating rather than merely increasing at the rate of inflation.

Gleaning a study commissioned by the Health Industry Manufacturers Association (HIMA), what is clear is that by the late twentieth century, a small number of firms had a high degree of control of the U.S. medical device and diagnostics industry. As 'the global leader' in terms of both innovation and exportation, total production in the industry amounted to U.S. $68 billion in 1999, of which close to 22 per cent was for export (Lewin Group: 2000, 12). The structure of the U.S. medical device and diagnostics industry and its division of labour are as follows.

Of the 5,998 medical device and diagnostics companies comprising the industry by the late 1990s, 733 companies, or 12 per cent of the total industry, accounted for some 80 per cent of sales, and a mere 2 per cent of the industry accounted for 45 per cent of total industry sales (Lewin Group: 2000, 16, 17). In terms of size, medical device and diagnostics companies at the top of the sales hierarchy each employed 100 or more workers. Companies employing less than 100 employees, and accounting for a far smaller portion of sales, were responsible for the largest expenditures (as a proportion of sales) in research and development (R&D). In 1998, R&D expenditures by firms with revenues of less than U.S. $5 million totalled 252 per cent of sales, while R&D by firms with revenues of more than U.S. $1 billion amounted to only 13 per cent of sales (Standard and Poor's Compustat data, presented in Lewin Group: 2000, 23).

As the Lewin Group explains, this rather extreme imbalance was functional for all involved, though more beneficial to some companies than others:

Start-up firms have been disproportionately responsible for the innovation and early development of truly novel devices, including angioplasty catheters, artificial joints, cardiac support devices, diagnostic ultrasound . . .

larger firms are more likely to pursue next-generation or incremental improvements, for example, by refining or building on current product lines . . .

Although small companies may be responsible for early innovation, many will ultimately collaborate with larger partners to bring their products to market. Larger companies offer steady funding, opportunities for technological synergy, manufacturing capability, marketing, distribution channels, and field service. More frequently than small ones, larger companies have the experience and capacity to conduct clinical trials and take on regulatory and payment hurdles. (Lewin Group: 2000, 24)

Though not precisely in the same form, the structure and division of labour in the twentieth century medical device and diagnostics industry fall within the dynamics of what Baran and Sweezy (1966) have termed *monopoly capital*. According to Baran and Sweezy, in contrast to the typical nineteenth-century firm that produced 'a negligible fraction of homogenous output for an anonymous market,' the typical business unit of the twentieth century was the large-scale enterprise producing a substantial share of the output of one or several industries. These twentieth-century business units were able to control their prices, production volumes, and the types and amounts of their investments (Baran and Sweezy: 1966, 6).

In being the first to innovate and patent early medical technologies, in the first half of the twentieth century, companies like Baxter International, Becton Dickinson, and Bausch and Lomb were well-placed to absorb other medical technology producers, and monopolize the patenting and selling of new final products by the second half of the twentieth century. A brief rendition of the growth of the now, multinational, medical technology producer and distributor, Becton Dickinson, helps to illustrate this growth strategy.

In 1898, Becton Dickinson acquired half rights to the patent on the all-glass syringe developed in France. The company then went on to produce a range of syringes and other medical devices, surgical instruments, and sterile disposable products. Along the way, Becton Dickinson absorbed various other enterprises involved in producing and distributing medical technology. These included the Philadelphia Surgical Company, acquired in 1904; the Surgical Supply Import Company in 1913; the Toronto-based distributor Norman S. Wright Company in 1951; Mexico-city based MAPAD S.A. CV in 1952; and AMI of France in 1955. Also in 1955, Becton Dickinson acquired the Baltimore Biological Laboratory. The acquisition of the latter launched Becton Dickinson into becoming a leading force in two major changes in medical practice: the conversion to sterile, disposable products and the emergence of diagnostic medicine (Becton Dickinson: 2009).

As the hospital market expanded substantially due to state-assisted medical technology consumption by hospitals, and increased health insurance coverage, circa 1950, an increasing but limited number of firms followed this model, concentrating on perfecting, producing and marketing the most promising technologies, and thereby coming to control the volume of production, types and amounts of investment, and prices of medical technology. All of this led to high levels of profitability in the medical devices and diagnostics industry, and high costs for hospitals.

Beyond productive power, an important element of this control is *extra-economic*. The power of large-scale enterprises to influence regulatory procedures and other political deliberations is crucial, particularly in the health care market. This point is exemplified by the strategizing of National Medical Care (NMC), which by the early 1980s was the largest provider of kidney dialysis treatment in the United States, as well as a producer of dialysis supplies, equipment, and testing analysis (Kolata: 1980, 379).

At the subnational level, prior to establishing kidney dialysis clinics, NMC typically created links with nephrologists, scientists within the academe, and state officials, allowing locally relevant individuals to appoint medical directors of NMC clinics (Kolata: 1980, 381). Such support was instrumental in politics at the national level. In 1978, for instance, a bill aimed at replacing costly treatment in clinics with home dialysis came before Congress, and NMC mobilized its medical directors across the country to fight the bill, in addition to hiring a former campaign director of Ronald Reagan. Using testimonies from its medical experts, NMC argued that home dialysis was not effective in achieving long-term survival rates. In turn, the bill that eventually passed into law did not specify any goals or targets to increase the use of home dialysis (Kolata: 1980, 382).

Through control, then, of (a) the direction of innovation, (b) the manufacturing, marketing, and expansion of product lines, and (c) industry relations with health sector regulators and hospitals, the major consumers of medical technology – a relatively small group of medical device and diagnostics producers – was able to expand the U.S. market for medical device and diagnostics into double-digit figures

Figure 3.1: U.S. Market Size for the Medical Device and Diagnostics Industry (billions of USD)

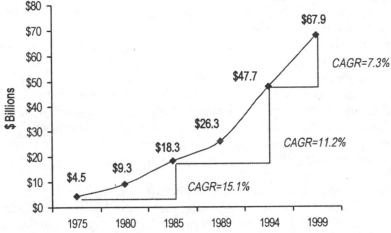

Source: U.S. Department of Commerce; figure reproduced from Lewin Group (2000, 13).

from 1975 to 1994 (see figure 3.1, where CAGR refers to 'compounded annual growth rate').

An examination of official national health expenditure data confirms that, along with the producers of pharmaceuticals (an industry more widely known for its monopoly structure and impact on health care costs), producers of medical devices and diagnostics played a leading role in U.S. health expenditure escalation between 1960 and 2006.

As shown in figure 3.2, the official category 'Retail Outlet Sales of Medical Products,' – which includes the products of both the pharmaceutical and medical device and diagnostics industries – ranks third in the top five areas accounting for some 80 per cent of U.S. health expenditures over time. The cost impact of the monopoly structure of the medical device and diagnostics industry can also be traced within the second highest area of health expenditures, 'Physician and Clinical Services' given that the large firms placing medical devices on the market are in many cases the main providers of the clinical and laboratory services that must accompany the devices.[11]

Looking exclusively at the subcategory of 'Durable Medical Equipment' under the category 'Retail Outlet Sales of Medical Products,' what becomes evident is a continual rise in national expenditures, over time, on commodities produced by the medical device and diagnostics

Figure 3.2: Leading Aggregate Amounts in National Health Expenditures, Selected Years (billions of USD)*

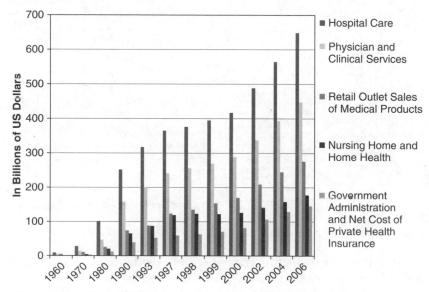

*All five areas are official categories or subcategories accounting for the largest proportions of national health expenditures, ranging from a total of 81 per cent (1960) to 85 per cent (2000).
Source: National Health Statistics Group (2007).

industry – the consumers of which are predominantly hospitals (see figure 3.3). Essentially what has been at play in the U.S. health care market is that hospitals, the major consumers of medical technology, have transferred monopoly-driven, high medical technology costs to consumers. Therefore, since 1960, 'Hospital Care' has consistently constituted the highest health expenditure category for the United States.

For the purpose of comparison, table 3.7 shows expenditures in each of the three subcategories under the official category, 'Retail Outlet Sales of Medical Products.' In addition to the subcategory, 'Durable Medical Equipment,' that of 'Other Non-Durable Medical Products' is affected by monopoly-driven prices given that producers of medical technology – Baxter International and United States Surgical, for example – are also involved in the production of the non-durable products required in the use of medical equipment.

Figure 3.3: National Expenditures, Durable Medical Equipment, Selected Years (billions of USD)

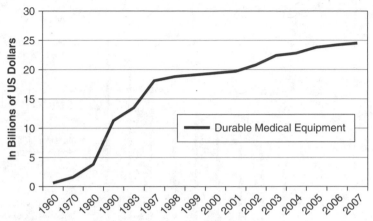

Source: National Health Statistics Group (2007).

All of this reveals that it was not simply the march of science that pushed up U.S. health expenditures in the second half of the twentieth century. Taken together, the monopoly structures of production of medical technology and pharmaceuticals demonstrate the ways in which capital has manipulated the opportunity provided by employer and public health insurance coverage – hard-won, no less, by working people – to expand profitability, regardless of the far-reaching costs involved for the U.S. state and U.S. society as a whole.

Casualty of Capitalist Logic: Nursing Labour Restructuring

As demonstrated in the policy discussions around U.S. health sector inflation, open discussion and thorough analysis of monopoly structures were essentially non-existent in dominant discourses of twentieth-century capitalism. In theoretical discussions, the notion of *economies of scale* was and continues to be used by economists as justification for *technical monopoly* in the production of medical and other technologies. A quote from Milton Friedman exemplifies this line of reasoning:

> Monopoly arises to some extent because technical considerations make it more efficient or economical to have a single enterprise rather than many. There is unfortunately no good solution for technical monopoly. (Friedman: 1962, 128)

Table 3.7
U.S. Expenditure on Retail Medical Products, by Subcategory, Selected Years (billions of USD)*

Official Subcategory	1960	1970	1980	1990	1998	2000	2007
Prescription Drugs	2.7	5.5	12.0	40.3	88.5	120.6	227.5
Durable Medical Equipment	0.6	1.6	3.8	11.3	18.8	19.4	24.5
Other Non-Durable Medical Products	1.6	3.3	9.8	22.5	28.2	30.2	37.4

*These are the three subcategories within the official category of 'Retail Outlet Sales of Medical Products,' which constitutes the third largest proportion of National Health Expenditures.
Source: National Health Statistics Group (2008).

The conscious or/and subconscious denial of the negative social implications of monopoly within twentieth-century capitalist discourse is emblematic of one of the major irresolvable conflicts within the fourth (U.S.) systemic cycle of accumulation. Where the survival of individuals becomes dependent on commodities and services produced by private interests, the control of production lies fundamentally with those private interests rather than with the state. The state – itself dependent on commodities and other outcomes of capitalist production – then defers primary decision-making around production to those private interests, regardless of the fact that profit accumulation, rather than collective good, is the end goal of private interests.

By the late 1980s, with the continuing escalation of costs in U.S. hospitals and the limited impact of health expenditure reduction measures focused on reducing hospital use, attention was turned to labour costs.[12] Adopting a micro-level solution to a macro-level problem, hospital administrators looked to the restructuring of nursing labour. The focus of administrators was on female hospital labour despite the fact that the cost of services of the male-dominated segment of health care – physician and clinical services – considerably surpassed the cost for the female-dominated segment (see figure 3.4). Rather contrary to logic, then, hospital labour cost-cutting occurred through the reorganization of the work of nurses, the health labourers providing the bulk of care in the hospital setting.

In a 1994 survey commissioned by the American Society for Healthcare Human Resources Administration and the Hay Group, 55 per cent of the 1,036 hospitals surveyed across the United States were actively

Figure 3.4: Labour Costs in National Health Expenditures, Selected Years (billions of USD)

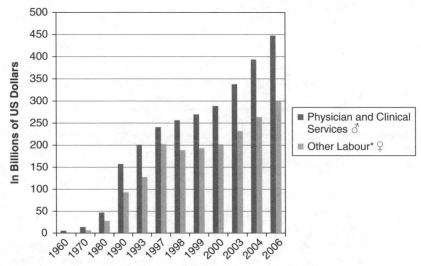

*Included here are the official categories of 'Other Professional Services,' 'Other Personal Health Care,' and 'Nursing Home and Home Health' – all of which are assumed to be female-dominated. Labour costs of hospitals are not included here as disaggregated figures are not available for the official cost category of 'Hospital Care.' It may be assumed, however, that the labour cost structure is quite similar within the hospital setting given a very similar composition of care services.
Source: National Health Statistics Group (2007).

involved in 'work redesign,' with a further 8 per cent having already completed work redesign initiatives. (Pierson and Williams: 1994, 30) In addition to 1,036 for-profit, non-profit, secular, religious, and public hospitals across the country, the Hay Hospital Compensation Survey covered 348,000 health professionals (Pierson and Williams: 1994, 29).

Of the 55 per cent of surveyed U.S. hospitals undergoing redesign initiatives, 42 per cent had created new team manager positions, 48 per cent had developed team care deliverer positions, and 35 per cent were 'enhancing' the role of registered nurses to include advanced technical care and management skills (Pierson and Williams: 1994, 30). Along with these work redesign initiatives, the Hay Hospital Compensation Survey reported that hospitals were replacing remuneration structured on base salaries with new 'compensation strategies' rewarding 'performance.' The 'Glossary of Compensation Strategies' included in the article by Pierson and Williams, 'Compensation via Integration' – a cover story for the trade journal *Hospitals and Health Networks* – features such 'strategies' as 'broadbanding,' or the grouping of jobs and roles into fewer but wider pay ranges; 'team-based pay'; 'gainsharing'; and 'pay for skills' (Pierson and Williams: 1994, 28).[13]

In order to fully understand the reorganization of work and compensation that was taking place in U.S. hospitals during the late 1980s and 1990s, it is useful to employ a labour lens, or methodological emphasis on the evolution of nursing work organization. According to Norrish and Rundall, 'team nursing' was the dominant model for nursing labour organization in U.S. hospitals prior to the 1970s (2001, 59). In this model, nursing tasks were divided among several workers with little regard for the nurse–patient relationship. In part as a result of the dissatisfaction expressed by nurses with the working conditions emanating from the team nursing model, hospitals shifted to 'primary nursing' in the 1970s (Norrish and Rundall: 2001, 60).

In the primary nursing model, registered nurses (RNs) were accorded responsibility for all decision-making relating to the care of their patients throughout their period of hospitalization (Norrish and Rundall: 2001, 60). Thus, starting in the 1970s, RNs provided direct care to individual patients and were no longer required to manage the work of other caregivers, as in the team nursing model. According to Norrish and Rundall, for nurses in the United States of America, primary nursing's reunification of tasks espoused the essence of nursing, allowing for a strengthening of the nurse-patient relationship (2001, 59).

Through the 1980s, as primary nursing expanded as a model of hospital work organization, the demand for RNs grew. Concurrently, between 1981 and 1985, 42,000 of 350,000 RNs joined labour unions, including major national unions such as the Service Employees International Union; the Retail, Wholesale, and Department Store Union; the American Nurses Association; United Food and Commercial Workers; and the Teamsters Union (Weiss: 1997, 61). Along with the continued unionization of RNs into the 1990s, the bargaining power of RNs increased – all against the backdrop of rising expenditures on medical technology. The rationale behind a new round of nursing work reorganization, in the late 1980s, may be explained as follows:

This rationale for restructuring emphasizes improving operational efficiency by reducing hospital costs through replacement of high-cost registered nursing staff with lower-cost license practical/vocational nurses and unlicensed assistive personnel. This type of restructuring specifically seeks to reduce the skill mix of RNs (the number of RNs providing patient care compared with the number of total patient-care givers) and to deploy substitutes for RN caregivers wherever possible. (Norrish and Rundall: 2001, 58)

The new 'compensation strategies' adopted by U.S. hospital administrations become more clear when one considers the increasing bargaining power of RNs and the evolution of nursing work organization. The return to the team nursing model in the late 1980s and early 1990s went along with the notion of offering rewards and incentives to particular individuals and groups of workers in place of pay structures negotiated through collective bargaining (Greiner: 1995). *Team-based pay* and *gainsharing*, therefore, went hand-in-hand with the redefining of RN roles to include management skills, the creation of team management positions, and the creation of team care deliverer positions. Similarly, *competency-based pay* and *pay for skills* were means of dividing a sector of increasingly unionized workers by favouring individual workers or/ and teams deemed exceptional by employers.

The increased use of temporary migrant nursing labour was part and parcel of the re-adoption of the team nursing model in U.S. hospitals. Migrant RNs were imported in increasing numbers from the early 1990s through to 2004 (see table 3.8), replacing RNs who were regarded as *high-cost* due to their salaries and working conditions, which were negotiated through collective bargaining. The 1989 Immigration Nursing Relief Act created the legal instrument (i.e., the H1A visa) through which employers were permitted liberal access to temporary migrant RNs from various countries for five-year periods. Another legal instrument, the TN visa, facilitated the temporary employment of Canadian nurses in the United States of America under the auspices of the 1988 Free Trade Agreement between the United States and Canada.

Through liberalized access to temporary migrant nurses during the 1990s, employers were able to further advance the reorganization of nursing work. They also implemented additional cost-cutting measures by offering differential rewards and working conditions to nurses on the basis of legal status and country of training.[14] To explain this in greater detail: temporary work permits necessitate temporary contracts, the combination of which makes for the relatively lower cost of migrant nurses, as their terms of employment may be determined by employers and states outside of the collective bargaining process.[15] This exemplifies the essence of the reserve army of labour argument

Table 3.8
Internationally Trained Nurses Admitted to the U.S. on Temporary Work Visas,
1991–2004

Visa Type	1985	1989	1990	1991	1992	1993	1994	1995
Registered Nurses (H1A visa)*	X	X	X	2,130	7,176	6,506	6,106	6,512
Registered Nurses (TN visa)**	X	X	X	2,105	2,946	3,967	3,293	19

	1996	1998	1999	2000	2001	2002	2003	2004
Registered Nurses (H1A visa)	2,046	551	534	565	627	1 145	924	7,795
Registered Nurses (TN visa)	9	9,133	6,809	1,150	4,380	N/A	N/A	N/A

*These numbers represent migrant nurses entering the United States, each time they enter. The numbers of H1A temporary work visas that are issued to nurses are available only for some years. Comparing the two sets of numbers where possible, the difference is not large. This is likely due to fact that it is not easy for migrant nurses to leave countries of employment for financial and work-related reasons. The year 2004 was the last year the H1A visa was in effect, though the Immigration Nursing Relief Act was replaced with the Nursing Relief for Disadvantaged Areas Act in 1999. The latter legislation created a quota of 500 H1C visas issued per year, significantly reducing employer access to temporary migrant nurses. It remains to be seen if and when American employers will be able to mobilize political support to reopen their access to temporary migrant nursing labour.
**These figures are an account of temporary visas issued annually to Canadian Registered Nurses under the provisions of 1988 Free Trade Agreement and cannot thus be tabulated and taken as an account of the number of Canadian RNs migrating temporarily. Figures for the years following 2002 are not available.
Source: Department of Homeland Security (2004; 2007).

discussed in chapter 2, a key element of the global integration of nursing labour markets. More specifically, with the multinational expansion of the reserve army of labour, the gains made by organized labour are further diminished through the employment of temporary workers from outside the national labour market – workers holding precarious legal status and few or unenforced rights entitlements. By way of comparison, between 1966 and 1978, prior to the rise of temporary migration schemes, some 10,717 nurses trained in the Philippines entered the United States as permanent residents (Choy: 2003, 98–9).[16] In the early 1990s, the United States became the largest demander of temporary migrant nursing labour trained in the Philippines. Approximately 80 per cent of nurses entering the United States under the Immigration Nursing Relief Act between 1989 and 2004 were from the Philippines (Sassen: 2000, 521).

As would be expected, despite the restructuring of the nursing labour market – that is, reducing hospital costs via a reduction of the wage bill of workers providing the most ongoing, and therefore essential, care for the ill – expenditures on hospital care in the United States continued to increase into the early twenty-first century (refer to figure 3.2). In addition to speaking to the poverty of solutions offered through capitalist reasoning, this medley of contradictions attests to the intertwined nature of structures of patriarchy, and structures of capital, in the fourth (U.S.) systemic cycle of capitalist accumulation.

Summation and Theoretical Reprise

As the world's largest importer of internationally trained nursing labour, the United States of America was key in giving rise to the upward shift in world demand for temporary migrant nursing labour when it began importing large numbers of temporary migrant nurses in the early 1990s. The global integration of nursing labour markets – a process of radical restructuring within the financial expansion of the fourth (U.S.) systemic cycle of accumulation – thus began to unfold as other states of the global North followed the approach of using temporary migrant nurses as a form of health care cost-cutting. With the reorganization of nursing work and the increased use of temporary migrant nursing labour in the United States from the late 1980s to the early 2000s, many of the social and economic gains made in the 1970s and 1980s were reversed. This restructuring of the nursing labour market thus made a casualty of both nurses based in the United States of America and internationally-trained nurses employed temporarily in the United States of America.

In greater detail, through the 1970s adoption of the primary nursing model and the growing unionization of RNs in the 1980s, women's caring labour gained value in both economic and social terms. Not only did increased unionization challenge the socially accepted level of RN wages, but in raising those wages – as negotiated agreements covering all workers of a specific occupation within particular workplaces tend to do – the historically undervalued caring labour of a predominantly female workforce gained social recognition. Recognizing the greater relative precarity faced by temporary migrant nurses in the United States, it may still be said that Sassen's (1998) *double-disadvantage* of sex and class is faced by the U.S. nursing labour force as a whole, and not only by temporary migrant nurses in the United States.

While Sassen (1998) would ascribe this reinforcement of women's inequality simply to economic globalization, what is argued here is that the causes are rooted in contradictions within the material expansion of Arrighi's (1994) fourth (U.S.) systemic cycle of accumulation. The contours of the process are as follows.

Starting in the 1950s, the union-made gain of employer-based health insurance coverage and the working-class victory of U.S. state health care programs created a new opportunity for capitalist accumulation. Mounting capitalist power resulting from the successful use of this opportunity by producers of medical technology and pharmaceuticals contributed significantly to increasing costs faced by U.S. hospitals, the latter of which, consequently, also became a new opportunity for capitalist accumulation. Unable to intervene, given the preponderant power of private interests within twentieth-century capitalism, the U.S. state facilitated the increased use of temporary migrant nursing labour from the late 1980s to the early 2000s, as part of the female-labour focused, cost-cutting solution identified by U.S. hospitals. The reorganization of nursing work, along with the increased use of temporary migrant nursing labour, falls within the post-1970s shift from a polity recognizing trade union and workers' rights to one based on flexible labour policies – an element of the restructuring and reorganization characterizing Arrighi's financial expansion in the fourth (U.S.) systemic cycle of accumulation of historical capitalism.

With regard to Arrighi's explanation of the early 1970s accumulation crisis – which pushed large capitals from productive to speculative activity, marking the transition from material to financial expansion – the particular instance of the U.S. medical technology industry differs significantly. Arrighi identifies the outpacing of gains in labour productivity by rising real wages in North America as one of the key forces in the major contraction of returns to capital, beginning in 1973. In the instance of the U.S. medical technology industry, the rate of profitability did not contract, and monopoly-driven profits, not wage pressure from unions, made for the adoption of labour cost-saving strategies in the hospital market. Other industry-specific studies such as this would shed light on the variety of forms of restructuring that have been unfolding in the capitalist world economy since the 1970s.

In contrast to Brenner's macro-level emphasis on competition between capitals of differing national origins as a cause of the accumulation crisis, this study brings out the dynamics and consequences of *collusion*. It also brings out the overlap of vertical and horizontal integration of firms within specific areas of production, particularly the U.S. medical technology and hospital industries. Other historically specific studies examining growth paths of particular capitalists at the micro-level would add to understandings of the rise, spread, power, and patterns of profitability of various industrial sectors and multinational corporations in the twentieth century.

Finally, in analysing industries underlying what have been seen as part of the hallmarks of the Golden Age – employer-paid health benefits and health programs of the welfare state – what becomes clear is the capital-driven nature of developments arising during the world historical process of Keynesianism. From the 1960s, the U.S. state has been subordinate to medical technology producers, regardless of anti-trust and other legislation, and those producers, rather than U.S. society as a whole, have drawn the greatest benefit from the expanded consumption of medical care.

4 The Global Integration of Nursing Labour Markets – The Canadian Instance

The phenomenon of labour shortage is commonly linked to that of labour migration, both as explanation and justification. Writing in 2004 about the Canadian instance of nurse migration, for example, Blouin et al. stated that 'cross border migration is central to the issue of the global shortage of nurses' (2004, 38). Writing a few years later, Kelly and D'Addorio projected that 50 per cent of Canadian nurses employed in 2001 would retire by 2016, leading to a shortfall of 113,000 nurses, and hence argued for the importance of Filipino and other internationally trained health workers in analysing the Canadian scenario (2008, 82). This explanatory linkage between labour shortage and migration is problematized here through a tracing of the nursing *labour process* in Canada, starting in 1960. Drawing from Kathryn McPherson's (1996) historical study *Bedside Matters: The Transformation of Canadian Nursing, 1900–1990*, it is argued that undervalued nursing labour has formed the basis of universal public health care in Canada, and that the increased entry and exit of temporary migrant nursing labour to and from Canada are two of several developments arising from this fundamental contradiction.

As in the analysis of the U.S. instance in the previous chapter, the overarching world historical framework is used here to trace the range of key forces in the Canadian health care system over time, including health care costs, state policies, the policies of hospital administrations (i.e., employers), and the efforts of organized labour. The public health care system in Canada is thus understood to be a part of the Keynesianism of the material expansion in Arrighi's fourth (U.S.) systemic cycle of accumulation of the world economy. Given the centrality, however, of the persistent undervaluing of nursing labour in explaining the exit and entry of migrant nursing labour in Canada, a socialist feminist lens is applied in this chapter.

The analysis is divided into three sections. The first section examines what was identified in the late 1980s and early 1990s as *the nursing crisis*. Also at this time, the notion of a *nursing shortage* arose in policy discussions and increases in nursing labour migration became significant. The second section provides an account of the reality of nursing work, starting from the 1960s, demonstrating that what appeared as a crisis in the 1990s was the outer expression of deeply rooted incongruences that had been present in the organization of Canadian, publicly funded health care from its very inception. The final section presents a long-run comparison of health care expenditures, linking them to the evolution of nursing work over the past fifty years.

The Nursing Crisis circa 1990

The notion of a nursing shortage broke ground as an issue in Canada with the publication of a 1988 study entitled *The Nursing Shortage*. Commissioned by the Registered Nurses Association of Ontario, the study identified supply as the key causal factor in the nursing shortage, arguing that the shortfall of nurses was due to reductions in nursing college spaces and that all of these problems would be solved by the market (Meltz: 1988, 65).

In an early 1990s article that provided a labour perspective on the issues, Jerry White turned the claim of a nursing shortage on its head by presenting figures drawn from the College of Nurses registration data on the employment status of nurses in Ontario for the period of 1983–1987 (refer to table 4.1). By contrasting the number of employed nurses with the number of nurses who were voluntarily unemployed, White demonstrated that some 23,582 nurses – or 30 per cent – had withdrawn from the profession in 1987. Citing a 1988 Ministry of Health report, he showed that the number of voluntarily unemployed nurses far outstripped the 1,143 unfilled nurse positions in Ontario at the time (White: 1993, 105). There was thus no 'absolute shortage of nurses' in Ontario, the province with the 'greatest reported shortages' in Canada, in the early 1990s (White: 1993, 105).

The key question to pose regarding the early 1990s, then, is: *Why were nurses withdrawing from the nursing labour market?* In answering this question, White uses data from interviews with nurses in Ontario, Alberta, and Saskatchewan, and nurse union demands in the 1980s,

Table 4.1
Nurses in Ontario, 1983–1987

Year	Total	Employed	New	Other*
1983	100,091	68,284	2,801	29,006
1984	100,171	70,411	2,962	26,798
1985	101,704	73,677	3,985	24,042
1986	103,517	75,935	3,005	24,577
1987	105,356	78,735	3,039	23,582

*This includes those who were voluntarily unemployed and a small number that had left the jurisdiction.
Source: College of Nurses of Ontario, Registration Data; table reproduced from White (1993, 105).

showing that across Canada changes in labour process were at the root of the withdrawal by nurses of their labour from the market. This withdrawal, or nurse resistance, took shape in nurse strikes and work stoppages, in addition to voluntary unemployment or part-time employment (White: 1993, 108).

Along the same lines, in a chapter entitled 'The Price of Generations: Canadian Nursing under Medicare, 1968–1990,' Kathryn McPherson points to a 'fundamental transformation' in the collective conscience of nurses to explain the spate of nurse strikes across Canada in the late 1980s (1996, 249). These include strikes in Saskatchewan and Alberta in 1988 – the latter lasting eighteen days – and the 1989 strikes by the British Columbia Nurses Union and La Fédération québécoise des infirmières et infirmiers, the former of which was joined by other health workers in British Columbia. Two forces were at play in this transformation: the rise of the feminist critique emphasizing society's persistent devaluation of women's work, and the increasing presence of female service workers in the Canadian labour movement (McPherson: 1996, 249).

Labour process may be defined as the location of 'the nexus of structure and human agency,' whereby the workplace is a zone in which practices shaped by historic social and cultural assumptions are eventually put into question by dissatisfied workers (White: 1993, 107). There were three key changes in the nursing labour process which constituted a shift that affected both personal and collective notions of the meaning of nursing by the 1990s (White: 1993, 111). This notion of a shift complements McPherson's assessment that there was a fundamental transformation in the collective conscience of nurses in the 1980s, leading to a first-time chain of nurses' strikes in various provinces in the late 1980s.

The first key change in the nursing labour process was the decreasing work satisfaction of registered nurses related to work intensification caused by increased acuity of patients. While in the late 1970s one-third of patients entered hospitals with severe symptoms, by the early 1990s this proportion had increased to nearly 90 per cent (White: 1993, 108). As patients entering hospitals were more severely ill, the care they required intensified. Combined with the increasingly common practice in hospitals of sending patients home to recuperate, nurses experienced far less satisfaction from their caring work (White: 1993, 108–9). This intensification of work, or increasing workload, was particularly pronounced in the 1990s when growing acuity was coupled with a reduction in the employment of nurses. An examination of changes in federal financing of health, education, and social programs helps to explain this decline.

In 1990, as part of the goal of deficit and debt reduction, the federal government imposed a ceiling on funds transferred to Canada's three largest and wealthiest provinces for health and post-secondary education programs – initially called the Established Program Financing, and later the Canada Assistance Plan (CAP). In other words, though costs to provincial governments were increasing for these programs, the federal government prevented the CAP from keeping pace with these increases. This was preceded by a 1986 change in the formula used to calculate CAP transfers, which resulted in reduced transfers for all provinces for the fiscal year 1990–1 (Yalnizyan: 2005, 33). In fiscal 1994–5, federal transfers in support of social programs and health care – now called the Canada Health and Social Transfer (CHST) – were further reduced by 15 per cent, followed by another 15 per cent in fiscal 1996–7 (Yalnizyan: 2005, 33). For the period 1994–7 alone, cutbacks for these programs amounted, according to calculations based on Public Accounts figures, to CAD $8.2 billion (Yalnizyan: 2005, 33).

Facing what may be phrased as a devolution in the responsibility for ensuring equal access to basic social services, education, and health care, provincial governments devolved part of the burden of reduced funding onto hospital administrations, which in turn chose salaried labour as the area for cost-cutting. As part of what Stasiulis and Bakan have called 'the casualisation of the hospital workforce,' just over half of the nursing positions in Ontario were transformed into part-time positions by the end of the 1990s (Stasiulis and Bakan: 2005, 120; Canadian Institute for Health Information, as cited by Armstrong and Armstrong, 2002, 108).

The second key change in nursing labour process was a new accent on *productivity*, whereby nurses' tasks and time came to be monitored by hospital managers using computerized patient classification systems (White: 1993, 109–10). *Productivity* thus replaced *care* as the orientation for nursing work, leading to further work intensification. Added to this reorientation of nursing work was another aspect of reorientation resulting from provincial funding reductions to chronic care budgets. Though they were not trained to care for the chronically ill, nurses in the early 1990s were charged with this work as chronically ill patients remained in hospitals due to a shortage of chronic care spaces elsewhere. In some Ontario hospitals, chronically ill patients constituted up to half of the total patients in a single work area (White: 1993, 111).

Changes in working space made up the third element of the shift in the nursing labour process. The management practice of rotating nurses to different hospital wards and work settings led to increased stress for nurses by the 1990s. This was due to nurses' resulting inability to become familiar with patients, machines, or/and storage systems in their constantly changing work spaces. This, combined with the other key changes, fed into growing resistance by nurses in the form of voluntary unemployment, voluntary part-time employment, strikes, and work stoppages (White: 1993, 111).

White's analysis, which is based on interviews and collective bargaining demands, is consistent with the findings of a study commissioned in the 1980s by the major Ontario nursing union. The study, *The Nursing Shortage in Ontario: A Research Report for the Ontario Nurses Association*, reported that one in seven of the nurses surveyed intended to leave nursing, and that burnout, exhaustion, long hours, heavy workload, understaffing, low pay, and lack of decision-making power were the main reasons behind nurses choosing to shift from full-time to part-time employment (Goldfarb: 1988, 30).[1] Similarly, in 1989, l'Ordre des infirmiéres et infirmiers du Québec reported that 78 per cent of nurses surveyed claimed to be working overtime 'without pay, staying late or reporting in early or by cutting short their rest periods and meal periods' (as cited by Stelling: 1994, 610).

Though the studies of White (1993) and McPherson (1996) do not incorporate the phenomenon of nurse migration, the emigration of

Table 4.2
TN Visas Issued to Canada-based Registered Nurses, 1991–2001*

Year	Total	Female	Male
1991	2,195	1,998	197
1992	2,946	2,643	303
1993	3,967	3,571	396
1994	3,293	2,927	366
1996	19	17	2
1997	9	5	4
1998	9,133	7,976	1,157
1999	6,809	5,975	834
2000	1,150	957	193
2001	4,380	3,759	621

*These figures are an account of temporary visas issued annually, and thus cannot be tabulated and taken as an account of the number of Canada-based RNs migrating temporarily for work in the United States for the period 1991–2001.
Source: Immigration and Naturalization Service; table reproduced from Blouin et al. (2004, 45).

Canadian nurses to the United States can be logically tied in here. Facilitated by the 1988 signing of the Free Trade Agreement between Canada and the United States – in which registered nurses were part of the list of occupations qualifying for prompt processing of temporary work authorizations, or TN visas – significant numbers of frustrated nurses left Canada in the early 1990s, opting instead for temporary contract employment in the U.S. As the effects of diminishing federal transfers through the CAP and CHST trickled down through the decade, an increasing number of TN visas were issued to Canadian nurses by the Immigration and Naturalization Service in the United States.

The pattern of registered nurse migration to Canada – both temporary and permanent – figures well into this explanation (refer to figure 4.1). Internationally trained nurses entered Canada in relatively large numbers in the late 1980s and early 1990s. Through the 1990s, the number of internationally trained nurses entering fell, as full-time nursing positions were eliminated by hospital administrations.[2] By the end of the decade, as an absolute shortage of nurses began to form, the entry of internationally trained nurses began to rise once again.[3]

Figure 4.1: Legal Status of Internationally Trained Registered Nurses Entering Canada, 1989–2007*

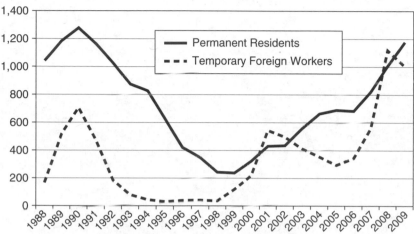

*Figures of the official category 'Temporary Foreign Workers' represent the number of entries, not the number of temporary work permits issued.
Source: Citizenship and Immigration Canada (2007).

The total number of nurses entering as permanent residents between 1988 and 2007 dropped to about half that of nurses entering as permanent residents in the previous twenty-one years (see figure 4.2). Between 1988 and 2007, 14,309 nurses entered Canada as permanent residents. Between 1966 and 1987, the number was about twice as large at 31,027. This reflects rising employer preference for temporary migrant labour. This preference is due to the fact that the employment of temporary migrant nurses contributes both directly and indirectly to cost-cutting efforts in health care expenditures. Upon entering Canada on temporary work authorizations, temporary migrant-registered nurses undertake full-time employment as registered nurses with all the responsibilities implied, but receive the lesser salaries and benefits of 'graduate nurses' until they have passed Canadian licensing exams.[4] Alternatively, temporary migrant-registered nurses, particularly from the Philippines, are employed as licensed practical nurses, as has occurred in Alberta.[5] This is despite the fact that internationally trained, registered nurses arriving in Canada are for the most part only accepted by recruitment agencies and Canadian hospital employers because they already possess some or several years of nursing experience.[6]

Figure 4.2: Graduate and Registered Nurses Entering Canada as Permanent Residents, 1966–2007*

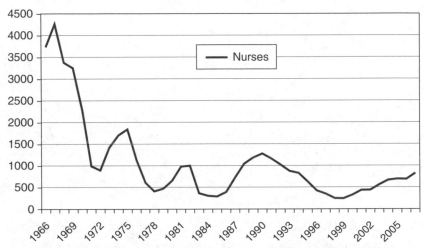

*The official category used for nurses entering between the years 1966 and 1987 is 'Graduate Nurses.' For the later period, the official category used is 'Registered Nurses.' Source: Manpower and Immigration (2005); Employment and Immigration Canada (2005); Citizenship and Immigration Canada (2007).

In more indirect terms, increased access to temporary migrant nurses allows employers to erode away the few gains that have been made over time by unions in the caring labour sector of Canada. In 2006, for example, a nursing bargaining unit of the British Columbia General Employees Union (BCGEU) saw the displacement of seventy of its members through state-approved employment of temporary migrant nurses by Park Place Seniors Living Limited. The latter employed a labour contractor, which offered the BCGEU members a significantly reduced wage and benefit package, claiming a labour shortage when the unionized workers refused. The labour contractor, Advocare, subsequently applied for and obtained permission to employ temporary migrant nurses for the same workplace through the federal Temporary Foreign Worker Program. The contract of these temporary migrant nurses included an hourly wage of CAD $15, reduced from CAD $20, and a significantly reduced benefit package eliminating the sick leave, long-term disability, paid vacation, and pension benefits previously held by BCGEU workers (Valiani: 2007a, 4–5).[7]

Since 2002, there has been a rising number of internationally trained nurses entering Canada as permanent residents. This is explained in part by the fact that, by this time, some internationally trained nurses on temporary work authorizations would have been selected by their employers to become permanent residents through Provincial Nominee Programs.[8] The importation of temporary migrant nurses to Canada will likely continue to rise – provided that there is ongoing public funding for hospitals – given the signing, in 2007 and 2008, of bilateral agreements between the Philippines state and the governments of British Columbia, Alberta, Saskatchewan, and Manitoba for the temporary migration of Filipina nurses. In 2008 and 2009, the number of internationally trained, registered nurses entering Canada per year on a temporary basis was only slightly different than the number entering per year on a permanent basis. In 2008, 1,118 RNs entered as temporary migrant workers while 1,006 entered as permanent residents. In 2009, 1,003 RNs entered on temporary work authorizations and 1,177 entered as permanent residents (Citizenship and Immigration Canada: 2010).

Additionally, at the federal level, instructions published by the Minister of Citizenship and Immigration have included registered nurses among the list of occupations prioritized for permanent residency under the Canadian Experience Class (CEC). The CEC is the newest immigration program in Canada and is indicative of the employer-driven approach mentioned in chapter 2. Under the CEC, skilled temporary migrant workers in Canada may apply for permanent residency after a two-year employment period, on the basis of employer approval.[9] Despite the growing need for nurses in Canada, it is preferable to employers to initially hire internationally trained nurses on temporary work authorizations so that they can assess workers prior to recommending them for permanent residency. Federal and provincial governments in Canada have accommodated this preference.

Though important, what must be underlined about both the number of nurses emigrating to the United States and the number of internationally trained nurses entering Canada is that these numbers are relatively small when compared to the number of nurses voluntarily unemployed in Ontario alone – around 25,000 through the 1980s (refer to table 4.1). What all of this suggests is that voluntary unemployment and underemployment of nurses in the 1980s, the chain of industrial actions by nurses unions in the late 1980s, migration of nurses to and from Canada at the end of both the 1980s and 1990s, and the absolute shortage of nurses materializing in Canada by the year 2000 – are all outcomes of intolerable working conditions resulting from the types of cost-cutting strategies adopted by hospital administrations prior to the 1980s.

The Nursing Status Quo, 1960–1990

Though embracing feminist perspectives in their accounts of Canadian nursing in the 1980s and 1990s, White (1993) and Stasiulis and Bakan (2005) take as given the choice of hospital administrators to cut costs in the area of salaried labour – in other words, the wages of the predominantly female caring labour in hospitals, including that of registered nurses. Similarly, in a slightly earlier article entitled 'Productivity in Canadian Nursing: Administering Cuts,' feminist analyst Marie Campbell states,

> Hospitals were forced into taking measures to economize on service provision. Within hospitals, nursing services, absorbing as they do a high percentage of the total budget, became an important focus for administrative efficiency measures. (Campbell: 1987, 464)

Though the category of salaries does figure as the highest category of hospital expenditures in Canada, an examination of the growth of other major hospital costs, over time, warrants the following question (refer to figure 4.3): *Why were hospital cost-cutting measures focused primarily on salaried service provision while from at least the mid-1970s, expenditures in the areas of physician compensation, medical supplies, and prescribed drugs were rising steadily?*

In order to answer this question, a long view is required, reaching at least as far back as the 1960s, to when health care became a public good in Canada. Though White (1993, 104) speaks of a 'fiscal crisis of the state' pushing changes in the nursing labour process and leading to the nursing crisis, the basic conditions underlying the nursing crisis were in place prior to the 1980s, and long before the major reductions of federal health and social transfer payments in the 1990s.

Citing the 1970 Task Force Reports of the federal Committee on the Costs of Health Services, Campbell argues that cost constraint has been a major preoccupation since the advent of public health care in Canada (1987, 463). Through the 1970s, federal transfers for health and post-secondary education were continually scaled down, leading to

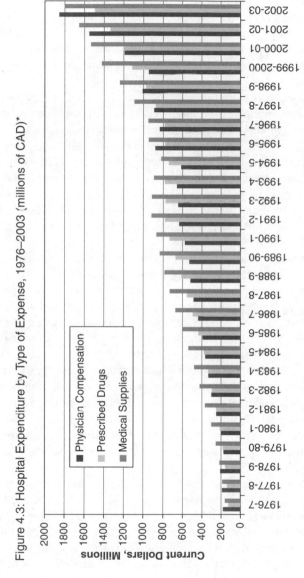

Figure 4.3: Hospital Expenditure by Type of Expense, 1976–2003 (millions of CAD)*

*Expenditure for official categories 'Salaries,' 'Benefits,' and 'Other Supplies and Sundries' are not included here.
Source: Canadian Institute for Health Information (2005a).

various health cost constraint policies at the provincial level. With Ontario as an example, Campbell points out that the provincial government capped grants made to hospitals and, by 1982, had adopted a policy of no cost overruns in hospital funding (Campbell: 1987, 463–4). According to Angus, cost containment strategies through the 1970s made for relatively stable health care expenditures, averaging around 7.3 per cent of gross national product throughout the decade (Angus: 1987, 57).

What this meant in hospitals was the rise of what Campbell calls 'sophisticated new management methods' that 'systematically devalue nurses' knowledge and displace their professional judgment' (1987, 463). Throughout the 1970s, document-based technologies were adopted by hospitals, shifting the responsibility for case-by-case determination of therapeutic interventions required by patients from nurses to supervisors and nurse managers (Campbell: 1987, 464). Hospital administrators were thus able to manipulate, on a daily basis, the definition of nursing work so as to coordinate nursing labour time with hospital budget choices.

More specifically, Patient Classification Systems were increasingly put into use in hospitals, whereby nurses' ideas of the care required by patients were transformed through computer programs into timing and costing by hospital management. Once patient information was entered by nurses, labour-time was allocated by the system in accordance with hospital budgeting, which was programmed into the system through management-determined formula. Campbell underlines that in order to 'make budgets stretch, staffing calculations [were] programmed as if untimed work were more or less unnecessary and nurses could drop it or hurry over it' (1987, 465). Such untimed work included walking between different hospital areas, communicating with doctors and patients' families, keeping records, relieving colleagues for breaks, and dealing with unexpected work (Campbell: 1987, 467–70).

Patient Classification Systems were in use in unaffiliated hospitals across Canada by 1980. A 1981 survey commissioned by the Canadian Nurses Association revealed that these systems were being used for staffing purposes in all provinces except Prince Edward Island (Campbell: 1987, 465). Similarly, an unpublished Ontario Hospital Association Survey, dated in 1982, reported that 64 of 165 responding Ontario hospitals were using Patient Classification Systems, while 42 others were planning to implement their use (Campbell: 1987, 465).

In the province of Quebec, as early as 1971, in an extensive pamphlet entitled *Le nursing québécois . . . malade* (Quebec Nursing . . . in Trouble), Les Infirmières et Infirmiers Unis/United Nurses, one of three nursing unions in Quebec at the time, raised issue with the compartmentalization of hospital caring work and the interrelated, narrow definition of tasks involved (Les Infirmières et Infirmiers Unis Inc.: 1971, 52). Linking this to the failure to recognize the importance of teamwork, the union underlined that the resulting lack of respect for the role of caring labour was carried and endured not only by nurses but also by all workers performing caring work in the hospital setting:

> Chez tout le personnel, sans doute à cause de la compartimentation et de la définition étroite des tâches, on observe peu d'échange sur le plan du travail. On ne perçoit point non plus l'existence d'un sentiment de solidarité. C'est l'anonymat qui prévaut: sur le plan du travail quotidien, de la reconnaissance par les autorités de l'importance de la participation des individus, et des relations humaines. (Les Infirmières et Infirmiers Unis Inc.: 1971, 52)

> [Among all the staff, no doubt due to the compartmentalization and narrow definition of tasks, we observe very little interaction in the workplace. A sense of solidarity is also lacking. Rather it is the impersonal which reigns: from the day-to-day relations among frontline workers, to the absence of recognition by management of the importance of human relations and the full participation of individual workers.] (Author's translation)

The United Nurses further connected all of this to the creation of a hospital climate that was discouraging for all: patients, visitors, and patients' families, as well as health care workers (Les Infirmières et Infirmiers Unis Inc.: 1971, 52). In line with this view, the 1970 Castonguay-Nepveu report – commissioned by the Quebec government to study the situation of health care – observed that 'the hospital climate was cold and impersonal, to the extent of being at times tense and ridden with difficulties' (as cited by Les Infirmières et Infirmiers Unis Inc.: 1971, 52, author's translation).

The same types of observations about hospital caring labour can be tracked in another part of the country a few years later. A job evaluation carried out in 1973 by the Canadian Union of Public Employees found that the labour of 98 per cent of the 936 female workers at the Winnipeg

Health Science Centre was being undervalued (McPherson: 1996, 255). The Anti-Inflation Board (AIB) in the province, however, subsequently ruled that a salary readjustment could not be implemented.

In the same pattern of these stories in Quebec and Winnipeg, by 1984 a Labour Canada study found that more than one-third of nurses in hospitals across Canada were experiencing symptoms related to stressful working conditions (as cited by Armstrong: 1993, 45).

It is through all of this that the impetus for the wave of nurse unionization, beginning in the mid-1970s, may be understood. Following the 1972 Supreme Court ruling in favour of the Service Employee International Union's right to organize nurses in Saskatchewan, nurses joined and formed autonomous unions across Canada, breaking from the pro-establishment, management-led nurse associations.[10]

The AIB ruling in Manitoba reflects the Canadian cultural tendency to persistently discount the undervaluing of female labour in the name of other priorities deemed larger and more essential. In the instance of the Winnipeg Health Science Centre, the goal of fighting inflation was deemed more important than rectifying the inadequate payment of female health care workers. Similarly, in the instance of public health care in Canada as a whole, the larger priority of providing universal access to health care was deemed more important than fairly compensating the workers doing the bulk of caring labour in Canadian hospitals (McPherson: 1996, 251).

Going yet further back in time, Campbell links the devaluing of nurses as skilled workers, and the undervaluing of nursing labour time through Patient Classification Systems, both of which occurred prior to and during the era of public health care. As she puts it, '[T]he contemporary approach to cost containment looks uncomfortably like the solution to hospital funding problems of an earlier era when nursing students provided unpaid labour' (Campbell: 1987, 463).[11]

This brief reference by Campbell reflects the thrust of Pat Armstrong's (1993) account of Canadian nursing, entitled 'Women's Health Care Work: Nursing in Context.' Tracing the political economy of health care starting in the late nineteenth century, Armstrong highlights the rise of the medical profession as central to the development of a hierarchical structure of health care provision in Canada. Due to the political power of the predominantly male, professional associations of doctors – not unrelated to their close class ties with society's decision-makers – the growth and protection of institutionalized health care was based on the biomedical model, the primary decision-making power of doctors, and the subordinate position for nurses and care work:

> . . . these efforts assured the dominance of medical, curative, hierarchical, and patriarchal form of medical practice. This allopathic approach empha- sized treatment rather than prevention and, not incidentally for nursing work, diagnosis rather than care. It was based on an engineering model of the body, which views the body like a machine made up of interconnected parts that can, to a large extent, be separately treated. While this model has allowed the refinement of techniques, the emphasis on body parts down- plays the importance of care of the whole person, the kind of approach still taught to nurses. (Armstrong: 1993, 23)

By the time the Hospital Insurance Diagnostic Act was passed in 1957, and with the 1966 passing of the Medical Care Act leading to the formal establishment of health care as a public good in Canada, doctors were able to make what McPherson calls 'dramatic' income gains through successful pressure for the adoption of fee-for-service payment under Medicare (McPherson: 1996, 255; Armstrong: 1993, 28). Consistent with the history of unpaid caring labour provided by nurse apprentices in hospitals, nurses did not enjoy anything close to the same gain in terms of compensation with the establishment of pub- lic health care. Instead, as demonstrated above and summarized suc- cinctly by Kathryn McPherson, 'professional commitment to patient care and the gender-specific tendency of women to absorb the extra tasks combined to ensure that nurses intensified their pace of work' (McPherson: 1996, 253).

This gender-specific tendency described by McPherson, together with the effects over time of the political clout of doctors as well as the Canadian cultural tendency to not prioritize full and fair recognition of female labour, form the structural basis for hospital cost-cutting focused on female caring labour. Put slightly differently, these three cultural and political forces provide, in large part, the answer to the question: *Why were hospital cost-cutting measures focused primarily on salaried service provision?* Though referring to the role of individual nurses within hos- pitals, the words of Marie Campbell may be applied at the macro-level of nurses within the Canadian health care system as a whole:

> In much the same way as mothers' work in the home is infinitely expand- able and variable to encompass what needs to be done to keep the family's

Figure 4.4: Percentage Distribution of Largest Health Expenditures in Canada, 1976–2000

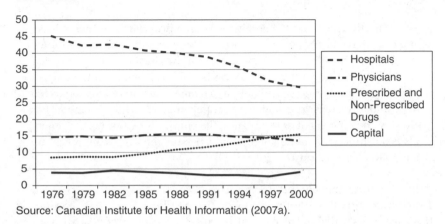

Source: Canadian Institute for Health Information (2007a).

interests and projects going so, too, the nurse must pick up the pieces of work that are not specifically somebody else's but need to be done. (Campbell: 1987, 470)

Successful Cost-Cutting: Crisis in Nursing, Crisis in Canadian Health Care

From the perspective of hospital administrators, cost-cutting in the area of salaried service provision was a success. Between 1976 and 2000, hospital expenditures decreased by 15 per cent while other major health expenditures in Canada remained steady or grew and health expenditures as a percentage of GDP increased slightly, in pace with most other OECD countries (see figure 4.4).

Though the Canadian Health Coalition, the Canadian Labour Congress, and others have highlighted, in recent years, rising national health expenditures on pharmaceuticals, as in the United States, few in Canada have questioned the size of continually rising expenditures on medical technology consumed by hospitals. Even less highlighted – despite Canada's dependency on U.S. medical technology – is the monopoly structure driving these rising expenditures, a rise which can be tracked particularly in the category of 'Medical Supplies,' in the expenditures of Canadian hospitals (refer to figure 4.3).[12] The lack of questioning around the importance and role of medical technology in Canadian hospital expenditures, as in the United States of America,

Table 4.3
Percentage Distribution of Largest Hospital Expenditures, Alternate Years, 1976–2000

Year	1976/7	1979/80	1982/3	1985/6	1988/9	1991/2	1994/5	1997/8	2000/1
Salaries*	69.7	69.0	67.2	66.4	65.4	63.8	62.1	61.1	59.0
Other Supplies and Sundries**	15.3	17.1	17.2	17.3	17.3	17.9	18.4	16.2	17.3
Benefits	6.6	5.7	7.3	6.8	7.0	8.4	9.7	10.1	9.7
Medical Supplies	2.9	3.4	3.5	4.0	4.2	3.9	3.7	4.8	5.5
Physician Compensation	3.3	2.3	2.5	2.6	2.8	2.7	2.8	3.9	4.2
Drugs	2.2	2.5	2.5	2.9	3.3	3.3	3.3	3.8	4.3

*Within this aggregate category, the 'Nursing Inpatient' subcategory accounts for approximately 30–40 per cent, while 'Administration and Support' accounts for approximately 20–30 per cent. These estimations are based-on break-downs contained within Hospital Trends in Canada: Results of a Project to Create a Historical Series of Statistical Data and Financial Data for Canadian Hospitals Over Twenty-Seven Years (Canadian Institute for Health Information: 2005a).
**From 1997, this category was divided in two: "Other Supplies' and 'Sundries.' For consistency, they are presented here together for 1997–2001.
Source: Canadian Institute for Health Information (2005a).

provides the remainder of the explanation for the tendency of hospital cost-cutting measures to focus on salaried service provision.

The decline in hospital expenditures from 1976 to 2000 was due primarily to reductions in expenditures on salaries (refer to table 4.3), of which, in 1993, nursing inpatient services constituted about 38 per cent, support services about 25 per cent, administrative services about 13 per cent, and operating and ambulatory services about 12 per cent.[13] Arguing for the centrality of nursing labour to the care function of hospitals, Stelling points out that 'among all hospital employees, it is nursing staff that is on the wards 24 hours a day, seven days a week' (1994, 609). At the same time, these subcategories of predominantly female, salaried hospital labour may also be seen as interrelated within the context of the intensification of hospital care work, its compounded undervaluing over time, and the changing definition of caring tasks, demonstrated here through the examination of the nursing labour process in Canada.

The overall result of successful hospital expenditure reduction through salaried services is the crisis in Canadian public health care, a crisis which is ongoing. In its 2008 publication, *A Renewed Call for Ac-*

tion: A Synthesis Report on the Nursing Shortage in Canada, the Canadian Federation of Nurses Unions (CFNU) makes ten recommendations, of which six address issues dating at least as far back as the 1970s, including workload, health and safety in the work environment, and lack of autonomy (Maddalena and Crupi: 2008, 65–72). As summarized in a 1987 press release of the Ontario Nurses Association, which is still valid today and which can be applied on a national scale,

> Nurses are required to endure working conditions that greatly reduce the amount of direct quality care they can give to their patients. These conditions include: too few support staff, excessive patient loads, increasing demands to perform non-nursing duties, poor work scheduling. These frustrating conditions, coupled with other working life frustrations – lack of recognition, poor employer support for extra education, little say in health care management – have created a crisis both for Ontario Nurses and its health care system as a whole. (As cited by Armstrong: 1993, 49)

Summation and Theoretical Reprise

In sum, the persistent undervaluing of female caring labour is the structural condition for the increased exit and entry of temporary migrant nursing labour in Canada. Nursing in twentieth-century Canada has evolved from an apprenticeship-based system, in which nurses-in-training were not paid a salary, to a post-1960s, publicly funded health care insurance and delivery system, in which paid nurses have been consistently undervalued and increasingly super-exploited through work intensification. All of this led, in the 1980s and 1990s, to registered nurses voluntarily withdrawing labour (on a partial or complete basis) from the Canadian health care system; this, despite attempts by nurses to use unionization, collective bargaining, and industrial action to improve working conditions and remuneration.

For the same reason that registered nurses based in Canada began withdrawing their labour from the Canadian health care system – an undervaluing of their work based on ongoing public funding constraints and an allocation system slanted against female caring labour – the Canadian health care system imported yet more undervalued labour in the form of temporary migrant nurses. These migrant nurses came in two waves: from 1989 to 1991, and from 1999 to present. That temporary migrant nurses have been prioritized for entry through bilateral labour mobility agreements since 2007 – and for permanent residency in Canada through Provincial Nominee Programs and the Canadian Experience Class since the late 1990s – demonstrates the growing importance of temporary migrant nursing labour in the Canadian health care system. Temporary migrant registered nurses are undervalued even more intensely than registered nurses based in Canada in that they are remunerated at the lesser wage rates of graduate nurses until they receive Canadian licensing, despite the nursing experience they bring to the Canadian health care system.

The Canadian instance differs from the U.S. American instance in various ways. Unlike in the United States, cost-cutting in the area of nursing labour has been and continues to be effective in reducing hospital expenditures, a strategy adopted virtually from the beginning of publicly funded health care. Though unionization of nurses in Canada began earlier than in the United States, the gains, in terms of both salary and working conditions, have been relatively greater in the United States. Due to the availability of appropriate and reliable data in Canada, the shift from permanent to temporary migration within the area of nursing labour is more easily identifiable (circa 2000).

The Canadian and U.S. American instances are similar in one principal respect: in both instances, the caring labour of doctors – regardless of the public/private funding difference – has been, and continues to be, relatively high value, with far higher levels of remuneration and work-related control for doctors than for nurses. This attests to the inability of welfare state ideals, specifically the notion of *universality* in Canadian health care, to break from the capitalist logic undervaluing female caring labour. A cherished public program aiming to serve the collective has thus been based, from the onset, on the super-exploitation of the majority of the workers sustaining it. This contradiction, which is inherent in the Keynesianism of the material expansion of the fourth (U.S.) systemic cycle of accumulation, is one of the structural forces creating the conditions for the increased circulation of temporary migrant nurses internationally. Canada began importing temporary migrant nurses in relatively large numbers in the late 1980s – thus setting the trend, along with the U.S., wherein countries of the global North increasingly began importing internationally trained nurses as temporary migrant nurses rather than permanent residents.

5 The Global Integration of Nursing Labour Markets – The Philippines Instance

In October 2008, the government of the Philippines hosted the second annual Global Forum on Migration and Development (GFMD). As mentioned in chapter 1, the GFMD is an intergovernmental gathering which emerged from discussions and proposals of certain states, private sector institutions, the International Organization for Migration (IOM), and the World Bank. The GFMD in Manila was attended by more than 600 delegates from 164 member countries of the United Nations and chaired by Philippines Undersecretary of Foreign Affairs for Migrant Workers' Affairs, Esteban B. Conejos Jr. That this global gathering was hosted by the Philippines was quite intentional. Priding itself on a policy of international labour deployment dating back to the 1970s, and presenting itself as a model for other states to follow, the Philippines state invested a great number of resources to host the second annual GFMD.

Concomitantly, the architecture of the Philippines's labour export policy is lauded by intergovernmental bodies and international development institutions as a model to be emulated. For instance, at a United Nations forum entitled 'Migration, Diaspora and Development' that was held in Addis Ababa in December 2008, Michele Klein Solomon, IOM Director of Migration Policy Research and Communications, stated that the newly established Ethiopian Expatriate Affairs Directorate within the Ministry of Foreign Affairs was a 'landmark achievement by the Ethiopian government' (quoted in *The Guardian*: 2008). Along the same lines, in January 2008 the government of Vietnam tasked its Ministry of Labour, Invalids and Social Affairs with developing a labour export policy (Ministry of Labour, Invalids and Social Affairs: 2009). In his study *Made in the Philippines: Gendered Discourses and the Making of Migrants*, geographer James Tyner (2004, 55) lists several countries that have sent government officials to receive orientations on the operations of the Philippines Overseas Employment Agency, including Bangladesh, Eritrea, Hong Kong, the Commonwealth of the Northern Mariana Islands, and Sri Lanka.

This chapter elaborates on the Philippines state as the leading international exporter of labour, tracing the lineage of labour exportation as a state policy and drawing out the elements of the labour export policy in the health sector in particular. Building on the work of specialists of Philippine migration Graziano Battistella (1999), James Tyner (2004), Pauline Barber (2008), Robin Rodriguez (2010), and others, the first section broadly depicts the state architecture underlying the export of labour and its development over time. The next section draws out particular elements of this process with regard to nursing labour force development.

Using the world historical framework, the last section aims to answer the question: *What made for the adoption of a labour export policy in the Philippines starting in the 1970s, and not before?* It is argued that the historically entrenched structure of the Philippines state led to the termination of domestically oriented, capitalist development in the newly independent Philippines of the 1950s and 1960s – and, in turn, to the shift to labour exportation as a key activity of the Philippines state. More specifically, the Philippines state's adoption of a labour export policy in the early 1970s is traced here as the outcome of contradictions arising from trade relations shaped under colonialism, severely unequal land distribution, and weighty U.S. political influence. These social relations are seen as underlying the Philippines state's choice to create an institutional framework for the export of temporary migrant workers, and this institutional framework is seen as underlying what neoclassical and other analysts see as the *choice* of individual workers to emigrate.

This explanation, rooted in a world historical political economy analysis, differs from those of post-structural analysts Tyner (2004), Barber (2008), Rodriguez (2010), and others, in which external debt servicing is identified as the primary motivation for the labour export policy of the Philippines state. In Tyner's formulation (2004, 66–7), the state's production and management of 'bodies' as 'migrants' is linked to what he calls the state's goal of 'capital accumulation,' or the collection of foreign exchange for the purpose of debt payments. For Barber (2008, 1270), the accumulation of external debt by the Philippines state is the result of increased world oil prices in the 1970s, corruption and economic mismanagement by the Marcos dictatorship, and faulty structural adjustment policies starting in the 1980s. McAfee (1991), Pomeroy (1992), and Stasiulis and Bakan (2005) underline that structural adjustment programs substantially increased low-wage employment in the Philippines from the 1980s, leading to greater numbers of workers *choosing* to emigrate. Rather than assuming the existence of external debt as an element of the Philippines location in the global economic hierarchy, or overemphasizing the role of international financial institutions and structural adjustment programs, as do most of these analysts, the explanation offered here seeks to reconstruct the cause of the perpetual indebtedness of the Philippines state, bringing out the underanalysed roles of Filipino and foreign bourgeoisies.

The Architecture of Labour Export

Branching away from the dominant view that labour migration is driven primarily by demand from wealthier countries (Martin et al.: 2006; Kuptsch and Pang: 2006; Connell: 2007; Piper: 2008; OECD: 2008b), Robyn Rodriguez (2010) emphasizes the role of the state in what she terms *labour brokerage*. In her groundbreaking book *Migrants for Export: How the Philippine State Brokers Labor to the World*, Rodriguez demonstrates how the Philippines state initiates the opening of markets around the world to labour from the Philippines. Using ethnographic material gathered in interviews with state officials, Rodriguez gives examples of how the Philippines state creates demand for migrant Filipino labour in a range of sectors and occupations, dating back over three decades.

In the 1970s, for example, Department of Labour and Employment (DOLE) officials organized 'marketing missions' in the United States, bringing U.S. American construction contractors together with private labour recruiters from the Philippines. The purpose of visiting the United States was of a strategic nature. Given that U.S. American companies were servicing the construction boom in Saudi Arabia and other parts of West Asia at the time, the DOLE preferred to orchestrate deals between the head offices of these companies and recruiters based in the Philippines, rather than leaving the migrant labour contracting to 'middlemen' based in West Asia (Rodriguez: 2010, 59).

In a more recent example, in the early 2000s the Labour Attaché of the Philippines Embassy in Brunei located an opportunity for labour

contracting in the garment manufacturing sector. This involved analysing the international trade commitments and export conditions of
Brunei and, in turn, identifying its garment manufacturing industry as
an area of possible expansion given an open quota for Brunei garment
imports in the U.S. (Rodriguez: 2010, 54). This illustrates how Philippines officials not only identify markets for migrant Filipino labour but
also contribute to the identification of areas of expansion for producers
outside of the Philippines based on Filipino migrant labour.

This range of what Rodriguez calls 'marketing efforts' fits well with
the description provided by Jose S. Brillantes, former ambassador of
the Philippines in Canada.[1] According to Brillantes – who, through his
various appointments, has both witnessed closely and helped to shape
the evolution of employment policy in the Philippines – there are three
pillars of Philippines foreign policy: political security, economic diplomacy, and protection and promotion of overseas labour. The last pillar – still quite unique in international terms to the foreign policy of
the Philippines – involves assessing which countries can provide jobs
to migrant labour from the Philippines and evaluating the potential
wages, working conditions, and problems that could arise. In Canada,
for example, consulates of the Philippines in Vancouver and other cities
work with local employers to create temporary migrant employment
conditions deemed appropriate by Philippines officials.[2]

Associated with this foreign policy pillar of promoting and protecting overseas labour is an institutional framework within the Philippines. In 1984, the Philippines Overseas Employment Administration
(POEA) brought together the functions of the Overseas Employment
Development Board and the National Seamen Board, both formed in
1974. The Overseas Workers Welfare Agency was formed in 1995, taking over the reintegration and relocation functions of the Welfare and
Training Fund, established in 1974. Finally, the Technical Education and
Skills Development Authority (TESDA) also plays a role in the state
objective of overseas employment.

This institutional framework, consisting of considerable state resources and commitments both within and outside the Philippines,
is what labour migration activists and Philippines advocates have
termed the Philippines's *labour export policy*. As analyst Graziano Battistella puts it, this policy found 'its highest formulation' in the 1974
Labor Code issued by President Marcos (legally known as PD442), 'and
was clearly aimed at promoting overseas employment and implicitly
at expanding the market for overseas Filipinos' (Battistella: 1999, 230).

Measured in its own terms, the success of the labour export policy may be observed through the absolute growth, over time, in the overseas deployment of workers from the Philippines (see table 5.1). In the period of twenty-five years between 1984 and 2009, there was a more than fourfold increase in the number of newly hired and rehired temporary migrant workers deployed from the Philippines, rising from some 300,000 to over 1,400,000. That *rehired* temporary migrant workers are included along with *newly hired* temporary migrant workers in official statistics of the Philippines state, underlines an aspect of temporary migration emphasized by advocates of migrants' rights. Though based on work authorizations for limited periods of time, temporary migration can consist of consecutive periods of temporary employment contracts and temporary legal status, leading to extended periods of precarious working and living conditions for migrant workers.

Of crucial importance to the success of the 'deployment of overseas workers,' as the Philippines state puts it, is the combined effort of the Philippines Overseas Employment Administration (POEA) and the Technical Education and Skills Development Authority (TESDA). A close examination of the POEA, its interconnections with the TESDA, and specific examples drawn from institutional documents and interviews with key officials shed light on this point.

The two major divisions of responsibility within the POEA are the Pre-Employment Services Office and the Seabased Projects Accreditation Division. The key functions within the Pre-Employment Services Office, the more important of the two major divisions, are laid out in the schema below.[3]

Pre-Employment Services Office
1. Accreditation Branch
2. Employment Contracts Processing Branch
3. Marketing Branch
   a. Market Promotions Division
   b. Market Research and Standards Division
4. Employment Branch
   a. Manpower Development Division
   b. Manpower Registry Division
5. Government Placement Branch
6. Welfare Services Branch

The following excerpts from the official descriptions of tasks within the Marketing Branch demonstrate the reach of the branch and bring out

Table 5.1
Overseas Deployment of Workers by the Philippines, New Hires and Rehires, 1984–2009

Year	Workers Deployed (New Hires and Rehires)
1984	350,982
1985	372,784
1986	378,214
1987	449,271
1988	471,030
1989	458,626
1990	446,095
1991	615,019
1992	686,461
1993	696,630
1994	718,407
1995	653,574
1996	660,122
1997	747,696
1998	831,643
1999	837,020
2000	841,628
2001	867,599
2002	891,908
2003	867,969
2004	933,588
2005	988,615
2006	1,062,567
2007	1,077,623
2008	1,236,013
2009	1,422,586

Source: Philippines Overseas Employment Administration (2010a);
House of Representatives: Congressional Planning and Budget
Department (2006).

the extent of state forces engaged in making possible the examples of labour brokerage cited above:

Market Promotions Division: Develops and implements marketing plans and programs for the promotion of overseas employment for Filipino workers; Coordinates and assists the private sector in its market development efforts; Organizes and manages special events to promote the employment of Filipino workers; Establishes cordial and harmonious relationships with foreign employers and embassies and other entities for the promotion of Filipino workers; Assists visiting foreign delegations interested in hiring Filipino workers . . .

Market Research and Standards Division: Conducts continuous studies and surveys here and abroad for formulation of standards on employment terms and conditions and practices; Monitors and studies developments in various worksites that affect the acceptability of Filipino labour; Conducts research studies for the continuing analysis of the overseas employment program; Integrates and analyzes statistical data on the overseas employment program . . .[4]

While the Marketing Branch has a reach that is principally international, the reach of the Employment Branch is both international and domestic. Coordinating the matching of occupations in demand (external) with labour in supply (internal), the POEA Employment Branch works with bodies such as the DOLE's Welfare and Employment Office, the Professional Regulation Commission (PRC), and TESDA. Each of these bodies compiles a registry of available labour in various skill types and levels – the DOLE for skilled labour, the PRC for professionally certified labour, the TESDA for labour of 'certified middle-level skill' – which the POEA combines and makes available to both local and international employers.[5]

Beyond data-gathering and analysis, the work of TESDA overlaps with that of the Employment Branch in the area of skills training. The blur between demand and supply, and between internal and external markets, becomes apparent in the following example provided by Irene Isaacs, executive director of the TESDA Qualifications and Standards Office:

In 2005 Australia needed 500 slaughter house workers. TESDA checked online and other sources for information on the qualifications required in

Australia for this occupation. We then approached private sector slaughter houses in the Philippines for training spaces because TESDA institutions could not provide adequate conditions for the training. Three slaughter houses opened their doors, and 500 workers were trained for Australia's slaughter houses.[6]

This example additionally brings out the external orientation of labour force development initiatives of the Philippines state. The development of this orientation has been supported by various other states through financing in the form of overseas development assistance. Australia has thus funded the formation of training regulations and competency-based training programs in the Philippines that are similar to those found in Australia. Germany has funded 'train-the-trainer' programs for industry-based skills training in the Philippines as it exists in Germany. And TESDA is currently facilitating discussions for the creation of training programs in Canada's Red Seal trades, a national system of skills training via the apprenticeship model – a model which has been underutilized within Canada over the past ten to fifteen years due to employer resistance to investment in training (Canadian Labour Congress: 2006, 7). The players involved in the latter TESDA initiative are Meralco, the largest electricity company of the Philippines; Meralco's MFI Technological Institute (Philippines); the Saskatchewan Institute of Applied Science and Technology (Canada); the Winnipeg Technical College (Canada); and the British Columbia Ministry of Trade (Canada).[7]

Moving beyond middle-level skilled labour, the same nature of developments can be detected at the highly skilled level. For example, according to Commissioner Ruth Padilla, head of the Professional Regulation Commission, in late 2008 there were seven new professional categories pending approval in the Philippines Congress and Senate, all of which had been created in response to international labour demand in these professions.[8]

On the whole, what becomes apparent here is that a host of functions and initiatives of the Philippines state, financially and technically supported by states of the global North – *core states*, in world historical language – are geared towards the objective of the temporary migration of portions of the Philippines labour force. As is quite rational in economistic terms, the Philippines state is interested in exporting skilled and highly skilled labour, given that this will ensure higher returns in the form of foreign exchange based on migrant wages entering the country. What remains unclear is the size of the portion of labour intended by the state for export. In other words, if employment possibilities are few or unattractive at home, and if the state does not actively help to create decent employment within the Philippines – as will be discussed in the last section of this chapter – then the portion of labour intended for export is continuously expandable. This implies a situation of state-sponsored skills training for export, and repeatedly renewed, state-promoted, temporary contracts for migrant workers; the latter is reflected in POEA deployment statistics, which, as pointed out earlier, include both newly hired and rehired temporary migrant workers.[9]

Regardless, then, of the state's proclaimed role of worker protection and assisting in the reintegration of migrant workers into Philippines society, more central to the work of not only the POEA, but also increasingly the TESDA, are the generation and preservation of overseas jobs for Filipino migrant workers and the production of skilled labour for markets outside of the Philippines. The POEA mission statement sets the order of priority as suggested in this reasoning:

> POEA connects to the world, and in partnership with all stakeholders, facilitates the generation and preservation of decent jobs for Filipino migrant workers, promotes their protection and advocates smooth reintegration into Philippine society.

Before moving on to an examination of the Philippines state's shaping of nursing labour force development and export, a portrayal of state requirements around migrant worker remittances is necessary to close the broad discussion around the architecture of the labour export policy.

According to the Department of Economic Statistics (2008, 9), 'overseas foreign worker remittances' for the year 2007 amounted to U.S. $14.5 billion.[10] In 2009, this figure increased to U.S. $17.3 billion (POEA: 2010b). These are vast increases from the 1990 remittance figure, U.S. $1.2 million, reported by the Bangko Sentral ng Pilipinas (as cited by Battistella: 1999, 232). As per the calculations of IBON, an independent think tank, for the year 2007 the total foreign exchange entering the Philippines in the form of worker remittances was twenty-two times greater than the amount entering as overseas development assistance (IBON: 2008, 14). In terms of gross international reserves, more than half of those received by the Philippines in 2007 were accounted for by overseas worker remittances (IBON: 2008, 14). The legal arrangements assuring the transfer of earnings by Filipino temporary migrant workers to banks in the Philippines are key to the long-standing success of the Philippines state in gathering this form of foreign exchange.

The year 2000 edition of *The Labor Code of the Philippines and Its Implementing Rules and Regulations* can be taken as a relatively recent version of the remittance-related rules and regulations of the world's largest labour export state. Rule XIII, entitled 'Foreign Exchange Remittance,' lays out detailed instructions applying to 'every contract worker and seaman recruit placed in overseas employment,' as well as licensed recruitment agencies, 'authority holders, and/or their foreign principals or employers' (Foz: 2000, 95). Particular sections of Rule XIII are worth citing at length in order to demonstrate the extent of state control involved:

> SECTION 2. **Obligation to Remit**. – It shall be *mandatory* for a worker or seaman to remit *regularly* a portion of his foreign exchange earning abroad to his beneficiary through the Philippine Banking system. *This obligation shall be stipulated in the following documents*:
>
> (a) Contract of employment and/or service between a foreign-based employer and a worker; (b) Affidavit of undertaking whereby a worker obligates himself to remit a portion of his earnings to his beneficiaries; and (c) Application for a license or authority to recruit workers; (d) Recruitment agreement and/or service contract between a licensed agency or authority holder and its foreign employer or principal; and (e) Application for accreditation of a principal or project.
>
> SECTION 3. **Amount of Foreign Exchange Remittances**. – The amount of foreign exchange referred to in Section 2 hereof, shall be *a minimum of 70 percent* of the overseas worker's basic salary in foreign exchange in the case of construction and sea-based workers, and *a minimum of 50 percent* in the case of other workers.
>
> SECTION 5. **Procedure of Remittance**. – (a) *The worker, prior to departure, shall open a deposit account for his mandatory remittance* in favor of his beneficiary in any Philippine bank. A foreign currency account may also be opened by the worker to be funded by savings in excess of the mandatory remittance. *The applicant shall inform the Bureau of Employment Services, the Overseas Employment Development Board or the National Seamen Board, as the case may be, his deposit account number.* (b) In the case of seamen, construction workers and other organized work crews involving at least twenty

five (25) workers, the foreign currency/peso account shall be opened by the employee with any Philippine bank upon the signing of the contract. The account shall be accompanied by a covering letter of nomination of beneficiaries and the date of payment of the allotment to the beneficiary as may be stipulated by the employee and the licensed agency, manning agent or construction contractor. (c) *At the end of every period . . . the licensed agency, construction contractor or manning agent shall prepare a payroll sheet* indicating the names of the workers covered by the scheme, their beneficiaries, their individual bank account numbers, the amount of foreign currency remitted and the peso equivalent thereof. This payroll sheet, together with peso check representing the remittance, shall be forwarded to the bank concerned . . . *A copy of the payroll sheet shall be furnished to the Bureau, OEDB, or NSB . . . on a monthly basis.* (Foz: 2000, 95, 96; emphases added)

In enforcing the regulation of remittances, as specified by legislation, on all parties involved – temporary migrant workers, their beneficiaries, recruitment agencies, banks of the Philippines, and certain employers – the Philippines state is able to maximize the collection of foreign exchange resulting from remittances of significant portions of workers' salaries, a symbol of which is the precise accounting and analysis of such remittances in the balance of payments and other state reports. Given the mandatory nature of these remittances, combined with the dependence of a growing proportion of Filipino workers on the arms of the state for employment overseas, international currency reserves received by the Philippines state through migrant worker remittances is one of, if not *the* most reliable and politically malleable supplies of foreign exchange available to the state.

Export-Oriented Nursing Labour Force Development

The labour market in which state-directed, export-oriented labour force development is most elaborate and established in the Philippines is that of nursing. In other words, in order to be the world's largest supplier of migrant nursing labour, the Philippines state has been and continues to be highly engaged in a range of functions. These include assessing general world demand for nurses; nurturing demand for Filipino nurses in specific national and sub-national markets; and re-structuring nursing training and work within the Philippines to accommodate the export of nursing labour. These functions are inter-related. Where nurses are observed, by the POEA and Labour Attachés, to be in demand in countries around the world, specific external nursing markets are studied by Labour Attachés and TESDA to ascertain the particularities of national or/and subnational demand and training requirements. Labour force development programs are then designed by TESDA to respond to demand for caring health labour.[11]

Clearly, the process is not as linear and neatly achieved in reality as these words imply. Political and other forces intervene and complicate the process. The scope and ambition of Philippines state planning in health care labour force development is, nevertheless, far-reaching and comprehensive. This is demonstrated below, principally through material gathered in interviews with key players involved: high-level Philippines state officials, leaders of the Philippines Nurses Association (PNA), health sector trade union leaders in the Philippines, and registered nurses involved in health care labour force development.

As shown in table 5.2, the number of nurses deployed internationally by the Philippines from the early 1990s is considerable, growing over the long run while reflecting fluctuations in world nursing labour demand.[12]

Paralleling this long-run growth is an increasing number, over time, of nursing colleges that have been licensed to train nurses by the Philippines state (Kelly and D'Addario: 2008, 86). (See figure 5.1.)

The existence of venues for nurse training and the state's intention to export professional nurses do not, however, assure that all or even a majority of students will successfully complete the Nursing Board Exam of the Philippines. As figure 5.2 demonstrates, during the period of 1980 to 2000, only about half the students training in private nursing colleges were able to pass the exam each year.

In concentrating, then, on increasing the numbers of nurse trainees, the Philippines state has given inadequate attention to regulating the quality of nursing education offered in the increasing number of nursing colleges (Xu: 2006; Yeates: 2009). Along these lines, according to Dr. Teresita Barcello, Manila Governor of the Philippines Nurses Association (PNA), the state is pressuring its top-performing College of Nursing – that of the University of the Philippines (UP) – to increase enrollment. Admitting only seventy students annually, the UP College of Nursing maintains that it cannot increase enrollment without forsaking the quality of nursing education it offers. This is due to a shortage of nurse educators resulting partially from retirement but also, not surprisingly, from emigration.[13] The state-proposed solution to the growing number of nurse trainees unable to qualify as registered nurses

Table 5.2
Professional Nurses Deployed Internationally by the Philippines,
New Hires and Rehires, 1992–2009

Year	Professional Nurses Deployed (New Hires and Rehires)
1992	5,747
1993	6,744
1994	6,699
1995	7,584
1996	4,734
1997	4,242
1998	4,591
1999	5,413
2000	7,683
2001	13,536
2002	11,867
2003	8,968
2004	8,611
2005	7,094
2006	13,525
2007	9,178
2008	11,495
2009	13,014

Source: Philippines Overseas Employment Administration (2010c).

through the Nursing Board Exam is revealing, in that it sheds light on the state's nursing labour force development strategy as a whole.

In 2002, a curriculum was introduced in the Philippines for the first-time training of licensed practical nurses (LPNs). Prior to this, such a curriculum did not exist due to the absence of the LPN designation in the Philippines health care system – and, in turn, the lack of demand for LPNs in the Philippines.[14] According to Irene Isaacs, TESDA executive director of the Qualifications and Standards Office, the introduction of the LPN curriculum was the result of a purported demand for LPNs in the United States. Two U.S. Americans partnered with Filipino capitalists – in compliance with foreign investment regulations – to offer LPN training programs that were approved by TESDA but did not have any

Figure 5.1: State-Licensed Nursing Colleges in the Philippines, 1920–2003

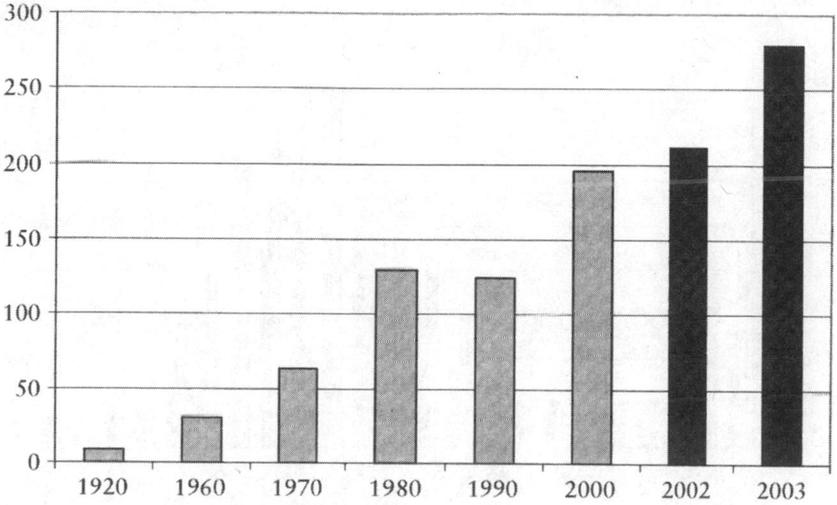

Source: Kelly and D'Addario (2008, 87).

'training regulations,' given the lack of domestic standards for LPN training.[15]

By 2008, some 20,000 LPNs had been trained in the Philippines, and the number of institutions offering the LPN curriculum had grown from two to forty-five.[16] It remains unclear in which particular countries LPN graduates of the Philippines have been employed, and in what positions.[17] Nonetheless, from the perspective of the PNA, the existence of the LPN curriculum is now being used by TESDA to argue for the introduction of a laddered training program that will produce various types of nursing labour.[18] More specifically, TESDA favours a system in which nursing students train for one year to obtain the designation of 'nurse aide,' one additional year for the designation of 'licensed practical nurse,' and two additional years for the designation of 'Registered Nurse.' Through such a system, existing students who have completed RN training but have not successfully passed the Nursing Board Exam would be designated as LPNs and nurse aides and placed in employment abroad.

In addition to solving the problem of the excess of graduate nurses inadequately prepared to pass the Nursing Board Exam, perhaps more important, laddered training would allow the Philippines state more ease in adjusting nursing labour force development to fluctuating and

Figure 5.2: Examinees and Passers of Nursing Board Exam, Philippines, 1980–2003

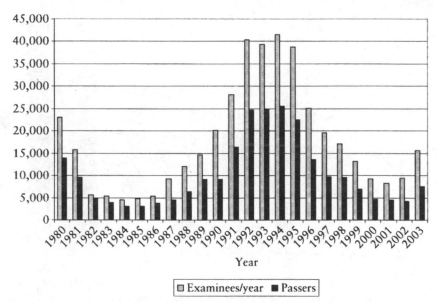

Source: Philippines Nurses Association; figure reproduced from Kelly and D'Addario (2008, 87).

changing external demand. As in the U.S. American instance examined in chapter 2, for example, demand for nursing labour shifted from registered nurses to nurse aides and licensed practical nurses in the late 1980s. To a certain extent, demand-sensitive nursing labour force development is already in play. The Department of Education makes adjustments to RN training in the Philippines as per the changing needs of the U.S. American and Canadian markets, such as adding more emphasis on psychiatric nursing or post-operative nursing when these specialized skills are required in North America.[19] Formalizing a laddered nurse training system, however, would require an amendment of the federal legislation – the Nurses Act (2000) – a political deliberation, the final outcome of which remains to be seen.

Democratic deliberation and final outcomes aside, the TESDA, in collaboration with the Australian Agency for International Development (AusAID, the overseas assistance agency of the Australian government), has already embarked on the beginnings of a new health care training system in the Philippines. Through its 'Human Resource

Development Facility' project in the Philippines, during the 2004–09 period, AusAID transferred some AUS $60 million mainly to TESDA, 'to improve the capacity of targeted institutions' in 'long-term training' and 'shorter-term human resource development activities' (AusAID: 2007). Among the groups of professional workers in the Philippines assisted to produce industry-specific, vocational training programs, highly experienced registered nurses were selected and assisted to produce competency-based training regulations, curricula, and assessment criteria for a range of health care designations new to the Philippines.[20]

The new health care designations created by the TESDA-erected, AusAID-funded Health Care Industry Training Council (HCITC) include 'caregiver'; 'health care assistant NC II'; 'barangay health worker NC II'; 'biomedical technician'; 'pharmacy assistant'; and 'massage therapist.'[21] While some of the new health designations are intended for export, others are clearly intended for the health care market of the Philippines. The contrasting amounts of skills training, instruction time, and remuneration attached to externally- and internally-oriented health care designations are glaring.

Following the vocational training and career ladder models of Australia, the 'health care services' and 'biomedical technician' designations are 'hospital-based' and geared to supply overseas health care labour markets.[22] These courses are two years in length and, in Australia, could be followed with university-level training. The caregiver designation consists of a six-month training course and, according to HCITC chair Elena Yu, tends to be pursued by RNs, and even physicians, who then take up caregiver positions in Canada and the United Kingdom where temporary migration of caregivers is facilitated by the state.[23]

In contrast, the barangay health worker NC II and pharmacy assistant designations are 'community-based' and geared to supply health care demand within the Philippines.[24] Both designations involve skills development in areas such as communication, safety, teamwork, and infection control.[25] While the barangay health service worker is responsible for the care of the entire barangay – a district of 2,000 to 5,000 people – the pharmacy assistant is assigned to work under a licensed pharmacist responsible for two barangays.[26] This rather thin spread of health care training and health care provision directed towards internal demand may be seen as a relatively new component of the reform of health care in the Philippines. Beginning in 1992, under the Republic

Act 7116, health care delivery was devolved from the national to local levels of government, including stringent cost-control measures.[27]

A brief comparison of course designs for the externally oriented health care assistant NC II and the internally oriented barangay health worker NC II further demonstrates the asymmetrical health care labour force development favoured by the Philippines state and its international partners, as exemplified by AusAID. In the case of the health care assistant NC II, designed to respond to international demand for hospital caring labour, a total of 996 training hours are required. The course covers 'core competencies' in preparing and maintaining beds, maintaining linen stocks, transporting patients, and providing 'biopsychosocial support.'[28]

In the case of the barangay health worker NC II, only 560 hours of training are required. Core competencies include working within a 'holistic community development framework,' providing 'primary residential care,' engaging community participation in health issues, and implementing 'health promotion and community intervention.'[29] Though it is a far more involved job description than that of the health care assistant in terms of tasks, skills required, and scope of responsibility, the training requirements for the barangay health worker are far less, and remuneration is symbolic. Barangay health workers must provide their labour voluntarily, with the majority receiving a daily honorarium of 50 Philippine pesos, or approximately U.S. $25 on a monthly basis.[30] This compares rather poorly with the U.S. $350 legislated monthly salary of public sector nurses in the Philippines.

Economic development, the social goal of most post-colonial states in the second half of the twentieth century, may be contrasted with *human development*, the social goal of the Venezuelan state within the framework of the Bolivarian Constitution. Taking a cue from the 1999 Bolivarian Constitution, Michael Lebowitz defines human development as 'the full development of human potential,' wherein the role of the state is to ensure overall human development (Lebowitz: 2008, 2, 3). Measuring the Philippines state against the social goal of human development, what can be observed is that the coordinating – indeed interventionist – role the state has designed for itself in the area of health care labour force development is far from strategic or rational. Linking in Eva Kittay's (1999) emphasis on the fundamental place of caregiving in human survival and the development of human societies, the Philippines's export-oriented health care labour force development strategy, with its severe underskilling, overburdening, and underpaying of the domestically oriented health care labour force, is in complete conflict with the social goal of human development. With regard to the short-term interests of the Philippines state, however, this policy is highly rational and effective. In order to help understand why, what follows is a historical sketch of post-colonial economic development in the Philippines, an instance of another dimension of material expansion in the fourth (U.S.) systemic cycle of accumulation of the capitalist world economy.

Lineages of the Philippines Labour Export Policy

The world historical process of Keynesianism, within the material expansion of the fourth (U.S.) systemic cycle of accumulation, took shape in import-substitution industrialization policies in much of the global South. For a myriad of interlocking and overlapping reasons, import-substitution industrialization (ISI) in most countries of the global South was unable to undo the deep structural inequalities of historical capitalism. Instances of ISI in the various countries of the global South must be traced world historically in order to understand why these processes did not tend to result in the positive social and economic outcomes experienced in most countries of the global North, where ISI processes unfolded earlier. These contradictions are among the several contradictions of the material expansion of the fourth (U.S.) systemic cycle of accumulation. In the instance of the Philippines – one of the first decolonized southern states of the twentieth century to embark upon import-substitution industrialization – a world-historical tracing of the ISI process is key to explaining the rise of the labour export policy.

Electing not to adopt the leading approach in neoclassical economics, in which ISI is dismissed virtually outright based on the assumption that state intervention in economic development is inefficient and should thus be minimal, Jennings (1991) offers a historical approach to compare ISI processes in Latin America and East Asia. Underlining that Singapore, South Korea, and Taiwan had initial periods of ISI before adding an emphasis on growth through exports, Jennings shows that these states promoted exports while protecting producers for the domestic market (1991, 199). At the time of Jennings's article, East Asian states had typically been seen by neoclassical economists and others as more successful than Latin American states because of emphasis on export-oriented industrialization by the former, and the lack of outward orientation of the latter – a juxtaposition which is untenable when examining the historical record.

Jennings argues that what is of central importance is the state's ability to steer the process of accumulation in accordance with the development needs of capitalism at crucial moments in history (1991, 224). Effective state intervention in the economy – leading to growth in gross domestic product, industrial output, industrial employment, and thus improved distribution – demands a well-structured state apparatus, consisting of cohesion among different government organizations and a tight bureaucracy. A 'triple alliance' between the state, foreign capital, and domestic capital is another aspect of this cohesion (Jennings: 1991, 203). Jennings stresses that this *triple alliance* cannot be taken for granted, as the determining element of the trio varies from country to country.

In an examination of ISI processes in the African continent and with a focus on the sphere of production, Mytelka (1989) observes that choosing the appropriate import substitutes is of importance in shaping socially beneficial ISI. Making a distinction between *import substitutes* and *import emulations*, Mytelka explains that a particular manufacturing 'logic' or 'process' evolves from the production of items socially necessary to those producing them (1989: 79). Transferring these 'metaphysical-material' systems is not obvious where import emulations are selected for ISI, and goods insufficiently linked to sociocultural specifics are put into production (Mytelka: 1989, 79).

Put another way, *market-based ISI*, where existing import data is used to determine which products are to be produced domestically, tends to lead to the production of consumer manufactures based on imported capital goods and technical expertise (Colman and Nixson: 1986, 281). Existing consumption patterns, however, may not be suitable to collectively oriented development aims or domestic factor endowments – particularly in formerly colonial societies, where development aims were rarely geared towards the needs of the majority. Production-based ISI, on the other hand, is based on the importation of the machine tools necessary to produce the capital and intermediate goods required to process locally abundant raw materials, and thus has the potential to put in motion ISI based on culturally, socially, and ecologically appropriate import substitutes (Colman and Nixson: 1986, 281).

Many of the themes discussed by Colman and Nixson (1986), Mytelka (1989), and Jennings (1991) are relevant in the instance of the Philippines, as demonstrated below. Though there was considerable cohesion within various organizations of the state engaged in ISI, the triple alliance between the state, foreign capital, and domestic capital was not present. The lack of such an alliance was further reinforced by competing sectors of domestic capital. Because the ISI experience was so short-lived in the Philippines, lasting only one decade, questions around the ability of the state to combine an outward orientation with the initial inward orientation of industrialization – or moving from market-based ISI to production-based ISI – cannot even be addressed.

The ISI experience is an aspect of post-independence Philippines that is rarely discussed, including by Philippines migration specialists. Far more recalled and elaborated are the politics of the rise and demise of the Marcos regime. Transnational migration specialist Pauline Barber (2008, 1270), for example, cites a 671 per cent rise in the number of Filipino applicants wanting to work abroad in the 1970s due to political instability and economic mismanagement under the Marcos regime. Writing in the late 1980s – almost twenty years after his arrest and imprisonment under the Marcos regime for imparting an anti-imperialist analysis of the Philippines economy – Alejandro Lichauco underlines the importance of understanding 'the origin and nature' of the crisis that brought Ferdinand Marcos to power in 1965 (Lichauco: 1988, 140). For Lichauco, a capitalist-turned-politician of the post-independence Philippines, the early 1960s elimination of foreign exchange controls was the cause of the economic crisis in the Philippines through which Marcos made his political ascent. Lichauco's account is useful in understanding the ISI process in the Philippines and beginning to uncover the structural inequalities which ultimately led to the development of the Philippines's labour export policy.

Beginning the story in the second half of the 1940s, Lichauco describes the context which gave rise to the adoption of capital controls in the Philippines. As a result of extensive damage from the Second World War – in which the Philippines, still a U.S. colony, opposed Japan – the U.S. state was pressured to provide compensation for losses endured by the Philippines. After delaying the payment of compensation with disputes over amounts, the U.S. state finally granted partial compensation to the Philippines in April 1946. The compensation, however, did not come without conditions. On 3 July 1946, one day prior to granting political independence to the Philippines, the U.S. colonial state succeeded in pushing the incoming administration to pass the Bell Trade Act, which, in Lichauco's words, extended 'the free trade arrangement that had characterized Philippine-American colonial relations' into the post-independence period (Lichauco: 1988, 141). The incoming administration agreed to pass the Bell Trade Act because payment of the remaining war compensation funds was tied to its passing. By 1949, this extended colonial-trade arrangement led to a balance of payments crisis, which in turn led the Philippines state to adopt capital controls.

In greater detail, as even the neoclassical economic historians Vicente Valdepeñas and Gemelino Bautista point out, the Bell Trade Act involved 'a number of things that seemed to infringe on Philippine sovereignty' (Valdepeñas and Bautista: 1977, 153).[31] The act thus prevented the Philippines state from levying export taxes or import duties; kept the Philippines state from adjusting the value of the peso in the best interest of the Philippines, obliging it to seek approval from the U.S. president prior to implementing changes in par value or convertibility; and provided equal treatment to U.S. and Filipino capitalists in the public utility and natural resource sectors of the Philippines, regardless of the 60 per cent Filipino ownership requirement enshrined in the country's 1935 constitution (Valdepeñas and Bautista: 1977, 154; Lichauco: 1988, 141–2). Bringing out the compliant attitude common among the Filipino elite of the time, which complemented U.S. imperiousness, parity for U.S. investors was extended over and above the provisions of the Bell Trade Act through an administrative ruling of the Secretary of Justice to the real estate sector (Lichauco: 1988, 142).

Within three short years of formal political independence, combined with the ongoing colonial trade relation, the Philippines faced a balance-of-payments crisis. This was the result of a mass of unlimited imports outweighing the supply of foreign exchange earned through exports (mainly copra and desiccated coconut), war compensation, and development assistance (Lichauco: 1988, 143; Valdepeñas and Bautista: 1977, 161). As Valdepeñas and Bautista remark, the few and short-lived export windfalls generated due to post-war world shortages of fat and oil were primarily absorbed by foreign investors (1977, 161). This undoubtedly contributed to shortfalls in foreign exchange, as foreign capitalists repatriated the cash-crop profits earned on the basis of Filipino labour. Between 1945 and 1949, the net change in international reserves moved from the positive figure of U.S. $256 million to the negative figure of U.S.-$160 million (Bell Mission Report figures, as cited by Valdepeñas and Bautista: 1977, 166–7).

The capital controls brought into full force by January 1950 allowed the Philippines Central Bank to manage all international exchange entering and exiting the Philippines. A system of priorities was established for the use of international exchange, and the international exchange earnings of both Filipinos and international residents of the Philippines were surrendered, at a fixed rate of 2 Philippines pesos to U.S. $1, to the Central Bank for rationing according to a periodically adjusted priority list of imports (Lichauco: 1988, 144). This policy change was subject to approval by the U.S. state, as per the stipulations of the Bell Trade Act. Moving away from its compliant attitude from a few years earlier, the Philippines state now asserted the right to impose capital controls. In Lichauco's words, 'it was largely through the assertiveness of then Finance Secretary Miguel Cuaderno that the President of the U.S. gave his consent to exchange controls' (1988, 144).

This assertiveness of the Philippines state was also expressed in a host of other policies from the early 1950s that promulgated industrialization. Attempting to shift away from an economy based on export-oriented, agricultural production, the Philippines state put in place measures used historically around the world to nurture industrial production by domestically based capitalists. The state thus sold its own corporations, at favourable prices, to capitalists in the Philippines, and it subsidized the purchase of raw material imports by rising, Philippines-based industrial capitalists (Valdepeñas and Bautista: 1977, 175). Through the Rehabilitation Finance Corporation, the state tilted resources gained through Japanese war reparations towards the provision of loans, capital goods, and services for industrialists of the Philippines. In the area of credit creation, the Central Bank of the Philippines was used to expand commercial bank credit and encourage lending to Philippines-based industrialists at low rediscount rates (Valdepeñas and Bautista: 1977, 175). The state also served as a guarantor, facilitating Filipino capitalists' access to credit markets in the United States. In the realm of fiscal policy, deficit spending was introduced to finance development and employment projects (Valdepeñas and Bautista: 1977, 177).

By the late 1950s, several changes had surfaced in the economy and society of the Philippines, most of which can be attributed to the state's program of import-substitution industrialization. Valdepeñas and Bautista render a lengthy list of the domestically produced manufactures which had become available, depicting the nature of these changes in very material terms:

Table 5.3
Growth of National Product, Manufacturing and Agriculture, Average Percentage
Changes (pesos, 1955 prices), 1948–1960

Period	Gross National Product	National Income	Value-Added, Manufacturing	Value-Added, Agriculture, Fishing, Forestry
1948–52	9.2	9.1	10.5	6.6
1952–6	7.7	7.6	12.9	6.3
1956–60	4.4	4.6	6.3	3.3

Source: National Economic Council; table reproduced from Valdepeñas and Bautista
(1977, 174).

> In 1955 . . . no dollar allocations were made for automotive storage batter-
> ies, ready-mixed paint, cotton and synthetic knitted fabrics, knitted jack-
> ets, sweaters, outwear, and all made-up garments of cotton and rayon. By
> 1956, such new products as smoking tobacco, cotton and rayon blankets,
> underwear, slips, nightgowns, gummed or painted labels, bags, sacks,
> tire-manufacturing and repair materials, automotive tires, abrasive, and
> emery paper and cloth [sic], corrugated aluminium sheets, plain sheets
> and foil were no longer imported because they were manufactured locally.
> (Valdepeñas and Bautista: 1977, 172–3)

At the macro-level, the growth rate of value added in manufacturing ranged from 6.3 to 13 per cent between 1948 and 1960, outpacing
growth of the agricultural sector and that of national income itself (see
table 5.3). As underlined by Valdepeñas and Bautista, the expansion
in manufacturing can thus be said to have been leading the rest of the
economy through the 1950s (1977, 173).

Taking a longer view, in just over one decade the Philippines had
shifted to a new pattern of development, for the first time in half a
century. Moving away from food manufacturing dominated by the
processing of primary products (i.e., sugar and coconut), which had
been central between the early twentieth century and 1938, by 1961 the
Philippines was producing a diverse range of industrial manufactures
(Valdepeñas: 1970, 12–14; Valdepeñas and Bautista: 1977, 125, 173–4).

This shift in the structure of production is reflected in data showing employment and wage patterns, in data tracing capital formation,
and in the industrial distribution of the labour force between 1950 and

Table 5.4
Real Daily Wage Rate in Industry and Agriculture (pesos, 1955 prices), 1950–1960

Year	Industry	Agriculture
1950	n.a.	2.05
1951	3.96	1.95
1952	4.47	2.28
1953	4.82	2.59
1954	4.96	2.73
1955	5.18	2.75
1956	5.12	2.38
1957	4.97	2.39
1958	4.81	2.37
1959	4.94	2.33
1960	4.73	2.28

Source: Central Bank of the Philippines; table reproduced from Ofreneo (1993, 148).

1960 (see tables 5.4 to 5.7). Though imperfect in many ways, the data reproduced here represent a consideration of various inter-related aspects of economic development – an approach largely missing in current economic development literature focusing on the Philippines. This is likely due to ongoing, politically charged ideological differences on the subject of state-led development.

Not only did wages and the aggregate level of employment rise (see tables 5.4 and 5.5), but also the distribution of the labour force changed. Most notably (see table 5.7), as stressed in the doctoral dissertation of Rene Ofreneo (1993) – later to become Undersecretary of Labour and Employment of the Philippines – between 1948 and 1961 the proportion of the labour force employed in manufacturing rose from 6.6 per cent to 11.5 per cent, while the proportion employed in agriculture fell from 71.5 per cent to 60.5 per cent. All of this marked a significant improvement from the hyperinflation, low wages, and resulting labour unrest of the early 1940s.

Furthermore, by the late 1950s, the Philippines had begun to tackle the issue of dependence on capital goods imports. Tax exemptions tied

Table 5.5
Employment and Unemployment (1000s of workers), 1949–1967

Year	Total Labour Force	Employed	Unemployed	Rate of Unemployment (percentage)
1949	7,529	6,408	1,121	14.5
1952	7,969	6,501	1,468	18.2
1955	8,489	6,962	1,527	17.7
1958	8,976	8,329	647	6.3
1961	9,713	9,095	618	7.2
1964	11,296	10,315	871	8.5
1967	11,955	11,107	858	6.7

Source: Bureau of the Census and Statistics; table reproduced from Valdepeñas (1970, 15).

Table 5.6
Growth of Real Capital Formation (pesos, 1955 prices), 1946–1967

Year	Capital Formation (million Pesos)	Capital Formation (percentage, real GNP)	Employment, (million persons)	Capital Formation per person employed (Pesos)
1946	194	8.1	6.1	31.8
1949	711	12.4	6.4	111.0
1952	434	6.1	6.5	66.8
1955	789	9.0	7.0	112.7
1958	935	9.5	8.3	112.6
1961	1,227	10.7	9.1	134.8
1964	2,355	17.3	10.3	228.8
1967	2,807	17.5	11.1	252.8

Sources: Various; table reproduced from Valdepeñas (1970, 13).

to the generation of local employment and use of indigenous inputs had proven to be effective by 1958. On average, tax-exempt firms had realized a net dollar savings of 44 per cent on imports displaced by domestic substitution, and had managed to generate one unit of employment for every 350 pesos of government net subsidy (Valdepeñas: 1970, 36). Between the early 1950s and 1958, tax-exempt firms had reduced their

Table 5.7
Industrial Distribution of Philippine Labour Force, 1948–1967 (percentages)

Industry	1948	1952	1955	1958	1961	1964	1967
Agriculture	71.5	72.0	72.5	62.8	60.5	58.2	57.0
Mining	0.3	0.6	0.4	0.2	0.3	0.4	0.2
Manufacturing	6.6	6.7	6.7	11.4	11.5	11.6	11.1
Construction	1.0	2.0	1.9	2.1	2.8	3.2	3.2
Transport & Communications	2.0	2.0	2.0	2.8	3.1	3.1	3.4
Trade	4.9	5.3	5.0	9.1	9.7	11.3	11.0
Government	3.6	4.7	3.6	5.6	5.9	5.4	7.0
Other Services	9.2	6.6	7.9	6.0	6.2	6.8	7.2

Source. Bureau of the Census and Statistics, table reproduced from Valdepeñas (1970, 14).

dependence on imported inputs by 10 per cent, from 76 per cent to 66 per cent (Valdepeñas: 1970, 36). Yet more concrete, in 1959, a cabinet decision was taken to erect a majority state-owned steel mill in order to lead the Philippines into a program of 'heavy industrialization' (Lichauco: 1988, 159).

Between 1960 and 1962, what Lichauco calls the 'decontrol program' was instituted by the Philippines state and the bourgeoning of a new structure of production geared towards domestic consumption and greater wealth distribution was reversed. Exchange controls that had been imposed to both encourage domestic manufacturing, and manage the volatile balance of payments, were eliminated, first through the introduction of a system of multiple exchange rates, then through the 1962 devaluation of the peso and introduction of a system of fluctuating exchange rates (Valdepeñas and Bautista: 1977, 188; Lichauco: 1988, 140). As underscored in *The Lichauco Paper* – which was published just before Lichauco's arrest and created a furor at the 1972 Constitutional Convention – devaluation, floating exchange rates, and tight monetary policies were adopted in the Philippines at a moment when even Latin American states, though allied politically to the United States, were resisting U.S. pressures to adopt such austerity measures (Lichauco: 1973, 55–6).

Full effects of the decontrol program can be traced from the second half of the 1960s onward. Indeed, this is why, in Valdepeñas's account

(1970), the moment of structural change in the development pattern of the Philippines is periodized from 1949 to 1967. In Ofreneo's (1993) labour-centred account, the period of positive change is slightly shorter, dating from the early 1950s to the early 1960s. Be that as it may, by 1965, domestic industrialists were severely lacking access to credit and faced unlimited competition from imported consumer goods; inflation was mounting; capital flight and increased luxury imports resulted from uncontrolled consumption of foreign exchange by agricultural export-ers; and manufacturing output grew by less than 1 per cent. Yet more tangibly, in 1966 some 1,500 firms failed, most of them new industri-alists, marking the resumption of growing unemployment (Lichauco: 1988, 165–6).

In terms of external debt, the Philippines state had moved from a pre-1962 debt level of U.S. $150 million to that of U.S. $600 million in 1965 (Lichauco: 1988, 172). An initial loan of U.S. $300 million had been made to the Philippines by the U.S. State Department and the Interna-tional Monetary Fund in 1962, in order to provide for the capital flight expected to result from the decontrol program. The combined effect of the decontrol measures and a loan double the size of the pre-existing external debt ultimately led to the quadrupling of the Philippine debt within three years, launching the country into a debt spiral which argu-ably continues to this day.

Why did the Philippines state abandon capital controls and import-substitute industrialization as a policy framework in the early 1960s, before most countries of Asia and Africa had even adopted such a pol-icy framework? Import-substitute industrialization, with its necessary controls over the foreign exchange entering and exiting the country, did not serve the interests of all layers of the Philippines elite. Exporters of traditional, as well as newer cash crops and raw materials did not favour exchange controls because the fixed exchange rate reduced the domestic value of export earnings and other controls applied limits to the overseas spending of those earnings. In 1956, as compared to 1938, timber exporters were earning eight times more; iron ore production had surpassed 1938 production levels by over 40 per cent; pineapple production had more than doubled; and copper production had in-creased more than six times over (Valdepeñas and Bautista: 1977, 156). Raw-material and cash-crop producers thus resisted capital controls from the onset. Already by 1953, these exporters – who were benefiting from increased international demand, including that caused by the Korean War – had won concessions from the state in the form of larger foreign exchange allocations (Valdepeñas and Bautista: 1977, 186).

Further concessions vis-à-vis foreign exchange allocations were made in 1957 due to continued clamouring by cash-crop and raw-material exporters (Valdepeñas and Bautista: 1977, 187). These same forces are at the root of a severely unequal distribution of land, formalized and fortified with the U.S. colonial state's establishment of landowner-based, municipal and provincial governance institutions in 1901 and 1907, respectively. As Valdepeñas and Bautista describe it, 'in less than ten years of American rule, the Philippines socio-economic elite, representing only 2.5 per cent of the population, got firmly entrenched politically' (1977, 111). The fact that, through state-supported, industrial development in the Philippines during the 1950s, a new, entrepreneurial layer was being added to the elite was no doubt a source of discomfort for the long-entrenched elite layer of landowners. Without making this suggestion, Valdepeñas and Bautista present evidence which supports it. More specifically, they cite a 1965 U.S. American study which estimates that 65 per cent of Filipino entrepreneurs emerging in the 1950s were from the 'lower stratum' of society, or from white-collar, lower white-collar, and manual labour backgrounds (Caroll: 1965, as cited by Valdepeñas and Bautista: 1977, 177).

U.S. American players were another contravening force to the expansion of diversified, domestically oriented production in the Philippines. As emblemized by the aforementioned Bell Trade Act of 1944, U.S. capitalists, with the support of the U.S. state, had long been invested in a Philippines economy tailored to U.S. capitalist accumulation and the repatriation of profits. As the Philippines state embarked upon its capitalist-friendly industrialization project, U.S. capitalists, though more accustomed to opposing industrialization in the Philippines, found ways to benefit. Further to the Bell Trade Act, U.S. capitalists managed to extend their rights through the Laurel-Langley Act of 1954, which awarded national status to all U.S. capitalists in the Philippines, thus extending to them all the credit and other facilities promoting domestic manufacturing (Lichauco: 1973, 49). At no point, however, did the U.S. state or U.S. capitalists in the Philippines – many of them involved in export and retail trade – fully concede to the Philippines state's adoption of capital controls (Lichauco: 1988, 178).

When Marcos defeated the U.S.- and landowner-supported President Macapagal in 1966 – amidst the economic mayhem caused by

Macapagal's decontrol program – state technocrats had already proposed a solution to the mayhem, but not one that was palatable in the anti-laissez-faire political climate of the time. As encapsulated in House Joint Resolution No. 2, popularly known as the Magna Carta of Social Justice and Economic Freedom, mass political sentiment rising from the effects of liberalized financial flows in the Philippines was decidedly in favour of domestically oriented, diversified development and a proactive state. Some of the rather clear wording of the Magna Carta, which was signed into law by Marcos in August 1969, is worthy of mention:

> the disposition of the nation's foreign exchange shall be subjected to a rigorous system of priorities; effort shall be undertaken to place all aspects of the distributive trade in the hands of Filipinos . . . all new institutions performing financial functions shall be owned and controlled by Filipinos . . . the government shall vigorously push through a program of industrial and agricultural pioneering and development . . . there shall be a national economic development authority with powers to plan and coordinate the nation's economic activities . . . basic and integrated industries essential to change the structure of the economy shall be established . . . (Cited by Lichauco: 1988, 186)

It was therefore only after his re-election in January 1970, with the help of Martial Law, that Marcos was able to implement the economic solution of the technocrats: the state removing itself from the industrialization of the Philippines and leaving the task to foreign investors.[32] From there it was not a far stretch – in terms of neither time nor policy – for the Philippines state to re-orient its energies from the elaborate architecture supporting import-substitute industrialization, to a similarly elaborate architecture supporting the export of labour. While the initial impetus for the export of labour came through an invitation to the Philippines state, by West Asian states, to provide temporary construction labour for the expansion flowing from the nationalization of oil by oil-rich states,[33] this led to the gradual formalization of the export of labour via legislative changes and the creation of corresponding regulations. As mentioned above, the foundation for all of this was created through changes brought to the Labor Code by the Marcos regime in 1974.

How did what started as a temporary situation of supplying labour for oil-related West Asian growth become a permanent fixture of state planning and activity? An examination of the pattern of foreign exchange earnings over time helps explain the impetus for the Philippines state to continue expanding its labour export functions after the 1970s. As shown in figures 5.3 and 5.4 below, the forces underlying the state's early 1960s shift away from the short-lived strategy of domestically oriented production – landowners, other primary product exporters, and foreign investors – are effectively the same forces which created the need for the concerted amplification of labour export policy.

Not only is it larger in absolute terms, but the growth rate of foreign exchange earnings via migrant worker remittances has also increased far more steadily than foreign exchange earnings entering the country through the top three official categories of agricultural and mineral exports. In order of size, as depicted in figures for the decade of the 1990s, the largest amount of foreign exchange entering the Philippines is via export sales of industrial commodities, the second largest amount is via remittances of migrant workers, with the top cash crops and raw materials following much further behind (see figures 5.3 and 5.4).

With a legislative architecture to ensure that migrant workers remit more than half the income they earn abroad – along with a policy emphasis on temporary migration that keeps the larger portion of families within the Philippines – remittances would become the most reliable supply of foreign exchange for a state facing what Filipino social policy analyst Noel Vasquez calls the 'chronic balance of payments problems' (Vasquez: 1992, 42). They would be a supply, in other words, which would remain in large part within international exchange reserve holdings of the Philippines until otherwise disbursed by the state, unlike the foreign exchange earnings of landowners, other primary product exporters, and the largely foreign manufacturers of export-oriented, industrial commodities.

With regard to the productive use of remittance-based foreign exchange by the state – one of the principal development benefits of migrant worker remittances put forward by international financial institutions and the GFMD – the following evaluation of IBON, one of the Philippines's foremost independent-policy think tanks, is quite clear:

> . . . it becomes relevant to ask to what ends the country's foreign exchange resources are used. Unfortunately these are not mobilized in the service of the country's development nor the people's welfare which have

Figure 5.3: Philippines Foreign Exchange Earnings, Various Sources, 1990–1999 (millions of USD)

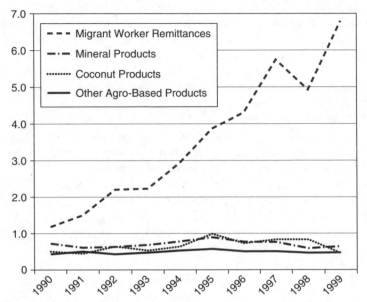

Source: Philippines Overseas Employment Administration (2010b); Bangko Sentral ng Pilipinas (2008a, 2008b).

been worsening even as the balance of payments (BOP) indicators have been improving. The country's foreign exchange is most of all used to be able to service the foreign debt, to pay for imports of foreign-dominated export-oriented industry, and to enable profit repatriation and capital flight by domestic elites. In this sense, the foreign exchange generated by overseas Filipinos remittances is being exploited for counter-productive ends. (IBON: 2008, 14)

A reading of the available Philippines balance of payments reports from the past several years substantiates this evaluation. Between 1999 and 2007, total annual imports were greater than total annual exports, with import growth consistently outpacing the growth of exports (Bangko Sentral ng Pilipinas: 2008a). Imports were dominated (some 60 per cent) by raw materials, intermediate goods, and capital goods required by foreign manufacturers of export goods (Department of Economic Research: 2004; 2008; 2009). Reflecting the complete reversal of

Figure 5.4: Philippines Foreign Exchange Earnings, Top Two Official
Categories Compared, 1990–1999 (millions of USD)

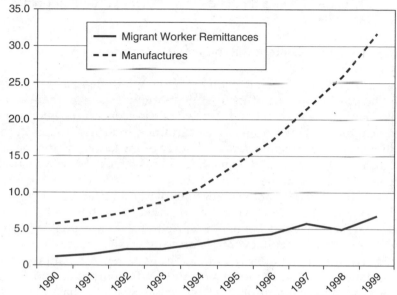

Source: Philippines Overseas Employment Administration (2010b); Bangko Sentral ng
Pilipinas (2008a, 2008b).

thinking and vision after the 1950s, such an expansion and distribution
of imports is considered by the state to be indicative of 'robust domestic
economic activity' (Department of Economic Research: 2004, 4). Investment income, including foreign direct investment income and portfolio
investment categories, has been steadily negative and growing in deficit since 1999 (Bangko Sentral ng Pilipinas: 2008b).

In terms of private capital outflow, using the World Bank definition
of the time, Vos estimates a total of U.S. $7.83 billion for the period
of 1971 to 1988[34] (Vos: 1992, 510). Using a broad definition of capital
flight, thus the net unrecorded capital outflow, Filipino scholar Edsel
Beja estimates a total of U.S. $16 billion in capital flight for the 1970s,
U.S. $36 billion for the 1980s, U.S. $43 billion for the 1990s, and U.S. $36
billion for the period of 2000 to 2002, reflecting the full-blown effects
of financial liberalization in the 1990s (Beja: 2006, 60).[35] Beja underlines a 'revolving-door process of capital flight and debt accumulation'
whereby capital inflows are consistently used to finance capital out-

flows (2006, 59). By the early twenty-first century, total capital flight – as defined by Beja – for the period of 1970 to 2002 amounted to U.S. $131 billion, or 2.8 times the total external debt of the Philippines in 2002 (Beja: 2006, 60).

Summation and Theoretical Reprise

After achieving political independence from the United States in 1946, the Philippines was one of the first post-colonial states in the African and Asian continents to take a proactive role in economic development. As such, the dynamics of import-substitution industrialization in the Philippines are instructive in tracing some of the key contradictions of the material expansion of the fourth (U.S.) systemic cycle of accumulation as experienced in the global South.

Due to the social and political confines of export-oriented, raw-material, and agricultural production based on the exploitation of landless peasants, the newly independent Philippines state was unable to sustain its program of capital controls and diversified, domestically oriented production. In the early 1960s, after some ten years of moderate but promising success in import-substitute industrialization and the effective use of capital controls to stabilize the balance of payments, the historically rooted elite regained control of the state and ended the program of capital controls and diversified domestically oriented production. The period of capital controls and domestically oriented capitalist production was brief, in world historical terms, and the redirecting of the Philippines state and economy failed synonymously due to deep class division in favour of the land-owning Filipino bourgeoisie and other capitalists benefiting from export-oriented production, as well as ongoing U.S. political influence in the post-colonial Philippines. All of these are relations emanating from historical structures of the stratified, capitalist world economy.

Starting in the early 1970s, the energies of the Philippines state were invested in organizing the exportation of nursing and other labour – part of the restructuring and reorganization of the financial expansion of the fourth (U.S.) systemic cycle of accumulation. Whether for the purchase of imports or repatriation of profits by U.S. and other foreign manufacturers in the Philippines, outward investment and consumption of international goods by Filipino landowning and other capitalists, or for the inter-related external debt servicing – the gathering of foreign exchange via the remittance of salaries by temporary migrant workers is crucial for the functioning of the Philippines state, hence its ongoing planning and implementation of export-oriented labour force development. Export-oriented nursing labour force development is one of the most advanced examples of such economic intervention and planning by the Philippines state. The Philippines thus set a trend in making available a supply of temporary migrant nursing labour internationally. Canada and the United States of America were in turn able, by circa 1990, to draw on this supply as a means of health care cost cutting. Given the subsequent shift in world demand for temporary migrant nurses created as other states of the global North followed the example of Canada and the United States of America, various states of the global South began emulating the Philippines in facilitating the export of temporary migrant nurses.

Export-oriented labour force development, supported by states of the global North, is a key element of restructuring in the capitalist world economy. As alluded to earlier, states as varied as Indonesia, India, Bangladesh, and Vietnam are redefining economic development to include the generation of foreign exchange through the exportation of temporary migrant workers – especially female migrants, who tend to remit larger sums with more consistency (Packer et al.: 2007, 31). What can be drawn from this is that notions of human development, and even less, the valuing of nursing and other caring labour have not gained ground in countries emulating the labour export model of the Philippines. What remains to be seen is how those countries in Latin America that are adopting the social goal of human development are able to combine the undoing of these and other gender inequalities with the undoing of other structural inequalities.

6 The Global Integration of Labour Markets and Deepening Unequal Exchange

From the 1940s to the 1960s, a host of movements for national independence were unfolding in countries of Africa and Asia – some achieving formal political independence during the 1960s, and others, like the Philippines, already in the process of attempting to construct economic independence. Within this context, Arghiri Emmanuel (1969) produced his seminal work *L'Echange inégal: essai sur les antagonismes dans les rapports économiques internationaux*, at l'Ecole pratique des hautes études of the Sorbonne. This work, published in English a few years later as *Unequal Exchange: A Study of the Imperialism of Trade*, was a key contribution to the critique of economic development theories arising in the 1950s. Like other works of socialists, Marxists, dependency theorists, and post-Marxists of both the global South and global North, Emmanuel's theory of *unequal exchange* questioned assumptions of economic development as an apolitical process contained within individual nations. Emmanuel's theory of unequal exchange was taken as a basic assumption in the core/periphery stratification of world systems theory formulated from different angles by Samir Amin, Andre Gunder Frank, Giovanni Arrighi, Terence Hopkins, and Immanuel Wallerstein during the 1960s and 1970s. All of these critical thinkers thus put the wealth of Western Europe and North America into historical perspective, linking economic development of what was then called the *First World* to military conquest, long-distance trade, and formal colonization of the Americas, Asia, and Africa.

Such a contextualization of Western European and North American wealth is highly relevant to more recent discussions of globalization, globalizing care economies, and the South-North migration of health workers – discussions which tend to be ahistorical and unlinked to a structural understanding of the capitalist world economy. Given this relevance, this chapter begins with a review of Emmanuel's theory of unequal exchange, linking it to concepts elaborated upon by world historical analysts. Emmanuel's theory of unequal exchange is demonstrated to be a useful tool for the systematic understanding of the economic losses and social costs of South-North labour migration, particularly that of nurses and other care workers. Dynamics of the global integration of nursing labour markets are then interpreted in world historical terms. Methodologically, this task of interpretation involves drawing out – from the particularities of the Philippines, Canadian, U.S. American, and other instances of the global integration of nursing labour markets – those elements which help situate the flow of nursing labour to the global North within the longer history of unequal relations between countries of the global North and global South. Following from this, the significance of the global integration of nursing and other labour markets is brought out with regard to current restructuring in the capitalist world economy.

Unequal Exchange and Historical Capitalism

Recalling the weight that David Ricardo's assumption of the *immobility of factors* across national borders carried within classical political economy, Arghiri Emmanuel underlines, in an elaboration of his theory of unequal exchange, the weakness of this assumption and offers significant improvements. Through to the mid-nineteenth century – regardless of the fact that the export of capital was occurring and on the rise – the assumption of the immobility of both capital and labour was used by classical political economists, as first presented in Ricardo's eighteenth-century theory of comparative costs (Emmanuel: 1972, 41). Only in 1873 did J.E. Cairns acknowledge that Ricardo's assumption of complete mobility of capital and labour within a nation, and complete immobility of capital and labour between nations, is 'false in both parts' (Emmanuel: 1972, 41). Cairns, however, maintained that the competition of factors is restricted by *relative immobility*, and this moderately amended assumption continued to be used in the twentieth century by most economists of Emmanuel's generation.

Concurrently – though in separate circles of discussion, as is reflected in Emmanuel's (1972, vii) lamenting over the lack of a common language – some economists of Emmanuel's time were in agreement around the tendency of international equalization of profits, which necessarily implies accepting the assumption that capital is mobile. Emmanuel gives the example of the neoclassical development economist par excellence, Arthur Lewis, who observed in the 1950s that many capitalists in *surplus labour countries* (commonly referred to, at the time, as *Third World* countries) invested their capital in England and the United States (Emmanuel: 1972, 43). Taking the mobility of capital as given, but keeping Ricardo's assumption of the *immobility of labour*, Emmanuel goes on to discuss the variance of wage levels across political frontiers.

Emmanuel argues that until the second half of the nineteenth century, subsistence wages were the norm internationally, with differences between countries reflecting differences in levels of subsistence. From the 1860s, according to Emmanuel, two distinctly separate categories of wages began to form – 'subsistence' and 'the rest' – due to the development of large-scale trade union movements in industrializing countries of the time (Emmanuel: 1972, 49).

Taking a more comprehensive analytic view, world historical analyst, Samir Amin, locates the separate categories of wages in the unequal exploitation of labour in the core and periphery of the world system (Amin: 2010b, 88). While the price of labour power or the real wage obtained by workers in the core increases in a manner more or less parallel to increases in productivity, the same is not true of the price of labour power in the periphery – despite the fact that production in both core and periphery is governed by the demands of world capitalist accumulation (Amin: 2010b, 89, 92). Labour has been and continues to be super-exploited in the periphery through extra-economic, coercive means because the exports of the periphery are constitutive elements of production in the core. For Amin, the low price of raw materials produced in the periphery based on the super-exploitation of peripheral labour was key to the rise of capitalist industrialization in the core, a process of which the late nineteenth-century development of trade union movements identified by Emmanuel is one element.[1]

For both Emmanuel and Amin, given the condition of two separate categories of wage levels, *unequal exchange* arises when goods without equivalent wage rates and *organic compositions of capital* are traded internationally (Emmanuel: 1972, 160). Differences in *organic composition of capital*, Emmanuel explains, using Marx's terms and rationale, are due to technical features of 'different branches of production' or industries (Emmanuel: 1972, 163).[2] Differences in wage levels are due to historically contingent forces, for example the concessions gained by workers from employers and the state in a given national context (Emmanuel: 1972, 163, 169).

The difference in wage levels based on historically contingent forces is of central importance in the perspective of Emmanuel and Amin and at the heart of their dispute with neoclassical economics. While in neoclassical economics, wages are determined by prices, for Emmanuel and Amin, the opposite holds true. Within capitalist production relations, prices are determined by wages that are created by historical and political circumstances and therefore constitute the independent variable of the system (Emmanuel: 1972, 70, 172).

As underscored by Emmanuel, unequal exchange is rooted in the 'immediate exploitation of one country by another' and the 'uneven development of different countries' (Emmanuel: 1972, 160), Referring back to Marx's assumption of perfect competition, in *Capital*, volume 1, Emmanuel stresses that Marx's law of value is 'distorted' by the reality that competition is not perfect.[3] Labour thus commands different prices, in different countries, due to 'the political fact' that the world is divided into different states (Emmanuel: 1972, 169).[4]

This *political fact*, as Emmanuel phrases it, that the world is divided into states as we know them today, is the outcome of a process which began, according to world historical analyst Anibal Quijano, with the constitution of the Americas following the arrival of Europeans. Central to this process is what Quijano calls the 'assemblage' of all forms of control and exploitation of labour, including systems of appropriation and distribution of the fruits of labour (Quijano: 2000, 3). Quijano's list of forms consists of *slavery, serfdom, petty-commodity-production, reciprocity*, and *wages*. For Quijano, these forms (other than *wages*) were reborn with European colonization of the Americas, through which they were articulated, individually and together, for the first time to capital and its growing world market. In Quijano's words:

> All of these forms of labor were historically and sociologically new: in the first place, because they were deliberately established and organized to produce commodities for the world market; in the second place, because they did not merely exist simultaneously in the same space/time, but each of them was also articulated to capital and its market. Thus they configured a new global model of labor control, and in turn a fundamental element of a new model of power to which they were historically and structurally dependent. (Quijano: 2000, 3)

A recasting of Marx's abstract notion of *socially necessary labour* may be tied in here. Marx's notion refers to the average labour time required to produce a particular commodity, under the general conditions of production (Marx: vol. 1). Given that Marx's notion is in the abstract, he assumes a general standard of the era in question, thus pertaining to *time*, and not *time and space* simultaneously. In concrete terms, through overseas trade – which rapidly and exponentially expanded due to increased liquidity resulting from European mining of precious American metals and other forces (to be discussed further below) – several modes of production, or forms of labour as Quijano puts it, were incorporated into a capitalist world economy. Recasting, then, Marx's abstract notion of socially necessary labour, socially necessary labour varies from one social formation, or state, to another; hence, the possibility of the existence, for example, of sharecropping as the dominant form of agricultural labour in the Philippines, from the late Spanish colonial period, through the American colonial period, to the present.[5]

Returning to Emmanuel's *unequal exchange*, Emmanuel draws out some of the subsequent effects of *unequal exchange* based on the difference of labour costs. Using algebra and numerical examples, it is demonstrated that in the twentieth-century world capitalist market, total value in Marxian terms – that is, the total of constant capital, variable capital, and surplus value[6] – and in turn, the *rate of accumulation* (or profit), are equalized for the rich and impoverished country involved in Emmanuel's hypothetical trading relationship (Emmanuel: 1972, 170–1).

The equalization of value and the equalization of the rate of profit occur regardless of the fact that total investment is larger in the hypothetical rich country and wages are lower in the hypothetical impoverished country. What results is a higher surplus value in the impoverished country (due to lower relative wage) and higher total profit in the rich country (due to higher relative price of production). All of this translates into more money in the pocket of the capitalist investing in the impoverished country, and more money available for tax collection by the state of the rich country.[7] With relatively more tax revenue available to it, the rich state is more able to augment the *social wage*, or physical and social infrastructures such as roads, schools, and social services. While Emmanuel underscores the importance of this difference in the level of economic and social development of the rich country relative to the impoverished, he does not include this outcome of the international trade relation within his definition of unequal exchange. Once again, Emmanuel's concept of unequal exchange is derived only from the difference in labour cost, whereby the products of rich or high-wage countries exchange at higher prices than those of impoverished or low-wage countries such that the latter earn less from exports while spending more on imports.

Beyond algebraic formulations, Emmanuel takes the concrete example of Sweden and its high standard of living. Where neoclassical economists would argue that Sweden's high standard of living is due to its large timber exports, Emmanuel argues that due to the 'social conquests' of the Swedish working class, the standard of living is high in Sweden and Swedish timber is, in turn, expensive on the world market (Emmanuel: 1972, 172). Emmanuel compares demand and prices for timber with those for petroleum, on a world scale, between 1913 and 1962. Though consumption of petroleum rose over the period, world petroleum prices fell. In contrast, world timber prices rose, though timber consumption fell. More specifically, between 1913 and 1962, world petroleum consumption rose from 50 million tons to 1,215 million tons, but the price index for petroleum fell from 100 in 1913, to 27 in 1962 (Emmanuel: 1972, 173). Conversely for timber, per capita consumption fell by about 10 per cent in Europe, and 25 per cent in the United States between 1913 and 1950, but the timber price index rose from 100 in 1913, to 559 in 1952 (Emmanuel: 1972, 173).

Accounting for differences in levels of productivity of petroleum and timber production, Emmanuel uses the factoral terms of trade, arguing that despite increases, over time, in petroleum production productivity, workers in major petroleum industries of the world earned only a subsistence wage (Emmanuel: 1972, 174). For timber production, on the other hand, a lower relative increase in productivity, over time, was accompanied by a twenty to forty-fold increase in timber worker wages (Emmanuel: 1972, 174). As Emmanuel summarizes:

> If it were the market that determined incomes, then timber, as such, would have no particular tendency to enrich Sweden, Finland, Canada, or Austria, any more than petroleum would have to impoverish the Middle East or Venezuela. If, however, it is incomes that determine the market, then everything is explained by the mere fact that timber happens to be a product of high-wage countries and petroleum of low-wage countries. (Emmanuel: 1972, 174)

Finally, Emmanuel takes the example of the rare species of timber produced and exported by countries of Africa and other *low-wage countries*. Taking into consideration both barter and factoral terms of trade, Emmanuel observes that 'precisely those timbers of superior quality,' produced almost solely by low-wage countries, are the only timber types facing falling prices in the world market (Emmanuel: 1972, 174).

Unequal Exchange and the Global Integration of Nursing Labour Markets

The conceptualization of unequal exchange of Emmanuel and Amin is based on the labour embodied within commodities exchanged between nations. Where labour itself is the commodity of international exchange, as in the export-oriented nursing labour force development policy of the Philippines, and where the state's use of foreign exchange generated through migrant worker remittances is structured as in the Philippines – the export of labour is an *absolute loss* in productive terms. In other words, the labour exporting country, responding to world demand, gains nil on a societal level from the export of labour and is thus in a position of *absolute unequal exchange*. This is fundamentally different from the international exchange of other commodities, where low-wage or peripheral countries gain relatively less from trade, but still gain something.[8]

Given the worldwide shortage of nurses and the growing demand for nursing labour to care for aging populations in high-income countries (Buchan and Calman: 2004, 20–1), even without a deliberate, export-oriented, nursing labour force development policy combined with a pattern of unproductive state usage of foreign exchange as in the Philippines, nursing labour-supplying countries are in a position of *deepened unequal exchange* because of the economic inability to compete with the world price of nursing labour. All of this further exacerbates the unequal distribution of nursing labour internationally. As mentioned in chapter 1, the reported average nurse-to-population ratio in countries of Western Europe and North America is 1,000 nurses per 100,000 population, the ratio in countries of Central and South-eastern Europe is 750 nurses per 100,000 population, and the ratio in countries of Africa, South-east Asia, and Latin America is 100 nurses per 100,000 population (Buchan and Calman: 2004, 11–12).

Absolute and deepened unequal exchange occurs on the basis of the direct and indirect labour involved in the production of migrant labour, all of which is lost by the labour-supplying country and gained by the labour-receiving country.[9] Combining the socialist feminist argument of the integral role of caring labour in the reproduction of capitalist societies with Marxian input-output analysis, this entails, in the instance of migrant nursing labour the unpaid labour of the predominantly female family members providing the nurturing and socializing of nurse-to-be-individuals; the labour of those producing the food and shelter for the nourishment and housing of nurses-to-be; the labour of those involved in transforming individuals into professional nurses (i.e., education and training costs incurred by individuals, families, and states); the labour time encapsulated in the work experience carried by professional nurses from the home country to the nurse-importing country; and the predominantly unpaid labour involved in reproducing the labour force in the form of the descendants of temporary migrant nurses – a cost typically borne by female family members in the home country, where descendants of temporary migrant nurses tend to reside.

Shifting to the concrete, the economic loss encompassed in absolute and deepened unequal exchange arising from the global integration of nursing labour markets is expressed in three principal ways. First, the loss of trained nurses may lead to the intensified undervaluing of health care labour in the labour-exporting country. This intensified undervaluing of health care labour occurs where the labour exporting country is unable to offer wages equivalent to or approaching the world price for nursing labour and, in turn, creates new forms of caring labour to supply domestic health care labour markets, as in the instance of the Philippines. The creation of the barangay health worker is a form of intensified undervaluing of health care labour. Though trained far below the standard of nursing labour in the Philippines and remunerated accordingly, at a monthly salary of approximately U.S. $25, individual barangay health workers are required to perform a wide range of caring tasks to meet the health needs of large portions of the Filipino population. This devaluation of health caring labour may, in turn, reflect back on the wage levels of nurses in the labour-exporting country. Some public sector nurses in the Philippines, for example, were earning less in 2008 than the minimum monthly salary set in the Nursing Act of 2002. More specifically, minimum monthly compensation for entry-level nurses is set in the act at 16,093 pesos (U.S. $350), while some public sector nurses were earning only 10,000 pesos (U.S. $220) in 2008 (Public Service International: 2008).

Second – unless resisted by organized labour in nurse-importing countries through insistence that collective agreements assure equal terms of employment for locally-based and temporary migrant nurses – the state-shaped, temporary nature of migration lends itself to the creation of lesser terms of employment for the temporary migrant nursing labour force.[10] Where the imported labour force consists of temporary migrant nurses of several different countries of origin, a hierarchy of employment terms results given the different location of states and the accompanying, race-based social classification system within the historically stratified, capitalist world economy. Moving beyond nursing labour, this would apply to the global integration of labour markets of any skill level or type based on temporary migration. This is illustrated by the ruling in a discrimination case filed in British Columbia, Canada by the Construction and Specialized Workers' Union (Local 1611) against the construction company SELI International, which was remunerating Western European migrant workers at higher wage levels than South American migrant workers performing the same tasks. The British Columbia Human Rights Tribunal ruling states:

> The members of the Complainant Group were especially vulnerable during their work here in British Columbia on the Canada Line project. They lived and worked here for up to two years. During that time, they were far from home and their families, and dependent on their employer, not only for their work and wages, but for meals, accommodation, travel to and from work, and travel back to their homes. The effect of the Respondents' actions was to treat them differently from, and adversely in comparison to, their European colleagues performing the same or substantially similar work. They were paid less, they were housed in inferior accommodation, they were given less choice about where and what to eat, and were made to account for every expense incurred, rather than being given an allowance to do with as they wished. In every aspect of their relationship with the Respondents, members of the Complainant Group were treated worse than members of the comparator group, not because of any differences in their experience and skills, but because of who they are and where they are from, *i.e.* characteristics related to the prohibited grounds engaged by the complaint. (British Columbia Human Rights Tribunal: 2008, 141)

Table 6.1
Temporary Migrant Nurses Entering Canada by Employment Category, Selected Years

Category	1989	1990	1991	2001	2002	2003	2004	2005	2006	2007	2008	2009
Head Nurses	–*	–	–	5	5	7	–	–	6	–	5	8
Registered Nurses	518	706	474	555	497	413	354	295	346	580	1,118	1,003

*The notation of '–' is used where the number of cases is less than five but more than zero.
Source: Citizenship and Immigration Canada (2007, 2010).

This leads to the third expression of economic loss encompassed in absolute and deepened unequal exchange: the undervaluing of skills and experience of internationally trained registered nurses. One example of this tendency is found in the Canadian instance of the global integration of nursing labour markets. Temporary migrant registered nurses assume the full slate of registered nurse responsibilities while earning the lesser salaries and benefits of graduate nurses until they are able to pass Canadian licensing exams. This is despite the fact that internationally trained registered nurses migrating on employer-sponsored, temporary work authorizations are able to do so because they have the applied nursing experience demanded by Canadian employers. As shown in table 6.1, a comparison of the numbers of temporary migrants entering Canada as 'head nurses' versus those entering as 'registered nurses' during the two major temporary migrant hiring waves for this sector further magnifies the point. Recalling the migration-related shortage of nurse educators in the Philippines mentioned earlier – a shortage faced in several nursing-labour-supplying countries (Buchan and Calman: 2004, 20) – the ratio of temporary migrant head nurses to temporary migrant registered nurses is extremely low.

An example of the undervaluing of skills of internationally trained health workers with permanent resident status in Canada is in the area of elderly care (i.e., care within the home as well as in institutions). In a research report based on surveys and interviews with employers, immigrant care workers, and care recipients in five major cities in Canada, 'many employers' state that a large number of their 'care aide,' or 'personal support worker' staff complements consist of internationally trained nurses and physicians (Bourgeault et al.: 2009, 75). Given the strong skill sets these workers bring – not unrelated to high levels of professional training – employers in elderly care sector state they prefer employing immigrant care workers.[11] The hourly wage of personal support workers in Canada's largest province, Ontario, ranged, in 2009, from CAD $10.35 (low wage) to CAD $19.40 (high wage) (Human Resources and Skills Development Canada: 2009; Valiani: 2011). This compares with the 2009 hourly wage of registered nurses in Ontario, which ranged from CAD $25.75 (low wage) to CAD $40.50 (high wage). The five largest source countries or source regions of internationally trained care workers in Canada, according to the study sample, are the Philippines (41.6 per cent), Eastern Europe (11.7 per cent), South America (9.1 per cent), Asia (6.5 per cent), and South-east Asia (6.5 per cent) (Bourgeault et al.: 2009, A-22).

Similarly, in the United Kingdom, overseas nursing experience is not recognized and internationally trained nurses tend to be placed at the bottom of their nursing grade or category (Yeates: 2009, 117). For black and Asian internationally trained nurses employed in the public health care system, this is an element of the discrimination resulting in the estimated loss of lifetime earnings ranging from 26,000 GBP to 35,000 GBP for female nurses and 30,000 GBP to 38,000 GBP for male nurses (Pudney and Shields: 1999, 23).

The manifestations of economic loss encompassed in absolute and deepened unequal exchange are manifold and profound. These manifestations are costs or/and consequences that may be described as both social and human, touching individuals, families, and entire societies. In her study entitled *Children of Global Migration*, Rhacel Parreñas documents that an average of 2,531 Filipinos leave the Philippines daily as temporary migrant workers (Parreñas: 2005, 12). This translates into approximately nine million Filipino children under the age of eighteen growing up without the presence of at least one migrant parent (Parreñas: 2005, 12). Parreñas uses Shellee Colen's (1995) concept of *stratified reproduction* to explain some of the contradictions faced by migrant mothers from the Philippines. As is made clear in the following citation, Colen's stratified reproduction, and the use of the concept by Parreñas, can be easily be applied to mothers of various origins who are temporary migrant workers, including temporary migrant nurses:

> . . . migrant women from the Philippines are subject to inequalities of reproduction, because they often face legal restrictions that exclude the members of their families from host societies whose next generation they are reproducing via their care work. Thus family reunification is not

always a choice, and transnational mothering becomes an inevitable outcome of migration. (Parreñas: 2005, 93)

Based on extensive surveys and in-depth interviews, Parreñas finds that the effects of migration on children of migrating mothers are negative, especially when compared to migration effects on children of migrating fathers. Of the 124 children of migrant fathers surveyed, 43 figured among the top 10 per cent of students in their schools in terms of academic and other performance. Among the surveyed children of migrant mothers, only 16 of 94 achieved the same (Parreñas: 2005, 95). Parreñas argues that this is due to the compensating efforts made by wives of migrant fathers and the corresponding lack of effort made by husbands of migrating mothers.

Regarding husbands of migrant mothers, Parreñas underlines that these men tend to reject both housework and the affective work of nurturing in the family, to the extent in many cases of moving away from the children to other towns or regions (Parreñas: 2005, 103). The family caring labour of the migrant mother is generally assumed by eldest daughters, 'over-extended' aunts, elderly grandmothers, and the migrant mother herself. Migrant mothers tend to provide emotional caring from a distance, while emotional and physical caring is provided by aunts, often with children of their own, or/and grandmothers, who often see themselves as too old to raise children (Parreñas: 2005, 114). Parreñas remarks that while fathers who are left behind tend to forgo the responsibilities of family care, mothers are increasingly expected to migrate to provide primary income for families, as well as fulfil traditional responsibilities of emotional caring from a distance (Parreñas: 2005, 98). This *expansion of mothering,* as Parreñas phrases it, is a manifestation of loss encompassed in absolute and deepened unequal exchange and has far-reaching cultural implications for all societies in which states are encouraging female migration, given the greater propensity of females to remit earnings home.

The use of HIV rapid tests in Kenya and Uganda is another example through which to understand the manifestations of loss encompassed in absolute and deepened unequal exchange. As mentioned in chapter 1, some 20,000 health workers migrate to North America and Europe from the continent of Africa each year, though African health workers represent only 3 per cent of the world's total health care labour force (Blanchet and Keith: 2006). In place of HIV testing by trained nurses, low-quality test kits are commonly used by 'non-medical staff' in

'Volunteer Counselling and Treatment Centres' in Kenya and Uganda (Kimani: 2009). A study of the effectiveness of the test kits was published in a 2009 issue of the *East African Medical Journal*, the key finding of which was that test kit results were inconsistent, faulty, or contradictory for over half of the cases examined (Kimani: 2009). Misdiagnoses such as these, the resultant spread of disease and deaths, and the very use of HIV test kits which are considered unreliable and hence no longer used in the global North – these are all manifestations of loss encompassed in the absolute and deepened unequal exchange resulting from the global integration of nursing labour markets.

The inter-governmental African Union (2003) estimates U.S. $60,000 and U.S. $12,000 as the costs of training one general practice doctor and one medical auxiliary, respectively, arguing that in total, through the migration of health workers, African countries subsidize high-income countries by some U.S. $500 million annually. Connell (2008) discusses the costs of health labour training to states in relation to the benefits of foreign exchange earnings resulting from health migrant worker remittances. Xu (2003, 271) justifies what she calls the 'semi-intentional' nursing labour export policy of the Philippines in that remittances from overseas nurses provide a significant portion of 'much-needed' foreign exchange. And Dilip Ratha and other analysts of the World Bank Development Prospects Group advocate the benefits of migrant worker remittances for economic development in labour-exporting countries (Ratha et al.: 2008).[12] A comprehensive accounting of absolute and deepened unequal exchange, the economic losses on a societal scale, and their subsequent effects, as exemplified here, presents a critical challenge to such studies and perspectives, as well as to the very proposition of analysing costs and benefits of foreign exchange accumulation via migrant health worker remittances. The challenge is simultaneously methodological, theoretical, ideological, and political.

More specifically, this examination – unlike those of the African Union (2003), the World Bank, or Connell (2008) – aims to account for the entirety of economic loss and human and social costs of some of the first skilled labour markets to begin the process of global integration. Furthermore, for the Philippines, the world's leading labour-exporter, this study traces historically the narrow class interests underlying the motivation for foreign exchange gathering via migrant worker remittances – a state motivation which is irrational, even in economistic terms. Given the use of the Philippines, internationally, as an exemplary model of development based on labour export and the gathering of foreign exchange via remittances, this study suggests that what is required for each state engaging with such a development model is a comprehensive accounting of deepened unequal exchange and historical examination of the root causes of foreign exchange deficits.

The Global Integration of Labour Markets in World Historical Perspective

In what may be seen as an economic history of British free trade and its world-scale political and social consequences, Karl Polanyi (2001), in *The Great Transformation: The Political and Economic Origins of Our Time*, discusses the process of the *universal mobilization of land*, which spread beyond Europe, starting from the mid-eighteenth century:

> The mobilization of the produce of the land was extended from the neighbouring countryside to tropical and sub-tropical regions – the industrial-agricultural division of labour was applied to the planet. As a result, peoples of distant zones were drawn into the vortex of change the origins of which were obscure to them, while the European nations became dependent for their everyday activities upon a not yet ensured integration of the life of mankind [*sic*]. With free trade the new and tremendous hazards of planetary interdependence sprang into being. (Polanyi: 2001, 190)

Free trade and the significantly reduced cost of transportation allowing for mass, cross-border transfers of grain and other agricultural raw materials are the principal vehicles of Polanyi's universal mobilization of land – both involving active intervention by the state. In a similar way, weakened social and legal recognition of trade unions, combined with the temporary migration policies of states, are the principal vehicles of the global integration of nursing and other labour markets. Borrowing from Polanyi's phrasing, the global integration of labour markets as envisioned by states may be broadly restated, for analytical purposes, as *the universal mobilization of labour*. Such a massive mobilization of labour – on a global scale, with global implications – has occurred only once in the history of the capitalist world economy, during or as part of the mercantilism of the second (Dutch) systemic cycle of accumulation. A look, therefore, at the pivotal role of African slave labour in the construction of Atlantic-centred production and commerce is useful in beginning to map what may lie ahead in terms of the world development implications of the *universal mobilization of labour*.[13] Given that the

Atlantic slave trade evolved over a period of some 300 years, this mapping is very preliminary, to be further historicized and theorized as the passing of time proves whether states and employers are successful in realizing the vision conceptualized here as the global integration of labour markets.[14]

In a ground-breaking study entitled *Africans and the Industrial Revolution in England: A Study in International Trade and Economic Development*, economic historian Joseph Inikori (2002) analyses long-term economic development through a methodology linking micro-scale production processes of different regions of the world.[15] Inikori's interest is in tracing the contributions of Africans – both continental Africans and diasporic Africans in the Americas – in the 'successful completion of the industrialization process in England' (Inikori: 2002, xvi). Included in the study is not only British America but also all of the Americas, given that African slaves were the principal source of labour power making for the possibility of Atlantic commerce, the whole of which, Inikori argues, laid the foundations for England's industrialization process (Inikori: 2002, 8).

For Inikori, coercion and timing are key to understanding the role of African labour in the growth of Atlantic trade. 'Forced specialization,' therefore, of 'enslaved Africans and their descendants in large-scale production of commodities' was key at a time when 'demographic, socio-economic and political conditions generally favoured small-scale subsistence production by independent, uncoerced producers' in the Americas (Inikori: 2002, 156, 157). Put another way, only slaves could be mobilized *en masse* by large capitalists for plantation production in the land-abundant Americas, where newly migrated European labour was legally free and geared towards production on small plots of state-provided land, cleared, for the most part, through forced movement and elimination of indigenous peoples.

Similarly, in the current historical moment, temporary migrant labour is the form of labour which allows employers to further alter production processes to meet their desired ends. The temporary nature of legal status combined with the temporary employment terms of the temporary migrant labour form is the twenty-first century version of coercion making possible *super-exploitation* by capitalists.[16] Enslavement, combined with geographical relocation, was the earlier version of coercion making African labour relatively more exploitable than other labour in the Americas during the seventeenth and eighteenth centuries.

Inikori highlights the island of Madeira as the first Atlantic island producing sugar for Europe – based on large-scale, African slave production – as early as the fifteenth century (Inikori: 2002, 165). By the end of the century, Madeira was the largest single supplier of sugar to Europe. Slave plantation sugar of the Canary Islands took over from Madeira as largest single supplier to Europe in the early sixteenth century (Inikori: 2002, 165). Inikori stresses this as the beginning of Atlantic commerce in that through what were initially experiments in Madeira and the Canary Islands – for both capitalists and states – the structures of Atlantic trade were erected, establishing the Atlantic Ocean as the nucleus of Atlantic commerce by the mid-seventeenth century.

Similarly, the contingent, increased use of temporary migrant nursing labour, which began circa 1990 with employers in Canada and the United States, is becoming a generalized practice among major nurse-demanding states around the world.[17] Following from this, employers of several skilled sectors, along with states and inter-governmental bodies, are deliberating on the notion of labour-force planning and skills development on a global scale, as most formally expressed in the 2007 formation of the Global Forum on Migration and Development (GFMD). States of the global North are increasingly framing overseas development assistance in terms of export-oriented skills development infrastructure in recipient countries, as in the AusAID-funded restructuring of health labour force development in the Philippines. Similarly, in Romania, subnational governments of northern Italy are funding the training of Romania-based nurses to work in the Italian language medium, and in accordance with nursing standards of Italy, for importation to Italy (OECD: 2009, 199). The OECD recommends further initiatives such as these, arguing they have the potential to create 'an international supply of workers in high-demand occupations' while generating 'a significant flow of remittances' back to home countries (OECD: 2009, 199).

More important than sugar, in terms of commodities in the sixteenth century, were gold and other precious metals, due to foreign exchange shortages in Europe and, ultimately, Asia (Frank: 1998; Arrighi: 1994; Inikori: 2002). After the rapid colonization of what is now known as Latin America, precious metals and gold became the major commodities imported by Europe between the fifteenth to eighteenth centuries.[18] Inikori argues that it was on the basis of slave sugar production, however, that the British Caribbean became the first economic challenge to Spanish America and Brazil in terms of control of Atlantic trade

Table 6.2
Per Annum Growth, by Period, of Slave-Produced Commodities, Atlantic Commerce
(British Pounds, GBP)

Year	1501–50	1651–70	1761–1780	1848–50
Yearly Growth	1.286 million	7.97 million	21.903 million	89.204 million

Source: Inikori (2002, 479).

(Inikori: 2002, 174). Combined with their successful use of naval power, the British managed to wrest control of Atlantic commerce from Portugal, Spain, and France in the seventeenth century, leading to Britain's expansion of slave-based mass production to a range of commodities including cotton, coffee, rice, and tobacco. Combining data and analysis from years of debates among economic historians, Inikori tracks the annual value of slave-produced commodities from the early sixteenth century, demonstrating that under British management, per-annum growth of the value of slave-produced commodities increased more than tenfold between the mid-seventeenth and mid-nineteenth centuries. (See table 6.2.)

Inikori posits that, in a variety of ways, it was through this expansion of the fruits of slave production that an amplification of Atlantic commerce occurred. The total annual value of Atlantic commerce was thus amplified from 3.241 million GBP in the 1501–50 period to 231.046 million GBP in the 1848–50 period (Inikori: 2002, 479). The fruits of slave production most relevant to this comparison are the formation of commodities of necessity for European working classes and the formation of instruments of finance in England.

Before drawing from each of these individually, an immediate comparison may be drawn between the slave-commodity-based amplification of Atlantic production and trade, and *the universal mobilization of caring labour* in the capitalist world economy today. The growing absorption of caring labour defined broadly – including both domestic labour and nursing labour – in countries with high rates of women employed outside the home and ageing populations, suggests that what may be in the making is the formal and perpetual production of caring labour in some countries for countries higher placed in the global hierarchy. This is due to the vital importance of caring labour for socialization, health maintenance, and social cohesion – the invisible labour within that which is understood as a country's standard of living. From a world historical perspective, this – rather than merely the increasing number of female labour migrants, as stressed by Piper (2008) and others – is the principal significance of the feminization of labour migration. The *world-stratified production and distribution of caring labour* can thus tentatively be taken as a budding tendency in restructuring world capitalism.

In proposing the *world-stratified production and distribution of caring labour as a budding tendency*, rather than a fully developed feature of restructured world capitalism, what is opened rather than answered here are two major questions for future research: *What role will China play as a major potential exporter or importer of temporary migrant nursing and other caring labour? How will this affect the pattern of world development flowing from the global integration of caring labour markets?* Will China become a major importer of migrant nurses, disrupting the absorption of caring labour by the global North – for example, to place nurses in the grassroots medical services system to which the Chinese state allocated 21.7 billion CNY in 2009 (Communist Party of China: 2010)? In greater detail, these funds were funnelled towards the construction of 986 county-level hospitals, 3,549 hospitals in central towns and townships, and 1,154 community health service centres – many of which will likely require nursing labour (Communist Party of China: 2010). Alternatively, will China become an increasingly important source of nursing labour for developed countries, as predicted by Fang (2007), with Chinese nurses replacing Filipina nurses as the largest group of internationally trained nurses in the United States, as suggested by Xu (2003)?

Explaining the role of enslaved African labour in the formation of commodities of necessity for European working classes, Inikori argues that expanded European consumption of plantation commodities was made possible by the combination of economies of scale and below-subsistence cost of labour. Over time, commodities of the Americas shifted from being luxury products of the European aristocracy to being necessities for all, feeding into what Inikori calls 'the phenomenal expansion of Atlantic commerce' (Inikori: 2002, 481). Relating this to the contemporary phenomenon of increasing use of migrant nursing labour, cost savings due to the importation of temporary migrant nurses are likely to feed into perpetuating the world-stratified consumption of medical technology and, in turn, monopoly profits of the corporations producing medical technology.

Finally, critical political economists and economic historians have long connected the creation of credit with the expansion of trade and production (Marx: 1966, vol. 3; Hobsbawm: 1975; Arrighi: 1994). Drawing out these connections with regard to long-term industrial development in England, Inikori demonstrates that textile industries of Northern England and the Midlands were able to further growth and innovation during the Industrial Revolution as a result of the growth of the credit economy (2002, 315, 316). Due to the 'peculiar risks and credit needs' of British Atlantic commerce, and the 'economics of slave plantation agriculture in the Americas,' banking houses, discount houses, insurance companies, and the stock exchange arose in England, mobilizing and circulating the funds of the rich like never before (Inikori: 2002, 316, 318). Bills of exchange were thus based on overseas trade, as exemplified in the commonly combined métiers of slave trader and banker, for instance, Benjamin Arthur Heywood of Liverpool; company bonds were dominated by the Royal African Company, the East India Company, and the South Sea Company; and the permanent national debt was established in the 1690s to provide the war-making capacity required to win control of slave-based, sea-borne commerce (Inikori: 2002, 320, 321).

A final parallel may be drawn here with current World Bank and GFMD discussions around the creation of remittance-based financial instruments. *Diaspora bonds* and other financial instruments are the creation of credit, by and for the state, in the name of economic development, on the basis of migrant worker savings. The 2008 GFMD statement of conclusions and recommendations thus speaks of creating 'partnerships' between source and destination countries to facilitate the best use of migrant workers' financial 'contributions,' through which states can 'harness diaspora assets beyond merely their income flows' (GFMD: 2008, 4). In addition to credit creation through the savings of increasingly poor, super-exploited workers, rather than through the savings of the rich, as in the seventeenth and eighteenth centuries, remittance-based financial instruments are being touted as a source of financing for small-scale projects to replace formerly existing public service systems. Along the same lines, this source of financing would replace, for the state, the now low-to-non-existent source resulting from taxation of the wealthy classes and collection of royalties from foreign investors. All of this is part of the redefinition of economic development in individualistic terms. Rather than a responsibility of the state on behalf of the collective whole, economic development is increasingly being framed as an outcome of 'human beings who are healthy, educated, employed, and able to care for their families' (GFMD: 2008, 3).

In closing, structurally similar to the mobilization of slave labour in Atlantic-centred world trade and production, the global integration of caring and other labour markets based on temporary migration has the potential to deepen stratification in the capitalist world economy. More specifically, given the historically uneven distribution of world wealth, certain states and societies are poised to benefit through increasingly dynamic combinations of skills if the universal mobilization of caring and other labour is achieved – to the detriment of human development in the world as a whole.

7 Capitalist Contradictions and World-Stratified Production and Distribution of Caring Labour – Roots and Flower of the Global Integration of Nursing Labour Markets

Presenting an alternative to the standard push-and-pull approach to questions of migration, this study examines historically, the increased world production, circulation, and use of temporary migrant nursing labour, one of the first skilled sectors to begin the process of integration on a global scale. Differing from most studies, which focus on a purported but poorly defined increase in international migration, this study emphasizes the 1990s rise of temporary labour migration as a new means of entry for internationally trained workers into core countries of the capitalist world economy. The shift from permanent residency to temporary labour migration is conceptualized as part of the shift from a social and economic policy framework built on notions of full employment and workers' rights to one built on the notion of flexible labour markets. The opening of a multinational reserve army of labour is exemplified through the relatively advanced instance of the global integration of nursing labour markets.

Combining world historical analysis with tools of Marxian economics and socialist feminism – all of which have been in use, though not by many scholars, for over fifty years – the sector-specific, multidimensional explanation offered here goes well beyond theories attributing increasing international labour mobility simply to globalization. Conditions giving rise to the global integration of nursing labour markets are explored relationally, in terms of dynamics between the core (the global North) and the periphery (the global South and formerly communist countries of Europe), the dynamics between capital and labour, the dynamics between capital and states, and the dynamics of patriarchy.

In greater detail, it is argued here that various contradictions in the material expansion of the fourth (U.S.) systemic cycle of accumulation

have led to increased world production, circulation, and use of temporary migrant nursing labour and, in turn, to the the global integration
of nursing labour markets. These contradictions are: health care cost
escalation caused by the monopoly structure of production of medical
technology; persistent undervaluing of nursing labour; and the inability to forge collectively oriented development due to a state structure
built on inequality. Through particular spatio-temporal instances of the
material expansion of the fourth (U.S.) systemic cycle of accumulation,
these contradictions are reconstructed historically, demonstrating the
forces creating the conditions for the increased world supply and demand of temporary migrant nursing labour. Seemingly separate processes, unfolding on a national scale, are shown here to be interrelated
and overlapping, leading to the global integration of nursing labour
markets – part of the radical restructuring of the financial expansion of
the fourth (U.S.) systemic cycle of accumulation.

The dynamics flowing from the monopoly of medical technology are
traced primarily through the U.S. American instance. More specifically,
hospital cost escalation, resulting from the monopoly structure of production of medical technology, led, by the late 1980s, to the adoption of
cost-cutting in hospitals via reduced employment of U.S.-based, unionized registered nurses; and increased employment of licensed practical nurses, vocational nurses, nurses' aides, and temporary migrant
nurses. The choice of hospitals – the employers of nurses – to counter
the workplace gains made by unionized registered nurses is seen as
part of the larger contradiction of the fourth (U.S.) systemic cycle of
accumulation, whereby workers around the world achieved greater
rights, but at the expense of employers – a redistribution which is ultimately unsustainable within a capitalist organization of the world
economy.

The U.S. American instance is of world historical importance in that
the United States is the world's largest absorber of internationally
trained nursing labour, as well as one of the first countries of the global
North to adopt the practice of hiring temporary migrant nurses in relatively large numbers. Additionally, the monopoly driven U.S. medical device and diagnostics industry is likely to have similar effects on
health care industries around the world.

The dynamics flowing from the persistent undervaluing of nursing
labour are traced primarily through the Canadian instance of the global
integration of nursing labour markets. Despite the well-intentioned establishment of health care insurance and provision as a public good,

the value of nursing labour in Canada – in contrast to male-dominated physician labour – has been persistently under-recognized, leading nurses to withdraw their labour from the Canadian health care system by the 1980s. This in turn led to both the exit of temporary migrant nursing labour from Canada and the increased employment of temporary migrant nursing labour within Canada. The Canadian instance is of world historical importance in that, along with the United States, it set the trend in the use of temporary migrant nurses in the global North. The Canadian instance also demonstrates that monopoly structures of production escalate health care costs, even under public provision of health care, compounding the undervaluing of nursing and other caring health labour, of which female workers are the main providers.

The causes and consequences of the inability to forge collectively oriented social and economic development – a major contradiction of the material expansion of the fourth (U.S.) systemic cycle of accumulation in the global South – are traced though the spatio-temporal instance of the Philippines. The increased production and circulation of temporary migrant nursing and other labour are outcomes of the political configuration of the Philippines state. Motivated by the need for politically malleable foreign exchange to sustain an economy rooted in colonial trade relations and highly polarized wealth distribution, in as early as the 1970s, the Philippines state elected to invest energy and resources in developing a complex architecture for the export of labour. The world historical importance of the Philippines instance is that this architecture is supported by core states, and is increasingly emulated by other states, due to its ability to generate both relatively lower cost labour in response to world demand, and politically malleable foreign exchange.

Moving from the range of contradictions at the root of the global integration of nursing labour markets, and extending the flower metaphor suggested in the title of this chapter, the *stem* may be described as the *re-intensified exploitation of female caring labour*. This re-intensification may be observed in all three spatio-temporal instances, though it takes shape differently in each. In the U.S. American instance, re-intensified exploitation of female caring labour began taking shape in the undoing of gains made by unionized registered nurses. In the Canadian instance, it takes shape in the undervaluing of skills and experience of temporary migrant nurses, as well as the state-sanctioned use of temporary migrant nursing labour by employers seeking to dodge elevated standards achieved through collective bargaining. In the Philippines instance, it takes shape in the undervalued caring labour of barangay health workers, female family members of migrant workers, and nurses employed in the Philippines.

In conclusion, a *budding tendency* in the restructuring of world capitalism is also proposed here. Given the historically under-recognized role of unpaid female labour within capitalist social relations, the global integration of nursing labour markets and the interrelated global integration of domestic care labour markets appear to be leading to a world-stratified distribution of caring labour, based on export-oriented production of caring labour in some countries of the world. This has the potential to concentrate crucial caring labour in the social reproduction of a dwindling fraction of world society, moving world society as a whole further away from the goal of human development. What remains to be seen is how processes in China may alter the patterns of *the universal mobilization of caring labour* that are conceivable today. Finally, though severely marginalized by capitalists and states over the past three decades, trade unions have an ever-important role to play in the current restructuring of relations between workers and employers of the world.

Notes

Foreword

1 I have elaborated on this vision in my article 'Globalization and the Agrarian Question' (Amin: 2006).
2 See my book, *Ending the Crisis of Capitalism or Ending of Capitalism?* (Amin: 2010).
3 See my book, *The Law of Worldwide Value* (Amin: 2010).

1. Introduction

1 Conceptual terms are italicized to emphasize the constructed nature of terms typically assumed to be merely descriptive words.
2 This statistic should be taken with caution. The proportion of permanent migrants is even smaller than it appears here given that individuals entering countries on temporary work permits of more than one year in duration, individuals entering on temporary work permits that are technically renewable, and individuals changing their legal status after initially entering on a short-term basis (for example, refugee claimants) are counted in this set of OECD data as 'permanent migrants.' In several countries, the aforementioned categories are counted separately, and not linked to categories referring to *permanency*. In short, definitions of *permanent migration* and *temporary migration* – and, in turn, the resulting statistical data – vary from state to state, and are subject to differing national experiences and manipulation for ideological purposes.
3 The following countries are members of the Organisation for Economic Co-operation and Development: Australia, Austria, Belgium, Canada, Czech Republic, Denmark, Finland, France, Germany, Greece, Hungary,

Iceland, Ireland, Italy, Japan, Korea, Luxembourg, Mexico, Netherlands, New Zealand, Norway, Poland, Portugal, Slovak Republic, Spain, Sweden, Switzerland, Turkey, United Kingdom, and the United States.

4 See, for example, *Care, Autonomy, and Justice: Feminism and the Ethic of Care* (Clement: 1996).

5 As of the early twenty-first century, particularly among critical policy analysts, the term *core* is used interchangeably with *global North* and *periphery* is used interchangeably with *global South*, though it remains unclear in the latter whether or not countries of the former Soviet Bloc are included in the term *periphery*. In this analysis, the term core will be used synonymously with the terms *rich countries* and *global North*, and the term *periphery* will be used to refer to the *global South* and formerly communist states.

6 While this study argues that processes of the Philippines, the United States, and Canada are of global importance and likely consist of elements relevant to other countries, the precise conditions of the ease of entry or levels of emigration of temporary migrant nurses vary from country to country and merit specific historical investigation.

7 Saudi Arabia began importing temporary migrant nurses in large numbers prior to 1990, but this demand alone was not enough to create a shift in world demand for temporary migrant nurses. In 1974, for example, 2,457 migrant nurses were employed in the public sector in Saudi Arabia, most of which were drawn from countries of West Asia and North Africa (Mejia et al.: 1979, 49). In contrast, in the United States, in 1991, the first year for which statistical data are available on temporary migrant nurses admitted to the United States, the figure was 4,325 (see table 3.8).

8 In this study, 'medical technology' refers to medical devices and diagnostics equipment. This industry, it is shown, has a unique history to that of the pharmaceutical industry, including an entirely different set of corporations.

2. Temporary Migration and the Global Integration of Labour Markets

1 This differs from the OECD (2008a) definition of permanent migration, which includes labour migrants entering on work permits of longer than one year in duration. The definition of permanent migration varies by country and by organization, mostly due to historical and political reasons. In the post–1492 history of North America, for instance, if permanent residency had not been the means of entry for the majority, population and labour force growth would have not amounted to what they are today.

2 For an analysis of Canada's shifting immigration policy and system, see 'The Shift in Canadian Immigration Policy and Unheeded Lessons of the Live-in Caregiver Program' (Valiani: 2009). For a historical view of the rising use of temporary migrant labour in Canada, see *Home Economics: Nationalism and the Making of 'Migrant Workers' in Canada* (Sharma: 2006). Though the latter is the most extensive study of temporary migration in Canada, the numbers tabulating various categories of temporary migrant workers are questionably large as compared to data now available for the same years. This is likely due to changes and improvements in counting methods of the Canadian state.

3 In the Canadian instance, for example, there were two major waves of immigration between 1946 and 1977. Family reunification and European immigration were emphasized in state policy in the first wave, and labour-force requirements and family reunification formed the policy basis for the second wave. Many non-European immigrants entered in the second wave, especially following the removal of discriminatory immigrant selection criteria in 1962. Both waves were characterized by *permanent migration*, or permanent residency (Pendakur: 2000). Pendakur underlines that 'permanent migration has constituted the cornerstone of Canadian immigration policy since Confederation' (Pendakur: 2000, 3).

4 For a close-up view of proposals in development by OECD policy experts, see the report on 'Fair Labour Migration: From Vision to Reality,' a seminar held at the OECD in Paris in 2007, in *Labour and Migration Update: Policy and Research News* (Valiani: 2007b).

5 The World Bank estimates that remittances to developing countries amounted to U.S. $251 billion in 2007. This figure differs from the one used here because the World Bank figure does not include countries of Eastern and Central Europe. The latter, however, are important to include given the high numbers of workers migrating from these regions as formerly socialist economies attempt to make the much vaunted *transition* to capitalism.

6 The term 'distribution' is used here in the Marxian sense, referring to the division of company income between capitalists (in the form of profits and interest) and workers (in the form of wages and public programs funded through the taxation of capitalists).

7 The 'International Migration and Development Initiative' emerged from discussions between the International Organization for Migration (an intergovernmental organization established in 1951), the private sector, the World Bank, and some governments.

8 For an analysis of the second intergovernmental Global Forum on Migration and Development, and a report of events occurring parallel to it,

see 'Labour and Migration Update: Policy and Advocacy News' (Valiani: 2008a), http://www.justicia4migrantworkers.org/pdf/MigrantLUpdate Nov08.pdf.

9 Ambet Yuson, Regional Representative, Building and Wood Workers' International – Asia/Pacific, presentation at Press Briefing of the Global Union Forum on Migration, Manila, 24 October 2008. See *Labour and Migration Update: Policy and Advocacy News* (Valiani: 2008a).

10 In figure 2.5, the number of temporary migrant doctors seems to be approaching that of permanent residents by 2005; this is due to the phenomenon of temporary migrant doctors and certain other migrants employed in Canada being permitted to transfer to permanent resident status upon nomination through employer-driven, Provincial Nominee Programs. See chapter 4 for further elaboration.

11 Not all internationally trained doctors are permitted to practice medicine in Canada on temporary work authorizations. Only those of the following countries are permitted to do so, as per the rules of the Royal College of Physicians and Surgeons of Canada: Australia, New Zealand, Hong Kong, Singapore, South Africa, Switzerland, and the United Kingdom. Temporary migrant doctors of these countries are given geographically specific licenses that allow them to practise only in the Canadian province offering the temporary employment contract (see 'Jurisdiction Approved Training,' Royal College of Physicians and Surgeons of Canada, accessed 28 August 2009, from http://rcpsc.medical.org/residency/certification/img_page2_e.php). The United States is not included in this list, most likely because when U.S. doctors migrate to Canada, they tend to be granted entry as permanent residents.

3. The Global Integration of Nursing Labour Markets – the U.S. American Instance

1 See, for example, *Medical Science and Medical Industry: The Formation of the American Pharmaceutical Industry* (Liebenau: 1987); *The Truth About the Drug Companies* (Angell: 2004); *L'envers de la pilule: les dessous de l'industrie pharmaceutique* (St-Onge: 2004); *The Pharmaceutical Corporate Presence in Developing Countries* (Tavis and Williams: 1993).

2 Prescription drugs consumed by patients in hospitals are for the most part billed separately from the cost of the hospital care, and are hence mostly reflected in the subcategory 'prescription drugs' within the category 'Retail Outlet Sales of Medical Products' in official national heath expenditure data. The cost of medical equipment, on the other hand, another

subcategory within 'Retail Outlet Sales of Medical Products,' is carried mostly by hospitals and included as part of the services comprising hospital care. As shown in figure 3.2, 'Hospital Care' is the largest U.S. health expenditure under the official category 'Personal Health Care,' which represents 85 per cent of national health expenditures.

3 Though mediated through private health insurers from the onset, Medicare covers most of the costs of in-patient hospital care, hospice care, medical nursing home care, and home health care for elderly Americans and certain persons with disabilities. Additionally, for these same groups, Medicare covers the costs of physician and outpatient hospital services, durable medical equipment, and other medical services and supplies (Weiss: 1997, 153).

4 The centralization of capital refers to the gathering of different forms of already-existing capital – in this case, most notably buildings, health care delivery operations, and medical technology – by a decreasing number of capitalists (see Sweezy for more on this Marxian term: 1942, 254–5).

5 The lead-up conference was entitled 'Effects of Inflation and Anti-Inflationary Policies on the Health Sector' and was organized by the National Center for Health Services Research. Conference papers and other key documents of this period of the policy debate are included in the edited volume, *Health: A Victim or Cause of Inflation?* (Zubkoff: 1976).

6 Newhouse notes that when using a higher-income elasticity of demand for medical care of 1.0 or more (as per international cross sections of developed countries), rising income accounts for just under one-quarter of the overall increase in U.S. health expenditures (Newhouse: 1992, 7).

7 Since its inception in the 1880s, Eastman Kodak has produced medical technology in addition to the basic photographic equipment more widely associated with the company. For example, at the same time that it produced the KODAK Pocket Camera in the 1890s, it also produced plates and paper for the newly developed X-ray process. From the 1920s through to the 1940s, Eastman Kodak developed further advances in X-ray paper, film, and processing techniques. In the 1970s, the company innovated in mammography systems and succeeded in creating one using half the patient exposure of older systems. In the 1980s, Eastman Kodak developed technology for dry chemistry clinical analysis, as well as for new clinical tests to detect T-cell leukemia and Acquired Immunity Deficiency Syndrome. In the 1990s, Eastman Kodak's medical technology innovations included a new laser imaging system for mammography (accessed 25 July 2009, from http://www.kodak.com/global/en/corp/historyOfKodak/historyIntro.jhtml?pq-path=2217/2687).

8 By 1985, Baxter International had become a broad-based distributor of health care products in addition to producing and distributing medical technology. It was named the leading company in medical products for the seventh time in the 1999 Dow Jones Sustainability Index (accessed 26 July 2009 from http://www.baxter.com/about_baxter/company_profile/sub/history.html).

9 Bausch and Lomb began as a spectacle vendor during the 1850s in Rochester, New York. By the early 1900s, the company was producing a range of optical products, leading to the innovation and production of cataract and vitroretinal surgery technology, as well as pharmaceutical products to treat eye diseases. Major brands of Bausch and Lomb intraocular lenses and surgical delivery systems include 'Crystalens,' 'SofPort,' and 'Akreos.' The company's major lines of phacoemulsification equipment are 'Stellaris' and 'Millennium.' Other surgical instruments and devices produced by Bausch and Lomb include the 'Storz' line of instruments (accessed 26 July 2009 from http://www.bausch.com/en_US/corporate/corp comm/general/about_bauschandlomb.aspx).

10 United States Surgical was formed in the 1960s, 'pioneering,' according to the company's own rendition of its history, 'minimally invasive and bariatric surgery.' The two product lines of United States Surgical, Autosuture and Syneture, have international reach in the production and distribution of surgical devices, laparoscopic instrumentation, biosurgery products, and suture technology. United States Surgical is now a business unit of Covidium (formerly Tyco Healthcare), an international manufacturer, distributor, and servicer of medical devices. The product portfolio of Covidium includes disposable medical supplies, monitoring equipment, medical instruments, and bulk analgesic pharmaceuticals (accessed 25 July 2009, from http://www.ussurg.com/ussurgical/pagebuilder.aspx?webPageID=151690, and http://www.covidien.com/covidien/pageBuilder.aspx?topicID=161270&page=AboutUs:OurStory).

11 See, for example, Rudolph Daniels's article 'Legislation and the American Dialysis Industry: Some Considerations about Monopoly Power in Renal Care' (1991).

12 In the mid-1980s, Newhouse et al. (1985) reported that, though they did cause a once-and-for-all reduction in cost, throughout the 1960s and early 1970s HMO costs increased at the same rate as fee-for-service costs. In the late 1980s, Feldstein et al. (1988) reported that compulsory utilization review programs instituted by a large private insurance carrier had resulted in an 11.9 per cent reduction of hospital expenditures

and an 8.3 per cent reduction of total medical expenditures. The study was based on an analysis of health insurance claims from 222 groups of employees and dependents over a two-year period, controlling for employee characteristics, health care market area factors, and benefit-plan features.

13 The survey in question was carried out by the Hay Group, a consulting firm, of which Pierson – one of the authors of the article – was regional director of health care consulting at the time of writing, and Williams – the other author – was managing director of international health care consulting in the firm's San Francisco office.

14 As with most capitalist cost-cutting strategies, the use of temporary migrant nurses at differential wage levels was not an entirely new idea. In *Empire of Care*, a study tracing the history of nurse emigration to the U.S. from the Philippines, Catherine Choy (2003) documents anecdotal evidence of some hospital administrators, in the 1950s and 1960s, assigning Filipina nurses the work of registered nurses while merely compensating them with the stipend required by the Exchange Visitor Program, through which they were entering the U.S. on a temporary basis. Demonstrating the wage differential, Choy documents that in 1960, the wage of a general-duty nurse in a Philadelphia non-state hospital was U.S. $71.50, as compared to U.S. $46.50, the wage of a Filipina nurse with temporary immigration status through the Exchange Visitor Program (Choy: 2003, 78, 79).

15 Given that collective agreements cover all domestically-based workers, internationally-trained nurses with permanent resident status who were employed fared better in the U.S. relative to temporary migrant nurses. This is not to say that internationally-trained nurses with permanent resident status did not face other forms of discrimination based on country of training and/or race. In a 2008 workshop entitled 'Health, Globalization and Migration: Issues and Struggles of Migrant Health Workers,' Naida Castro of the National Alliance for Filipino Concerns (USA) detailed several complaints of workplace discrimination filed by temporary migrant nurses and Filipina nurses with permanent resident status at the U.S. Equal Employment Opportunities Commission (International Assembly of Migrants and Refugees, Bayview Hotel, Manila, Philippines, 30 October 2008). See also Mireille Kingma's *Nurses on the Move: Migration and the Global Health Care Economy* (2006).

16 In 1967, the Philippines became the largest source country of internationally trained nursing labour for the United States, followed by Canada and Britain (Choy: 2003, 98).

4. The Global Integration of Nursing Labour Markets – The Canadian Instance

1 According to Census data, between 1970 and 1985, the percentage of registered and graduate nurses employed part-time rose from 38.2 per cent to 61.6 per cent (Kerr and MacPhail: 1996, 201).

2 Stasiulis and Bakan emphasize that temporary migrant nurses were 'the first to be laid-off' in the early 1990s (2005, 118). Such an outcome is consistent with the overall argument made in this study regarding increasing employer preference of temporary migrant labour as a particularly flexible workforce. Given the scale of casualization of the hospital workforce implemented in the 1990s, however, it is deemed inappropriate here to reproduce the emphasis of Stasiulis and Bakan.

3 Government data in figure 4.1, specifically the number of internationally trained nurses entering with the official status of 'temporary foreign worker,' differs from data gathered earlier for the same category by the same government department, Citizenship and Immigration Canada (see figure 2.4). The differences reflect inconsistencies in data gathered by the state workers of an under-resourced public service within the context of quickly expanding temporary labour migration.

4 Leah Primitiva G. Samaco-Paquiz, National President, Philippines Nurses Association, personal communication with the author, 11 January 2009.

5 Irene Isaacs, Executive Director, Qualifications and Standards Office, Technical Education and Skills Development Authority, interview with the author, Manila, the Philippines, 10 November 2008. According to data of Citizenship and Immigration Canada (2008), in 2008 there were 196 nurses admitted into Alberta on temporary work authorizations in the category of 'licensed practical nurses and registered nursing assistants' (National Occupation Classification category 3233).

6 Annie Enriquez Heron, General Secretary, Public Services Labor Independent Confederation, interview with the author, Manila, the Philippines, 21 October 2008.

7 For another example, see the story of nursing home workers in the Canadian Union of Public Employees (Valiani: 2007b).

8 For a detailed discussion of this process of temporary migration leading to permanent residency, a relatively new but growing phenomenon in Canada, see Valiani (2008), *The Temporary Foreign Worker Program and Its Intersection with Canadian Immigration Policy* (Ottawa: Canadian Labour Congress).

9 For an elaboration of the CEC and the new system of selecting applications for permanent residency, see Valiani (2009), *The Shift in Canadian Immigration*

Policy and Unheeded Lessons of the Live-in Caregiver Program, http://www.
progressive-economics.ca/wp-content/uploads/2009/02/temppermlcpfi
nal.pdf.

10 The process of unionization for the purpose of collective bargaining had
   already begun in Ontario in 1971. (For more detail of this history in Ontario, see the website of the Ontario Nurses' Association, http://www.ona.
   org/aboutus/ourhistory.html.)

11 Unlike apprenticeships in male-dominated sectors, such as carpentry and
   tool and dye operation, wages and union membership were not part of the
   nursing apprenticeship system.

12 In an article entitled 'Medical Technology in the United States and Canada:
   Where are we going?' Dewar (1997) argues that Canada depends on the
   U.S. for medical technology, given its extremely low expenditures on
   health research. Vicente Navarro (1989) argues that similar epidemiological
   patterns of diseases and interwoven medical education systems imply consensus between Canada and the USA in the use of technology-based health
   care. Additionally, in the year 2000, the Health Manufacturers Industry
   Association in the U.S. projected that Canada would be among its top ten
   consumers of medical devices by 2005 (Lewin Group: 2000).

13 This disaggregation of the service salary category is derived by the author
   from CIHI and Statistics Canada figures on the distribution of hospital expenditure by functional centre (Canadian Institute for Health Information:
   2005a, 27).

5. The Global Integration of Nursing Labour
Markets – The Philippines Instance

1 Since the 1970s, Jose S. Brillantes has served in various politically ap-
   pointed positions, including Secretary of the DOLE (1995–6), Labour Attaché in Canada (1990–1 and 1972–6), Labour Attaché in the U.S. (1986–90),
   and Labour Attaché in Germany (1977–86).

2 Jose Brillantes, Ambassador of the Philippines to Canada, interview with
   the author, Ottawa, 11 September 2008.

3 This schema is taken from an internal government document entitled
   'POEA Functional Description, January 4, 2005/meme.'

4 Ibid., 6–7.

5 'Demand and Supply Analysis of Landbased Workers for Overseas
   Employment,' internal document prepared by the POEA Manpower
   Development Division, accessed at the POEA Documentation Room,
   7 November 2008.

6 Irene Isaacs, executive director of TESDA Qualifications and Standards Office, interview with the author, Manila, 10 November 2008.

7 Ibid.

8 The Honourable Ruth Rana-Padilla, Commissioner, Professional Regulation Commission, interview with the author, Manila, 5 November 2008.

9 In contrast to this, Tyner (2004, 59) claims that the 'development strategy' of the Philippines state is the overseas employment of 'surplus labour,' which assumes that only labour which is not needed within the Philippines is exported.

10 U.S. $14,956,000 is the amount reported for the official category 'Overseas Foreign Worker Remittances' in the current account section of the Philippines Balance of Payments (Bangko Sentral ng Pilipinas: 2008b). Included in these figures are remittances of both resident and non-resident overseas workers of Filipino origin.

11 As in the U.S. American instance, it is demonstrated below that the instance of the Philippines health care sector requires the methodological inclusion of a range of types of nursing and caring labour in the health sector.

12 Prior to the 1990s, the single largest importer of temporary migrant nursing labour from the Philippines was Saudi Arabia.

13 Dr. Teresita I. Barcelo, governor of the Philippines Nurses Association, interview with the author, Manila, 24 October 2008.

14 Ibid.

15 Isaacs, interview.

16 Ibid.

17 The PNA has posed these questions repeatedly to POEA and TESDA officials, and has not been answered. Irene Isaacs of TESDA, while admitting there was never an external demand for LPNs identified by the POEA, claims she cannot answer the question with certainty but 'has heard' that Filipina LPNs have been hired in Alberta, Canada.

18 Barcelo, interview.

19 Brillantes, interview.

20 Jossel I. Ebesate, RN, secretary general of the Alliance of Health Workers, interview with the author, Manila, 29 October 2009.

21 Elena Page Yu, chair of the Health Care Industry Training Council and retired chief nurse (Philippines General Hospital), and Evangeline E. Raphael, treasurer of the Health Care Industry Training Council, and department chair of Paid Patient Services (Philippines General Hospital), Manila, interview with the author, 5 November 2009.

22 Yu and Raphael, interview.

23 In the Philippines, the migration of registered nurses as caregivers to Canada, as well as to other countries of the global North, is a well-known phenomenon. Teresita Barcelo, Elena Yu, Evangeline Raphael, Jossel Ebesate, and Annie Geron – the registered nurses and union leaders actively involved in the Philippines nurse training and migration issues interviewed in this study – all confirm this phenomenon. While Canadian government statistics do not track the proportion of registered nurses sponsored by employers under the Live-in Caregiver Program (LCP), a Government of Canada document entitled 'Application Kit for Live-in Caregiver – Canadian Embassy, Manila' confirms that the practice is sanctioned by the Canadian state, and even encouraged. The second point in a list of requirements states:

> Six months of continuous full-time training or 12 months of experience in paid employment in a caregiving field or occupation related to the job you are seeking as a live-in caregiver.
>
> The training or experience may have been gained in early childhood education, geriatric care, or pediatric nursing, to name just a few areas. Licensed registered nurses, with experience, are normally considered to meet this requirement. (Accessed 10 April 2009, from http://geo.inter national. gc.ca/asia/manila/pdf/lcp_checklist-en.pdf)

24 Ibid.
25 Ibid.
26 There are over 41,000 barangays in the Philippines.
27 Jose Basas, chief health program officer, Bureau of Local Health Development, interview with the author, Manila, 10 November 2009.
28 Technical Education and Skills Development Authority (n.d.b), 1.
29 Technical Education and Skills Development Authority (n.d.a), 1.
30 Nery Buban, board secretary of the Public Services Labour Independent Confederation (PSLINK), personal communication with the author, 25 March 2009. The PSLINK is the Filipino union that has initiated the process to unionize and win collective bargaining rights for barangay health workers.
31 Though the perspective in Valdepeñas and Bautista's study (1977) is markedly neoclassical, an earlier study by Valdepeñas, *The Protection and Development of Philippine Manufacturing* – based on his doctoral thesis and published in 1970 – is far more Keynesian in perspective, offering a positive assessment of import-substitute industrialization in the Philippines. Evidence from both studies is used here.
32 See the section 'Imperialism and Our Political Establishment' in *The Lichauco Paper* for an elaboration of CIA and other U.S. intervention in the political and bureaucratic realms of the Philippines throughout the 1950s.

33 Brillantes, interview. In the words of Brillantes, who served as a Labor
Attaché in the 1970s, 'Governments of the Middle East looked to the Philippines to supply the workers because Filipino labour was seen as ideal:
trained in a U.S.-style education system dating back to colonial days and
fluent in English.'

34 The World Bank (1985) definition of *private capital outflow* is the sum of net
(short-term) foreign asset acquisition by the banking sector and the private, non-banking sector (Vos: 1992, 506).

35 In greater detail, Bejas's definition of *total capital flight* is net additions to
external debt + net foreign direct investment + net portfolio and other
investment assets, minus current account deficits + accumulation of international reserves, including central-bank-sanctioned uses of foreign
exchange. This equation is adjusted for the impact of exchange rate fluctuations, long-term external debt, trade misinvoicing, and unrecorded
remittances (Beja: 2006, 56).

6. The Global Integration of Labour Markets and Deepening Unequal Exchange

1 One example of industrial production in the core spurred by super-exploitation of labour in the periphery is the Mourid brotherhood in Senegal,
which was 'the most important vector' for the expansion of the groundnut
economy in the late nineteenth century. The submission of peasant producers to the goals of this economy – increased production of groundnuts
for oil processing in Europe – was achieved through a reinterpretation of
Islam by the Mourid brotherhood. As an expression of faith and loyalty to
the Mourids, peasants accepted and found new measures to increase their
production of groundnuts while receiving wages that were stagnant relative to the increases in the productivity of their labour (Amin: 1973, 192).

2 Marx's conceptualization of the organic composition of capital has been
significantly improved upon through discussion and theorization of *the
transformation problem*. Briefly put, for Marx, the organic composition of
capital – or the ratio of technology to labour – has the tendency to increase
due to what Marx assumed to be the continually rising degree of mechani-
zation in production. In better understanding the transformation of *values*
into *market prices*, debate around the transformation problem revealed that
the organic composition of capital varies from industry to industry and
cannot be generalized to be continually rising given that machines themselves are embodiments of labour, thus carrying different relative values
making for multi-directional ratios of technology to labour. None of this

significantly alters Emmanuel's propositions given that the central force in Emmanuel's unequal exchange relation is difference in labour cost.

3 Under the assumption of perfect competition, Marx's law of value – that all identical commodities, including labour, command the same exchange value (as symbolized by price) under capitalist social relations – holds true. Use values, or goods, in Marx's theory of value, become commodities only where they are the products of the labour of individuals carrying on work and earning independently of each other (rather than collectively).

4 The lack of perfect competition is also seen through the dynamics of pharmaceutical and medical technology production in the U.S. American and Canadian instances examined earlier.

5 Intal (2003) discusses the emergence and growth of export-oriented, mass agricultural production in the Philippines, beginning in 1870, under Spanish colonial rule. Valdepeñas and Bautista (1977) demonstrate the persistence and inequality of the share-cropping relation through the U.S. colonial period. Ofreneo (1989, 9) confirms the persistence of this structure for the approximate 5.1 million agricultural workers registered by the Philippines National Statistics Office as 'own account' (self-employed) workers.

6 Briefly put, *constant capital* refers to land and machines employed by the capitalist in a given production moment, *variable capital* refers to labour employed in a given production moment, and *surplus value* refers to the value produced by the worker which exceeds the wage earned. The wage is understood here as covering only the cost of the worker's basic needs.

7 The higher surplus value in the impoverished country helps explain the role of U.S. capitalists in the Philippines instance examined in chapter 4.

8 Stated slightly differently for the instance of the Philippines, wages remitted home by migrant workers provide for the basic needs of families in the Philippines, which alleviates the Philippines state from investing in job creation and public services. This in turn allows the historically existing polarized distribution of wealth to continue, which is seen here as socially inacceptable.

9 In terms of the country supplying nursing labour in the world market, this holds true whether nurses are migrating on a temporary or permanent basis. The differences, as elaborated below, are in the degree of loss incurred, whereby individuals and families in situations of temporary migration incur greater economic losses and social costs.

10 For a comprehensive discussion of the role of trade unions in responding to increased employer use of temporary migrant workers in the Canadian context, see the policy position paper of the Canadian Labour Congress, 'Analysis, Solidarity, Action: A Workers' Perspective on the Increasing

Use of Temporary Migrant Labour in Canada' (Valiani: 2007a). For a more
global approach to the role of trade unions in responding to increased
employer use of temporary migrant labour internationally, see 'Labour
Migration and Development: Towards a North-South Vision for Change'
(Valiani: 2008b).

11 The authors interviewed 23 employers, 75 immigrant care workers, and 29
care recipients in Montreal, Toronto, Hamilton, Vancouver, and Victoria.
These are cities which draw the majority of immigrants to Canada. Surveys
were also collected from 149 employers, 102 of which answered the full
set of questions relating to the employment of immigrant care workers
(Bourgeault et al.: 2009, 4).

12 See, for example, Ratha, Mohaptra, and Plaza (2008), *Beyond Aid: New Sources
and Innovative Mechanisms for Financing Development in Sub-Saharan Africa*.

13 The Atlantic slave trade is estimated to have involved fifteen million
people, while indenture or the coolie labour system, extending from the
mid-nineteenth century to the mid-twentieth century, is estimated to have
involved thirty-two million people (Potts: 1990). Though it involved a
larger estimated number of people transported globally for the purpose of
performing work at a relatively cheaper cost to employers, the indentured/
coolie labour system is not conceptualized here as a *mass mobilization of labour* of world systemic consequence; this is because indentured labour was
not a strategic commodity of international exchange and capital accumulation from the mid-nineteenth to mid-twentieth centuries. During the period
of the indenture/coolie system, iron and metal minerals were the commodities of international exchange that were of strategic importance. In contrast
to indentured labour, slave labour, as is demonstrated here, was a strategic
commodity of international exchange and capital accumulation in the seventeenth and eighteenth centuries, given the key role of slaves in producing
plantation crops which spurred industrial development in England.

14 Emmanuel notes in his study of unequal exchange that his motivation is
to 'analyze exchange from the standpoint of commodity economy itself'
(Emmanuel: 1972, 168). He cites Marx to explain further: 'What you think
is just or equitable is out of the question. The question is: What is necessary and unavoidable with a given system of production.' Similarly here,
the comparison based on the role of African slave labour in the formation
of the Atlantic-centred capitalist world economy is a tool of analysis rather
than the articulation of a political position, or a tabulation of that lost and
gained through the Atlantic slave trade.

15 Inikori's methodology differs from that of Polanyi in one key way: though
incorporating historical forces of Europe, it is not centred on Europe. In

this sense Inikori's study brings us closer to understanding world economic history relationally.

16 Super-exploitation is the Marxian term describing the process whereby some capitalists are able to draw more surplus value from some workers relative to others (for example, women versus men).

17 Though it has not gained much attention in the global North, throughout the 1990s several states of the global South attempted to call attention to the phenomenon of brain drain and the problems caused within the global South by health worker emigration.

18 Slave labour in the form of indigenous peoples of the Americas, as well as Africans, was used to mine these metals in South America and Africa.

References

Abella, Manolo. 2006. 'Global Competition for Skilled Workers and Consequences.' In *Competing for Global Talent*, edited by Christiane Kuptsch and
Eng Fong Pang, 11–32. Geneva: International Labour Organisation.

Abelson, Julia, Miata Giacomoni, Pascale Lehoux, and Francois-Pierre Gauvin.
2006. 'Bringing "the Public" into Health Technology Assessment and Coverage Policy Decisions: From Principles to Practice.' *Health Policy* 82:37–50.

African Union. 2003. *The Role of the African Diaspora in the Development of Their
Countries of Origin*. First Ordinary Session of the African Union, Labour and
Social Affairs Commission, Conference Report, 10–15 April 2003, Port Louis,
Mauritius (XXVI, LSC/9).

Aiken, Linda, Julie Sochalski, and Gerard Anderson. 1996. 'Downsizing the
Hospital Workforce.' *Health Affairs* 15:88–91.

Alboim, Naomi. 2009. *Adjusting the Balance: Fixing Canada's Economic Immigration Policies*. Toronto: Maytree Foundation.

Altman, Stuart, and Joseph Eichenholz. 1976. 'Inflation in the Health Industry:
Causes and Cures.' In *Health: A Victim or Cause of Inflation*, edited by Michael
Zubkoff, 7–30. New York: Milbank Memorial Fund.

Amin, Samir. 1973. 'Underdevelopment and Dependence in Black Africa:
Their Historical Origins and Contemporary Forms.' *Social and Economic
Studies* 22:177–96.

– 2006. 'Globalization and the Agrarian Question.' In *Globalization and the
Third World: A Study of Negative Consequences*, edited by B.N. Ghosh and
H.M. Guven. New York: Palgrave Macmillan.

– 2010a. *Ending the Crisis of Capitalism or Ending of Capitalism*. Oxford: Pamba-
zuka Press.

– 2010b. *The Law of Worldwide Value*. 2nd ed. New York: Monthly Review.

Anderson, Elaine, and Mark Ginsberg. 1986. 'The Health Care Marketplace: Perspectives on a System in Transition.' *Policy Studies Review* 5:654–62.

Anderson, Odin, Patricia Collette, and Jacob Feldman. 1963. *Changes in Family Medical Expenditures and Voluntary Health Insurance: A Five-Year Resurvey.* Cambridge: Harvard University Press.

Angell, Marcia. 2004. *The Truth About the Drug Companies.* New York: Random House.

Angus, Douglas. 1987. 'Health-Care Costs: A Review of Past Experience and Potential Impact of the Aging Phenomenon.' In *Health and Canadian Society – Sociological Perspectives,* 2nd ed., edited by David Coburn, Carl D'Arcy, and George Torrance, 57–72. Markham: Fitzhenry and Whiteside.

Armstrong, Pat. 1993. 'Women's Health Care Work: Nursing in Context.' In *Vital Signs: Nursing in Transition,* edited by Pat Armstrong, Jacqueline Choiniere, and Elaine Day, 17–58. Toronto: Garamond Press.

Armstrong, Pat, and Hugh Armstrong. 2002. *Wasting Away: The Undermining of Canadian Health Care.* 2nd ed. Toronto: Oxford University Press.

Armstrong, Pat, Jacqueline Choiniere, and Elaine Day. 1993. *Vital Signs: Nursing in Transition.* Toronto: Garamond Press.

Arrighi, Giovanni. 1994. *The Long Twentieth Century.* London: Verso.

AusAID. 2007. *Aid Activities in the Philippines.* Commonwealth of Australia. Accessed 30 July 2011. http://www.ausaid.gov.au/country/cbrief.cfm?DCon=1148_8702_9418_7487_8517&CountryID=31

Ball, Rochelle. 1997. 'The Role of the State in the Globalisation of Labour Markets: The Case of the Philippines.' *Environment and Planning* 29:1603–28.

– 2004. 'Divergent Development, Racialised Rights: Globalised Labour Markets and the Trade of Nurses: The Case of the Philippines.' *Women's Studies International Forum* 27:119–33.

Bangko Sentral ng Pilipinas. 2008a. *Philippines: Balance of Payments 1990–1999.* Manila: Bangko Sentral ng Pilipinas.

– 2008b. *Philippines: Balance of Payments 2008.* Manila: Bangko Sentral ng Pilipinas.

Baran, Paul, and Paul Sweezy. 1966. *Monopoly Capital.* New York: Monthly Review.

Barber, Pauline. 2008. 'The Ideal Immigrant? Gendered Class Subjects in Philippine-Canada Migration.' *Third World Quarterly* 29:1265–85.

Battistella, Graziano. 1999. 'Philippine Migration Policy: Dilemmas of a Crisis.' *Soujourn* 14:229–48.

Battistella, Graziano, and Anthony Paganoni. 1992. *Philippine Labour Migration: Impact and Policy.* Quezon City: Scalabrini Migration Center.

Bausch and Lomb. 2009. *About Bausch and Lomb*. Accessed 26 July 2009. http://www.bausch.com/en_US/corporate/corpcomm/general/about_bausch andlomb.aspx.

Baxter. 2009. *History*. Accessed 26 July 2009. http://www.baxter.com/about_ baxter/company_profile/sub/history.html.

Becton Dickinson. N.d. *BD Milestones*. Accessed 29 July 2009. http://www.bd.com/aboutbd/history.

Beja, Edsel Jr. 2006. 'Capital Flight and the Hollowing Out of the Philippine Economy in the Neoliberal Regime.' *Kasarinlan: Philippine Journal of Third World Studies* 21:55–74.

Beneria, Lourdes. 1979. 'Reproduction, Production and the Sexual Division of Labour.' *Cambridge Journal of Economics* (September):203–25.

Bezanson, Kate, and Meg Luxton, eds. 2006. *Social Reproduction: Feminist Political Economy Challenges Neo-Liberalism*. Montreal: McGill-Queen's University Press.

Blanchet, Karl, and Regina Keith. 2006. 'L'Afrique Tente de Retenir ses Medecins.' *Le Monde Diplomatique* 633 (December):13.

Blouin, Chantal, Heather Gibb, Maire McAdams, and Ann Weston. 2004. *Engendering Canadian Trade Policy: A Case Study of Labour Mobility in Trade Agreements*. Ottawa: Status of Women Canada.

Bortolotti, Marguerite. 2004. *The Political Economy of Nursing in the Industrialized World: Impacts of Caring, Professionalism and State Policy on the Everyday Practice of Nurses*. Unpublished PhD dissertation: Carleton University.

Bourgeault, Ivy L., Jelena Atanackovic, Jane LeBrun, Rishma Parpia, Ahmed Rashid, and Judi Winkup. 2009. *The Role of Immigrant Care Workers in an Aging Society*. Ottawa: University of Ottawa Press.

Braudel, Fernand. 1980. *On History*. Chicago: University of Chicago Press.

Brenner, Robert. 1998. 'The Economics of Global Turbulence.' *New Left Review* no. 229:1–264.

Briones, Leah. 2009. *Empowering Migrant Women*. Surrey: Ashgate.

British Columbia Human Rights Tribunal. 2008. *C.S.W.U. Local 1611 v. SELI Canada and others*, No. 8, December 3, BCHRT 436, 1–177.

Buchan, James, and Lynn Calman. 2004. *The Global Shortage of Registered Nurses: An Overview of Issues and Actions*. Geneva: International Council of Nurses.

Campbell, Maria. 1987. 'Productivity in Canadian Nursing: Administering Cuts.' In *Health and Canadian Society: Sociological Perspectives*, 2nd ed., edited by David Coburn, Carl D'Arcy, and George Torrance, 463–75. Markham: Fitzhenry and Whiteside.

Canadian Institute for Health Information. 2005a. *Hospital Trends in Canada: Results of a Project to Create a Historical Series of Statistical Data and Financial*

Data for Canadian Hospitals Over Twenty-Seven Years. Ottawa: Canadian Institute for Health Information.

– 2005b. *National Health Expenditure Database*. Ottawa: Canadian Institute for Health Information.

– 2007a. *National Health Expenditure Database*. Ottawa: Canadian Institute for Health Information.

– 2007b. *Total Health Expenditure by Use of Funds, Canada, 1975 to 2007 – Current Dollars (Percentage Distribution)*. Ottawa: Canadian Institute for Health Information.

– 2008. *Drug Expenditure in Canada 1985–2007*. Ottawa: Canadian Institute for Health Information.

Canadian Labour Congress. 2006. *Submission by the Canadian Labour Congress to the House of Commons Standing Committee on Human Resources, Social Development and the Status of Persons with Disabilities*, November 28. Ottawa: Canadian Labour Congress.

Canadian Nursing Advisory Committee. 2002. *Our Health, Our Future: Creating Quality Workplaces for Canadian Nurses*. Ottawa: Health Canada.

China Daily. 2004. *Working Age Population to Hit 940 Million by 2020*. Beijing: China Daily.

Chochrane, Allan, and Kathy Pain. 2004. In *A Globalizing World? Culture, Economics, Politics*, 2nd ed., edited by David Held, 5–46. London: Routledge.

Choy, Catherine Ceniza. 2003. *Empire of Care*. Durham: Duke University Press.

Citizenship and Immigration Canada. 2007. *RDM, Facts and Figures*. Ottawa: Citizenship and Immigration Canada.

– 2008. *Entry of Temporary Foreign Workers by National Occupation Classification and Province, 2004–2008*. Ottawa: Citizenship and Immigration Canada.

– 2010. *RDM, Facts and Figures*. Ottawa: Citizenship and Immigration Canada.

Clement, Grace. 1996. *Care, Autonomy, and Justice: Feminism and the Ethic of Care*. Boulder, CO: Westview Press.

Colen, Shellee. 1995. ' "Like a Mother to Them": Stratified Reproduction and West Indian Childcare Workers and Employers in New York.' In *Conceiving the New World Order: The Global Politics of Reproduction*, edited by Faye Ginsberg and Rayna Rapp, 78–102. Berkeley: University of California Press.

Colman, David, and Frederick Nixson. 1986. *Economics of Change in Less Developed Countries*. Oxford: Philip Allan Publishers.

Communist Party of China. 2010. *Progress in China's Human Rights in 2009*. Government White Paper. Accessed 28 December 2010. http://english.cpc. people.com.cn/66102/7150905.html.

Connell, John, ed. 2008. *The International Migration of Health Workers*. New York: Routledge.

Connell, John, and Barbara Stilwell. 2006. 'Merchants of Medical Care: Recruiting Agencies in the Global Health Care Chain.' In *Merchants of Labour*, edited by Christiane Kuptsch, 239–53. Geneva: International Institute of Labour Studies.

Covidien. *Our Story*. N.d. Accessed 25 July 2009. http://www.covidien.com/covidien/pageBuilder.aspx?topicID=161270&page=AboutUs:OurStory.

Dalla Costa, Mariarosa, and Selma James. 1972. *The Power of Women and the Subversion of the Community*. London: Falling Wall Press.

Daniels, Rudolph. 1991. 'Legislation and the American Dialysis Industry: Some Considerations about Monopoly Power in Renal Care.' *American Journal of Economics and Sociology* 50 (April):223–42.

Davis, Karen. 1986. 'Aging and the Health-Care System: Economic and Structural Issues.' *Daedalus* 115:227–46.

Dayton-Johnson, Jeff, Louka Katseli, Gregory Maniatis, Rainer Munz, and Demetrios Papademetriou. 2007. *Gaining from Migration: Towards a New Mobility System*. Paris: Organisation for Economic Co-operation and Development.

Department of Economic Research. 2004. *Balance of Payments Developments – Fourth Quarter 2003 Developments*. Manila: Bangko Sentral ng Pilipinas.

– 2008. *Balance of Payments Developments: Fourth Quarter 2007 Developments*. Manila: Bangko Sentral ng Pilipinas.

– 2009. *Balance of Payments Developments: Fourth Quarter 2008 Developments*. Manila: Bangko Sentral ng Pilipinas.

Department of Economic and Social Affairs (DESA). 2005. *The Inequality Predicament: Report on the World Social Situation*. New York: United Nations.

– 2006. *Trends in Total Migrant Stock: The 2005 Revision*. Geneva: United Nations.

Department of Finance Canada. 2007. 'A Stronger Canada through a Stronger Economy.' In *Budget Plan*, 147–248. Ottawa: Department of Finance Canada.

Department of Homeland Security. 2004. 'Table 24: Nonimmigrants admitted by class of admission: selected fiscal years 1981–2004.' *Yearbook of Immigration Statistics*. Washington, DC: Department of Homeland Security.

– 2007. 'Characteristics of Speciality Occupation Workers (H-1B).' *INS Statistical Yearbook of the Immigration and Naturalization Service, 2000–2006*. Washington, DC: Department of Homeland Security.

Dewar, Diane. 1997. 'Medical Technology in the United States and Canada: Where are we going?' *Review of Social Economy* 60:359–79.

Di Matteo, Livio. 2000. 'The Determinants of the Public-Private Mix in Canadian Health Care Expenditures: 1975–1996.' *Health Policy* 52:87–112.

Directorate for Employment, Labour, and Social Affairs Group on Health. 2006. *Health Workforce and Migration Study: Preliminary Findings*. Paris: Organisation for Economic Co-operation and Development.

Directorate for Employment, Labour, and Social Affairs Health Committee. 2008. *How Can OECD Countries Achieve a Sustainable Health Workforce?* Paris: Organisation for Economic Co-operation and Development.

Dunlop, David, and Michael Zubkoff. 1976. 'Inflation and Consumer Behaviour in the Health Care Sector.' In *Health: A Victim or Cause of Inflation*, edited by Michael Zubkoff, 84–114. New York: Milbank Memorial Fund.

Eastman Kodak. 2009. *History of Kodak*. Accessed 25 July 2009. http://www.kodak.com/global/en/corp/historyOfKodak/historyIntro.jhtml?pq-path= 2217/2687.

Ebesate, Jossel. 2008. *Migration of Health Workers and Professionals: The Philippines Experience*. Presentation Notes, Health, Globalization and Migration Workshop, International Assembly of Migrants and Refugees, Manila, October 30.

Emmanuel, Arghiri. 1969. *L'Echange inégal: essai sur les antagonismes dans les rapports économiques internationaux*. Paris: F. Maspero.

– 1972. *Unequal Exchange: A Study of the Imperialism of Trade*. New York: Monthly Review Press.

Employment and Immigration Canada. 2005. *1977–1987 Immigration Statistics*. Ottawa: Minister of Supply and Services.

Fang, Zhiwu. 2007. 'Potential of China in Global Nurse Migration.' *Health Services Research* 42:1419–28.

Feder, Judith. 1977. *Medicare: The Politics of Federal Hospital Insurance*. Lexington: Lexington Books.

Fee, Terry. 1976. 'Domestic Labour: An Analysis of Housework and its Relation to the Production Process.' *Review of Radical Political Economics* 8:1–8

Feldstein, P.J., T.M. Wickizer, and J.R. Wheeler. 1988. 'Private Cost Containment. The Effects of Utilization Review Programs on Health Care Use and Expenditures.' *New England Journal of Medicine* 318:1310–14.

Fortune. 1967. 'The 500 Largest Industrials: Who Did Best (and Worst) Among the 500.' *Fortune*, 15 June, 172–3.

– 1968. 'The 500 Largest Industrials: Who Did Best (and Worst) Among the 500.' *Fortune*, 15 June, 204–7.

– 1972. 'The 500 Largest Industrials: Who Did Best (and Worst) Among the 500.' *Fortune*, May, 206–9.

– 1974. 'The 500 Largest Industrials: Who Did Best (and Worst) Among the 500.' *Fortune*, May, 252–5.

– 1976. 'The 500 Largest Industrials: Who Did Best (and Worst) Among the 500.' *Fortune*, May, 338–41.

– 1981. 'The 500 Largest Industrials: Who Did Best (and Worst) Among the 500.' *Fortune*, 4 May, 345–6.

– 1982. 'The 500 Largest Industrials: Who Did Best (and Worst) Among the 500.' *Fortune*, 3 May, 280–4.

– 1984. 'The 500 Largest Industrials: Who Did Best (and Worst) Among the 500.' *Fortune*, 30 April, 296–322.

– 1986. 'The 500 Largest Industrials: Who Did Best (and Worst) Among the 500.' *Fortune*, 28 April, 202–8.

– 1991. 'The 500 Largest Industrials: Who Did Best (and Worst) Among the 500.' *Fortune*, 29 July, 276–8.

– 1992. 'The 500 Largest Industrials: Who Did Best (and Worst) Among the 500.' *Fortune*, 20 April, 262–88.

– 1995. 'The 500 Largest Industrials: Who Did Best (and Worst) Among the 500.' *Fortune*, 15 May, F1–F22.

Foz, Vicente B, ed. 2000. *The Labor Code of the Philippines and Its Implementing Rules and Regulations*. Manila: Philippine Law Gazette.

Frank, Andre Gunder. 1969. *Latin America: Underdevelopment or Revolution*. New York: Monthly Review.

–1998. *ReOrient: Global Economy in the Asian Age*. Berkeley: University of California Press.

Friedman, Milton. 1962. *Capitalism and Freedom*. Chicago: University of Chicago Press.

Gilpin, Robert. 1987. *The Political Economy of International Relations*. Princeton: Princeton University Press.

Ginsburg, Paul. 1976. 'Inflation and Hospital Capital Investment.' In *Health: A Victim or Cause of Inflation*, edited by Michael Zubkoff, 164–78. New York: Milbank Memorial Fund.

Global Forum on Migration and Development (GFMD). 2008. 'Government Meeting, Conclusions and Recommendations.' Philippines: GFMD. Accessed 27 November 2008. http://government.gfmd2008.org/conclusion_recommendations.html.

Goldfarb Corporation. 1988. *The Nursing Shortage in Ontario, a Research Report for the Ontario Nurses Association*. Toronto: Ontario Nurses Association.

Goldfield, Michael. 1987. *The Decline of Organized Labour in the United States*. Chicago: University of Chicago Press.

Goldsmith, Jeff. 1984. 'Death of a Paradigm: the Challenge of Competition.' *Health Affairs*, 3 (Fall):5–19.

Government of Canada. 2007. *Application Kit for Live-in Caregiver: Canadian Embassy, Manila*. Accessed 10 April 2009. http://geo.international.gc.ca/asia/manila/pdf/lcp_checklist-en.pdf.

Grabel, Illene. 2008. *The Political Economy of Remittances: What Do We Know? What Do We Need to Know?* Working Paper No. 184. Amherst: Political Economy Research Institute.

Greiner, Ann. 1995. *Cost and Quality Matters: Workplace Innovations in the Health Care Industry*. Washington, DC: Economic Policy Institute.

The Guardian (Tanzania). 2008. 'Pressure on Migrant Workers Puts East Africa on Edge.' *The Guardian*, 26 December, Business and Foreign Section, i.

Heron, Craig. 1996. *The Canadian Labour Movement: A Short History*. 2nd ed. Toronto: Lorimer and Company.

Heyzer, Noeleen. 1994. 'Introduction: Creating Responsive Policies for Migrant Women Domestic Workers.' In *The Trade in Domestic Workers: Causes, Mechanisms and Consequences of International Migration*, edited by Noeleen Heyzer, Geertje Lycklama à Nijeholt, and Nedra Weerakoon, xv–xxx. Kuala Lumpur: Asian and Pacific Development Centre/Zed Books.

Heyzer, Noeleen, Geertje Lycklama à Nijeholt, and Nedra Weerakoon, eds. 1994. *The Trade in Domestic Workers: Causes, Mechanisms and Consequences of International Migration*. Kuala Lumpur: Asian and Pacific Development Centre/Zed Books.

Hobsbawm, E. 1975. *The Age of Capital 1848–1875*. New York: Charles Scribner's Sons.

Hochschild, Arlie. 2000. 'Global Care Chains and Emotional Surplus Value.' In *On The Edge: Globalization and the New Millennium*, edited by Will Hutton and Anthony Giddens, 130–46. London: Jonathan Cape.

Hopkins, Terence. 1979. 'The Study of the Capitalist World-Economy: Some Introductory Considerations.' In *The World-System of Capitalism*, edited by Walter Goldfrank, 9–38. Beverly Hills: Sage Publications.

Hopkins, Terence, Immanuel Wallerstein, and Associates. 1982. *World Systems Analysis: Theory and Methodology*. Beverly Hills: Sage Publications.

House of Representatives, Congressional Planning and Budget Department. 2006. *Facts in Figures*, May (No. 1).

Human Resources and Skills Development Canada. 2009. 'Labour Market Information, Wages and Salaries.' Accessed 19 April 2011. http://www.labourmarketinformation.ca.

IBON. 2008. *Facts and Figures: OFWs, Remittances and Philippine Underdevelopment*. Special Release, 31 (9&10, 15&31 May). Quezon City: IBON.

Les Infirmières et Infirmiers Unis Inc. 1971. *Le Nursing Québecois . . . Malade*. Montreal: Les Infirmières et Infirmiers Unis Inc.

Inikori, Joseph. 2002. *Africans and the Industrial Revolution in England: A Study in International Trade and Economic Development.* Cambridge: Cambridge University Press.

Intal, Ponciano. 2003. *Essays on the Philippine Colonial Economy.* Manila: De La Salle University Press.

International Fund for Agricultural Development (IFAD). 2007. *Sending Money Home: Worldwide Remittance Flows to Developing and Transition Countries.* Rome: International Fund for Agricultural Development.

International Labour Office. 2005. *Migration of Health Workers: Country Case Study Philippines.* Geneva: International Labour Organization.

International Labour Office, Bureau for Workers' Activities. 2008. *In Search of Decent Work: Migrant Workers' Rights: A Manual for Trade Unionists.* Geneva: International Labour Organization.

International Labour Organization (ILO). 1949. C97 Migration for Employment Convention (Revised). Accessed 24 July 2011. http://www.ilo.org/ilolex/cgi-lex/convde.pl?C097.

– 2008. *World of Work Report 2008: Income Inequality in the Age of Financial Globalization.* Geneva: International Labour Organization.

International Organization for Migration. 2005. *World Migration 2005: Costs and Benefits of International Migration.* Geneva: International Organization for Migration.

– 2006. 'Global Labour Mobility: A Catalyst for Development.' *Policy Focus* (September): 1–2.

International Trade Union Confederation. 2007. *Annual Survey of Violations of Trade Union Rights.* Brussels: ITUC.

Jennings, R. 1991. 'The Political Economy of Industrialization: A Comparison of Latin American and East Asian Newly Industrializing Countries.' *Development and Change* 22:197–231.

Johnson, Donald, and Vince diPaolo. 1981. 'Multihospital System Survey.' *Modern Healthcare II* (April): 80–99.

Kalb, Paul. 1990. 'Controlling Health Care Costs by Controlling Technology: A Private Contractual Approach.' *The Yale Law Journal* 99:1109–26.

Kardulias, P., and Thomas Hall. 2007. 'A World-Systems View of Human Migration Past and Present: Providing a General Model for Understanding the Movement of People.' *Forum on Public Policy: A Journal of the Oxford Round Table* (Summer):1–24.

Kelly, Philip, and S. D'Addorio. 2008. ' "Filipinos Are Very Strongly into Medical Stuff": Labour Market Segmentation in Toronto, Canada.' In *The International Migration of Health Workers*, edited by John Connell, 77–98. New York: Routledge.

Kerr, Janet, and Jannetta MacPhail. 1996. *Canadian Nursing: Issues and Perspectives*. 3rd ed. St. Louis: Mosby-Year Book.

Khoo, Siew-Ean, Elsie Ho, and Carmen Voigt-Graf. 2008. 'Gendered Migration in Oceania: Trends, Policies and Outcomes.' In *New Perspectives on Gender and Migration*, edited by Nicola Piper, 101–36. New York: Routledge/United Nations Research Institute for Social Development.

Kimani, Dagi. 2009. 'Kenya, Uganda: VCT Centres Turning in Thousands of False HIV-positives.' *The East African*, 14 March. Accessed 30 July 2011. http://www.africafiles.org/article.asp?ID=20406.

Kingma, Mireille. 2006. *Nurses on the Move: Migration and the Global Health Care Economy*. Ithaca, NY: Cornell University Press.

Kinkhead, Gwen. 1980. 'Humana's Hard-Sell Hospitals.' *Fortune*, 17 November, 68–81.

Kittay, Eva. 1999. *Love's Labor*. New York: Routledge.

Kofman, Eleonore, and Parvati Raghuram. 2006. 'Gender and Global Labour Migrations: Incorporating Skilled Workers.' *Antipode* 38:282–303.

Kolata, Gina. 1980. 'Human Thrives Selling Dialysis.' *Science* (New Series) 208:379–82.

Kuptsch, Christiane, ed. 2006. *Merchants of Labour*. Geneva: International Institute for Labour Studies.

Kuptsch, Christiane, and Eng Fong Pang, eds. 2006. *Competing for Global Talent*. Geneva: International Labour Organisation.

Lebowitz, Michael. 2008. 'The Only Road is Practice: After the Venezuelan Referendum Defeat.' *Monthly Review* 60 (June):1–10.

Lerguia, Isabel, and John Dumoulin. 1972. 'Toward a Science of Women's Liberation.' *Political Affairs* 6:40–52.

Levit, Katherine, et al. 1991. 'National Health Expenditures, 1990.' *Health Care Financing Review* 13:29–54.

Lewin Group. 2000. 'Outlook for Medical Technology Innovation: The State of the Industry.' Unreleased report commissioned by the Health Manufacturers Industry Association.

Lichauco, Alejandro. 1973. *The Lichauco Paper*. New York: Monthly Review Press.

– 1988. *Nationalist Economics: History, Theory and Practice*. Quezon City: Institute for Rural Industrialization Inc.

Liebenau, Jonathan. 1987. *Medical Science and Medical Industry: The Formation of the American Pharmaceutical Industry*. Basingstoke: Macmillan, in association with Business History Unit, University of London.

Lindorff, Dave. 1992. *Marketplace Medicine: The Rise of the For-Profit Hospital Chains*. New York: Bantam Books.

Maddalena, Victor, and Amanda Crupi. 2008. *A Renewed Call for Action: A Synthesis Report on the Nursing Shortage in Canada*. Ottawa: Canadian Federation of Nurses Unions.

Manga, Pran. 1989. 'Cost-Containing Medical Technology.' *Healthcare Management Forum* (Spring):26–31.

Manpower and Immigration. 2005. *1966–1976 Immigration Statistics*. Ottawa: Canada Immigration Division.

Martin, Philip, Manolo Abella, and Christiane Kuptsch. 2006. *Managing Labor Migration in the Twenty-First Century*. New Haven: Yale University Press.

Marx, Karl. 1966. *Capital*, vol. 3: *The Process of Capitalist Production as a Whole*. Moscow: Progress Publishers.

– 1973. *Grundrisse*. London: Penguin Books.

– 1976. *Capital*, vol. 1: *A Critique of Political Economy*. London: Penguin Books.

– 1995. *Capital: A New Abridgement*. Oxford: Oxford University Press.

Massey, Doreen. 1995. *Spatial Divisions of Labor*. 2nd ed. New York: Routledge.

McAfee, Kathy. 1991. *Storm Signals: Structural Adjustment and Development Alternatives in the Caribbean*. London: Zed Books and Oxfam America.

McMahon, John, and David Drake. 1976. 'Inflation and the Hospital.' In *Health: A Victim or Cause of Inflation*, edited by Michael Zubkoff, 130–48. New York: Milbank Memorial Fund.

McMichael, Philip. 1990. 'Incorporating Comparison within a World-Historical Perspective: An Alternative to Comparative Method.' *American Sociological Review* 55 (June):385–97.

McPherson, Kathryn. 1996. *Bedside Matters: The Transformation of Canadian Nursing: 1900–1990*. Toronto: Oxford University Press.

Mechanic, David. 1984. 'The Transformation of Health Providers.' *Health Affairs* 3 (Spring):65–72.

Mejia, Alfonso, Helena Pizurki, and Erica Royston. 1979. *Physician and Nurse Migration*. Geneva: World Health Organization.

Meltz, Noah. 1988. *The Nursing Shortage*. Toronto: Registered Nurses Association of Ontario.

Ministry of Labour, Invalids, and Social Affairs. 2009. *Provision of a Policy Paper to Support Future Implementation of the Labour Export Policy under Resolution 30a*. Ho Chi Minh City: 18 June.

Moody, Kim. 1988. *An Injury to All: The Decline of American Unionism*. London: Verso.

Moses, Jonathon. 2006. *International Migration: Globalization's Last Frontier*. Black Point: Fernwood Publishing.

Mytelka, L.K. 1989. 'The Unfulfilled Promise of African Industrialization.' *African Studies Review* 32:77–137.

Nash, June, and Maria Patricia Fenandez Kelly, eds. 1983. *Women, Men and the International Divison of Labour*. Albany: State University of New York Press.

National Health Statistics Group. 2007. *National Health Expenditures by Type of Service and Source of Funds, CY 1960–2006*. Washington, DC: U.S. Department of Health and Human Services. Accessed 16 November 2008. http://www.cms.gov/nationalhealthexpenddata/02_nationalhealthaccountshistorical.asp

– 2008. *National Health Expenditures by Type of Service and Source of Funds, CY 1960–2007*. Washington, DC: U.S. Department of Health and Human Services. Accessed 30 July 2011. http://www.cms.gov/nationalhealthexpenddata/02_nationalhealthaccountshistorical.asp

Navarro, Vicente. 1989. 'A National Health Program is Necessary.' *Challenge* (May/June):36–41.

Newhouse, Joseph. 1976. 'Inflation and Health Insurance.' In *Health: A Victim or Cause of Inflation*, edited by Michael Zubkoff, 210–24. New York: Milbank Memorial Fund.

– 1992. 'Medical Care Costs: How Much Welfare Loss?' *Journal of Economic Perspectives* 6:3–21.

Newhouse, Joseph, William Schwartz, Albert Williams, and Christina Witsberger. 1985. 'Are Fee-for-Service Costs Increasing Faster than HMO Costs?' *Medical Care* 23:960–6.

Norrish, Barbara, and Thomas Rundall. 2001. 'Hospital Restructuring and the Work of Registered Nurses.' *The Millbank Quarterly* 79:55–79.

North-South Institute. 1999. *Time for Work: Linkages between Paid and Unpaid Work in Human Resource Policy*. Ottawa: North-South Institute.

O'Cleireacain, Carol. 1989. 'Hospital Workers and the Health Care Crisis.' *Journal of Public Health Policy* 10:178–86.

Ofreneo, Rene E. 1989. *A Divided Economy, a Divided Labor Force and a Divided Labor Movement*. Professorial Lecture, July 15. Document accessed at the School of Labor and Industrial Relations Library, University of the Philippines, Quezon City, November 2008.

– 1993. *Labor and the Philippine Economy*. Doctoral Diss., College of Social Sciences and Philosophy, University of the Philippines-Diliman, Quezon City.

Organisation for Economic Co-operation and Development (OECD). 2007. *International Migration Outlook*. Paris: OECD.

– 2008a. *International Migration Outlook*. Paris: OECD.

– 2008b. *OECD Health Committee Papers*. Paris: OECD.

– 2009. *International Migration Outlook*. Paris: OECD.

– 2010. *International Migration Outlook*. Paris: OECD.

Özol, Cengiz. 1992. 'The Dual Theory of Value and the Theory of Exploitation.' *METU Studies in Development* 19:529–47.

Packer, Corinne, Ronald Labonté, and Denise Spitzer. 2007. *WHO Commission
on Social Determinants of Health: Globalization and Health Worker Crisis.* Ottawa: Institute of Population Health.

Panitch, Leo. 1981. 'Trade Unions and the Capitalist State.' *New Left Review* 125
(January/February):21–43.

Parreñas, Rachel. 2000. 'Migrant Filipina Domestic Workers and the International Division of Reproductive Labour.' *Gender and Society* 14:560–81.

– 2001. *Servants of Globalization: Women, Migration and Domestic Work.* Stanford: Stanford University Press.

– 2005. *Children of Global Migration: Transnational Families and Gendered Woes.*
Stanford: Stanford University Press.

Pendakur, Ravi. 2000. *Immigrants and the Labour Force: Policy, Regulation, and
Impact.* Montreal: McGill-Queen's University Press.

Philippines Overseas Employment Administration (POEA). 2010a. *Overseas
Employment Statistics: Deployment Statistics, Compendium of OFW Statistics.*
Manila: Philippines Overseas Employment Administration.

– 2010b. *Overseas Employment Statistics: Other OFW-Related Statistics, OFW Remittances.* Manila: Philippines Overseas Employment Administration.

– 2010c. *Overseas Employment Statistics: Deployment Statistics, Deployment per
Skill per Sex.* Manila: Philippines Overseas Employment Administration.

Pierson, David, and James Williams. 1994. 'Compensation via Integration.'
Hospitals and Health Networks 68:28–38.

Piper, Nicola. 2008. 'International Migration and Gendered Axes of Stratification.' In *New Perspectives on Gender and Migration,* edited by Nicola Piper,
1–18. New York: Routledge and United Nations Research Institute for Social
Development.

Polanyi, Karl. 2001. *The Great Transformation: The Political and Economic Origins
of Our Time.* 2nd ed. Boston: Beacon Press.

Pomeroy, William. 1992. *The Philippines: Colonialism, Collaboration, and Resistance!* New York: International Publishers.

Potts, Lydia. 1990. *The World Labour Market: A History of Migration.* London: Zed.

Public Service International. 2008. *Filipino Nurses Still Underpaid.* Ferney-
Voltaire, France: Public Service International. Accessed 16 April 2008.
http://www.world-psi.org/Template.cfm?Section=Home&CONTENTID=
21104&TEMPLATE=/ContentManagement/ContentDisplay.cfm.

Pudney, Stephen, and Michael Shields. 1999. *Gender and Racial Discrimination
in Pay and Promotion for NHS Nurses.* IZA Discussion Paper No. 85. Bonn:
Institute for the Study of Labor (IZA).

Quijano, Anibal. 2000. 'Coloniality of Power, Eurocentrism, and Latin America.' *Nepantla: Views from the South* 1:1–48.

Quijano, Anibal, and Immanuel Wallerstein. 1992. 'Americanity as a Concept, or the Americans in the Modern World-System.' *International Social Science Journal* 44:549–57.

Raj-Hashim, Rita. 1994. 'Review of Migration and Labour Policies in Asia.' In *The Trade in Domestic Workers: Causes, Mechanisms and Consequences of International Migration*, edited by Noeleen Heyzer, Geertje Lycklama à Nijeholt, and Nedra Weerakoon, 119–33. Kuala Lumpur: Asian and Pacific Development Centre/Zed Books.

Ratha, Dilip, Sanket Mohapatra, and Sonia Plaza. 'Beyond Aid: New Sources and Initiative Mechanisms for Financing Development in sub-Saharan Africa.' Policy Research Working Paper No. 4609. The World Bank, Development Prospects Group, Migration and Remittances Team. Accessed 30 July 2011. http://elibrary.worldbank.org/docserver/download/4609.pdf?expires=1312026182&id=id&accname=guest&checksum+E41289A7A2F966C88822405BEEF24A2F.

Richman, Louis. 1983. 'Health Benefits Comes Under the Knife.' *Fortune* 107 (May 2):95–6.

Rodriguez, Robyn. 2010. *Migrants for Export: How the Philippine State Brokers Labor to the World*. Minneapolis: University of Minnesota Press.

Royal College of Physicians and Surgeons of Canada. 2009. *Jurisdiction Approved Training*. Accessed 28 August 2009. http://rcpsc.medical.org/residency/certification/img_page2_e.php.

Russell, Louise. 1976. 'Inflation and the Federal Role in Health.' In *Health: A Victim or Cause of Inflation*, edited by Michael Zubkoff, 225–44. New York: Milbank Memorial Fund.

– 1979. *Technology in Hospitals: Medical Advances and Their Diffusion*. Washington, DC: The Brookings Institution.

San Martin, Laura. 2004. 'Chile Source Report.' In *Women and International Migration in the Health Sector*, edited by Kim Van Eyck, 32. Ferney-Voltaire, France: Public Service International.

Sassen, Saskia. 1988. *The Mobility of Labour and Capital*. Cambridge: Cambridge University Press.

– 1998. 'Toward a Feminist Analytics of the Global Economy.' In *Globalization and Its Discontents*, 81–105. New York: New Press.

– 2000. 'Women's Burden: Counter-Geographies of Globalization and the Feminisation of Survival.' *Journal of International Affairs* 53:503–24.

Sen, Kasturi, ed. 2003. *Restructuring Health Services*. London: Zed Books.

Shaikh, Anwar. 1999. 'Explaining the Global Economic Crisis.' *Historical Materialism* 5:103–43.

Sharma, Nandita. 2006. *Home Economics: Nationalism and the Making of 'Migrant Workers' in Canada*. Toronto: University of Toronto Press.

Silver, Beverly. 2003. *Forces of Labor: Workers' Movements and Globalization since 1870*. New York: Cambridge University Press.

Silver, Beverly, and Giovanni Arrighi. 2001. 'Workers North and South.' *Socialist Register* 37:53–76.

Stalker, Peter. 1994. *The Work of Strangers: A Survey of International Labour Migration*. Geneva: International Labour Office.

Starr, Paul. 1982. *The Social Transformation of American Medicine*. New York: Basic Books Incorporated.

Stasiulis, Daiva, and A. Bakan. 2005. *Negotiating Citizenship: Migrant Women in Canada and the Global System*. Toronto: University of Toronto Press.

Stelling, Joan. 1994. 'Staff Nurses' Perceptions of Nursing: Issues in a Woman's Occupation.' In *Health, Illness, and Health Care in Canada*, 2nd ed., edited by B. Singh Bolaria and Harley Dickinson, 609–25. Toronto: Hartcourt Brace and Company.

Stiller, Calvin. 1989. 'High-tech Medicine and the Control of Health Care Costs.' *Canadian Medical Association Journal* 140 (April 15):905–8.

St-Onge, Jean-Claude. 2004. *L'Envers de la Pilule: Les Dessous de l'Industrie Pharmaceutique*. Montreal: Éditions Écosociété.

Sweezy, Paul. 1942. *The Theory of Capitalist Development*. New York: Monthly Review.

Tavis, A., and Oliver Williams, eds. 1993. *The Pharmaceutical Corporate Presence in Developing Countries*. Notre Dame: University of Notre Dame Press.

Technical Education and Skills Development Authority. N.d.a. 'Course Design: Barangay Health Service.' Manila: TESDA.

– N.d.b. 'Competency-based Curriculum: Health, Social and Other Community Development Services.' Manila: TESDA.

Technical Review Panel on the Medicare Trustees Reports. 2000. *Review of Assumptions and Methods of the Medicare Trustees' Financial Projections* (December):i–70.

Thomson, Grahame. 2000. 'Economic Globalization?' In *A Globalizing World? Culture, Economics, Politics*, 1st Ed., edited by David Held, 85–109. London: Routledge.

Tilly, Charles. 1990. *Coercion, Capital, and European States, AD 990–1992*. Cambridge: Basil Blackwell Limited.

Tyner, James. 2004. *Made in the Philippines: Gendered Discourses and the Making of Migrants*. London: Routledge Curzon.

United States Surgical. 2009. *About Us*. Accessed 25 July 2009. http://www.ussurg.com/ussurgical/pagebuilder.aspx?webPageID=151690.

Valdepeñas, Vicente B. 1970. *The Protection and Development of Philippine Manufacturing*. Manila: Ateneo University Press.

Valdepeñas, Vicente B., and Gemelino M. Bautista. 1977. *The Emergence of the Philippine Economy*. Manila: Papyrus Press.

Valiani, Salimah. 2002. 'Towards a History of Top Profiteers: Multinational Capitalists in the Twentieth Century.' *VIKALP Alternatives, Special Issue: Another World is Possible* X (December):15–44.

– 2007a. *Analysis, Solidarity, Action: A Workers' Perspective on the Growing Use of Migrant Labour in Canada*. Ottawa: Canadian Labour Congress.

– 2007b. *Labour and Migration Update: Policy and Research News*. Ottawa: Canadian Labour Congress.

– 2008a. *Labour and Migration Update: Policy and Advocacy News*. Toronto: Justicia for Migrant Workers.

– 2008b. 'Labour Migration and Development: Towards a North-South Vision for Change.' *Just Labour: A Canadian Journal of Work and Society* 12 (Spring):23–9.

– 2009. *The Shift in Canadian Immigration Policy and Unheeded Lessons of the Live-in Caregiver Program*. Ottawa: No One is Illegal.

– 2011. *Valuing the Invaluable: Rethinking and Respecting Caring Work in Canada*. Toronto: Ontario Nurses' Association.

Van Eyck, K. 2004. *Women and International Migration in the Health Sector*. Ferney-Voltaire, France: Public Service International.

Vasquez, Noel. 1992. 'Economic and Social Impact of Labor Migration.' In*Philippine Labor Migration: Impact and Policy*, edited by Graziano Battistella and Anthony Peganoni, 41–112. Quezon City: Scalabrini Migration Center.

Vos, Rob. 1992. 'Private Foreign Asset Accumulation, Not Just Capital Flight: Evidence from the Philippines.' *The Journal of Development Studies* 28:500–37.

Wallerstein, Immanuel, ed. 1975. *World Inequality: Origins and Perspectives on the World System*. Montreal: Black Rose Books.

Walston, Stephen, Lawton Burns, and John Kimberly. 2000. 'Does Reengineering Really Work? An Examination of the Context of Outcomes of Hospital Reengineering Initiatives.' *Health Services Research* 34 (February): 1363–88.

Wang-Bae, Kim. 2004. 'Migration of Foreign Workers into South Korea: From Periphery to Semi-periphery in the Global Labor Market.' *Asian Survey* 44:316–35.

Weisner, Martha Luz Rojas, and Hugo Angeles Cruz. 2008. 'Gendered Migration in the Americas: Mexico as Country of Origin, Destination and Transit.' In *New Perspectives on Gender and Migration*, edited by Nicola Piper, 189–245. New York: Routledge and United Nations Research Institute for Social Development.

Weiss, Lawrence. 1997. *Private Medicine and Public Health.* Boulder, CO: Westview Press (Harper Collins).

White, Jerry. 1993. 'Changing Labour Process and the Nursing Crisis in Canadian Hospitals.' *Studies in Political Economy* 40 (Spring):103–34.

Willis, David, and Michael Zubkoff. 1976. 'Foreword.' In *Health: A Victim or Cause of Inflation*, edited by Michael Zubkoff, vii–xiv. New York: Milbank Memorial Fund.

World Trade Organization. 2008. *Services Signalling Conference: Report of the Chairman of the TNC*. Geneva: 30 July.

Xu, Yu. 2003. 'Are Chinese Nurses a Viable Source to Relieve the U.S. Nurse Shortage?' *Nursing Economics* 21:269–79.

– 2006. 'From Diplomacy to National Development: Chinese Policy on Transnational Mobility of Nurses.' *Harvard Health Policy Review* 7:121–32.

Yalnizyan, Armine. 2005. *Canada's Commitment to Equality: A Gender Analysis of the Last Ten Federal Budgets (1995–2004)*. Ottawa: Canadian Feminist Alliance for International Action.

Yeates, Nicola. 2009. *Globalizing Care Economies and Migrant Workers*. London: Palgrave MacMillan.

Young, Kate, Carol Wolkowitz, and Roslyn McCullagh, eds. 1981. *Of Marriage and the Market: Women's Subordination in International Perspective*. London: CSE Books.

Zubkoff, Michael. 1976. 'Health Report to the White House Summit on Inflation – Rapporteur's Report on HEW's Pre-Summit Conference on the Impact of Inflation on Health.' In *Health: A Victim or Cause of Inflation*, edited by Michael Zubkoff, 1–4. New York: Milbank Memorial Fund.

Index

absolute unequal exchange, 21, 132–9. *See also* unequal exchange
accumulation (systemic cycles of): accumulation crisis, 42–4, 57, 71–2; financial expansion of the fourth (U.S.) systemic cycle of accumulation, 18, 20, 21, 29–31, 44, 70, 71, 124; four systemic cycles of accumulation, 13–15, 17–18, 43; phase of financial expansion, 13, 14 fig 1.1, 43; phase of material expansion, 13, 14 fig. 1.1, 43; third (British) systemic cycle of accumulation, 13, 27. *See also* Arrighi, Giovanni; material expansion of the fourth (U.S.) systemic cycle of accumulation
Africa: African slave labour, 17, 139–42, 143, 144–5, 163n13, 163n14, 164n18; Ethiopian Expatriate Affairs Directorate, 92; European migration to South Africa, xii; and European Union migration policies, xv; and feminization of migration flows, 4–5; and global nursing care chains, 11; health worker emigration from Africa to the global North, 5, 137–8; import-substitution industrialization (ISI) in, 110, 118; and increasing remittances, 25, 26 fig. 2.1; and inequality in health migration, 7; Mourid brotherhood in Senegal, 161n1; movements for national independence in, 126; nurse-to-population ratio in, 7, 132; societies of the periphery in, xv; supply of migrant nurses from, 32, 33 fig. 2.2, 137–8; use of HIV rapid tests in Kenya and Uganda, 137–8
Alliance of Health Workers, xviii, 159n20
Altman, Stuart, and Joseph Eichenholz, 47–8
American Medical Holdings, 48–9
American Medicorp, 49
Amin, Samir, 126, 128, 129, 132, 161n1
Anderson, Elaine, and Mark Ginsberg, 46, 47, 52
Anderson, Odin, Patricia Collette, and Jacob Feldman, 46
Angus, Douglas, 84
'anti-market,' 13, 16
Armstrong, Pat, 86–7